营销原理、策略及应用

（汉英对照）

龚梦雪　著

ZHEJIANG UNIVERSITY PRESS
浙江大学出版社
·杭州·

图书在版编目（CIP）数据

营销原理、策略及应用：汉英对照 / 龚梦雪著. —
杭州：浙江大学出版社，2022.6
　　ISBN 978-7-308-22600-4

　　Ⅰ．①营… Ⅱ．①龚… Ⅲ．①市场营销学－汉、英
Ⅳ．①F713.50

中国版本图书馆CIP数据核字(2022)第077741号

营销原理、策略及应用：汉英对照

龚梦雪　著

策划编辑　吴伟伟
责任编辑　杨　茜
责任校对　许艺涛
封面设计　周　灵
出版发行　浙江大学出版社
　　　　　　（杭州市天目山路148号　　邮政编码　310007）
　　　　　　（网址：http://www.zjupress.com）
排　　版　杭州林智广告有限公司
印　　刷　广东虎彩云印刷有限公司绍兴分公司
开　　本　710mm×1000mm　1/16
印　　张　20.5
字　　数　388千
版印次　2022年6月第1版　2022年6月第1次印刷
书　　号　ISBN 978-7-308-22600-4
定　　价　68.00元

What Is Marketing?

何为营销?

1.1　Marketers and Role of Marketing 营销人员及营销角色

Do you remember those who try to get your attention by engaging you scan their products' QR codes and reward you with a small gift? Or the person who warmly introduces a university to you in order to get you enrolled? They are all marketers. They are the ones who identify goods and service desired by the customers, as well as advertise and sell those products on behalf of their organizations.

你还记得那些为了吸引你的注意，让你扫产品二维码，然后塞给你小礼物的人吗？记得那些为了让你入学，热情地向你介绍一所大学的人吗？他们都是营销人员。他们是能够发现消费者想要的商品和服务，并代表企业向消费者推销和售卖的人。

Ideal marketers would be balanced equally with analytical and verbal abilities, with excellent communication skills, including listening. Distinguished marketing practitioners should be well-organized, self-motivated, conscious of time, and somewhat aggressive; emphatic, understanding, and solution-oriented, with a solid grounding in the behavioral science; and imaginative, creative, expressive, and persuasive. The ideal practitioner would be easy to work with, and would truly enjoy meeting new people in new places.

完美的营销人员同时具有分析和口头表达能力，掌握卓越的沟通技巧，懂得倾听。出色的营销实践人员有条理，能自我激励，有时间观念，有闯劲；富有同情心、同理心、擅长解决问题，有扎实的行为科学专业背景；有想象力、创造力、表达力、说服力。和他们一起工作很愉快，他们非常喜欢在新领域结识新朋友。

However, nobody possesses all these qualities, but everyone has some. Honestly, everyone can be a marketer.

然而，一个人不可能拥有所有这些特质，但是每个人都具备其中某些特质。坦白说，每个人都可以成为营销人员。

Thus, where do the marketers come from? You may find that they come from all kinds of background such as business, law, IT, economics, linguistics, and even literature. Just to name some, advertisers usually have a degree in foreign languages. Brand managers often excel in law. Fashion marketers may have training experience in design. Digital marketers are skillful at information technology. Graduates from mathematics can help modeling consumer behavior. Whether students earn a marketing degree or not, or ever take marketing courses or not, they may end up doing marketing jobs, because it always helps while doing marketing jobs.

营销人员是从哪里来的？你可以发现他们具有各种专业背景，比如商科、法律、信息技术、经济学、语言学，甚至文学。举例来说，广告人通常有张外语方面的学位证书，品牌管理者通常钻研法律，时尚营销者在设计领域受过训练，数字营销人员擅长信息技术，数学专业的毕业生可以为消费者行为建立模型……无论他们是否有一张营销专业的学位证书，或者是否上过营销课程，他们可能最终都做了营销工作，因为拥有某一领域的专业知识或实践经验对营销工作总是很有帮助。

Marketers are scattered in every industry, so that you can see them anywhere and everywhere. Marketers work in consumer goods companies such as Nestlé and Coca-cola, service companies such as Air China and Alibaba, and nonprofit organizations such as churches, universities, the Red Cross.

营销人员分布在每个行业，随处可见，比如在雀巢和可口可乐之类的快消品公司、中国航空和阿里巴巴这样的服务型企业，或者教会、大学、红十字会等非营利机构。

Marketing department plays a vital role in promoting business in an organization. Marketing is responsible for most tasks that are hopefully profitable to an organization. For the nonprofit organizations, marketing is responsible for attracting customers to support the nonprofit's mission, such as raising donations or supporting a case. For both types of organizations, it is unlikely that they can survive without a strong marketing effort. All the other departments, such as human resources, financial, and IT, more or less, spend money the earned by the marketing department.

在一个组织中，营销部门在推进业务方面起到了关键作用。营销部门承担了大多数可能产生利润的工作。对于非营利组织来说，营销负责招揽客人来实现组织目标，比如募捐或支持一个项目。无论在哪种组织里，它们都不可能脱离营销而存在。而其他部门，如人力资源部、财务部、技术部，某种程度上都在花营销人员挣来的钱。

Unfortunately, not all companies realize what marketing really means to them. Some companies are very marketing oriented, whereas others may put it at a lower priority. A company can survive with or without those departments which produce cost, but without marketing departments, it will not be long before the company fails.

不幸的是，不是所有企业都能意识到营销对它们来说意味着什么。一些企业非常重视营销，但是另一些就让营销靠边站。没有那些产生成本的部门，企业或许还能生存，但倘若没有了营销部门，这家企业不久就会倒闭。

Marketing department is not necessarily called "Marketing Department" in real life. Sometimes it is decomposed as "advertising" or "sales", and sometimes they use the term "marketing" when they are actually doing promotion job. Marketers are not called "marketers", especially in not-for-profit organizations. They have their job titles, to name just a few, marketing data analyst, online product manager, digital marketing strategist, e-commerce marketing director, public relation manager, SEO specialist, email marketer, etc. Like CEO and CFO, there are Chief Marketing Officers, called CMO.

在现实中，营销部门不一定叫作"市场营销部"，有时候会被分解成"广告部"或"销售部"，有时候用市场营销部来命名，而实际上只是做推销的工作。营销人员不会被叫作"营销人员"，特别是在非营利组织。他们有自己的职位名称，举例来说，如营销数据分析师、线上产品经理、数字营销战略员、电子商务营销主管、公共关系经理、搜索引擎专员、电邮营销员，等等。类似于 CEO（首席执行官）、CFO（首席财务官），还有首席营销官，即 CMO。

1.2 Marketing Activity 营销活动

Many people think that marketing is all about advertising and selling. That is somewhat true, for we're bombarded with a great deal of TV commercials, newspapers ads, direct-email offers or even sales calls, in almost every single day. People are always trying to sell their products to us. It seems unable to escape from the overwhelming promotion at all.

许多人认为营销就是打广告和卖东西。某种意义上确实是这样。因为我们几乎每天都要受到电视广告、报纸广告、直邮广告的轰炸，或接到推销人员的电话，总是有人试图把产品卖给我们。我们似乎根本无法从铺天盖地的推销中逃离出来。

However, as you learn this subject, you will find that marketing in our sight, like advertisement, is just the tip of the iceberg. The huge mountain underwater can sometimes be more important. As a matter of fact, as the concept of marketing evolves over time, marketing nowadays cannot be purely understood as promotion or advertising activities. How to understand the marketing concept has an impact on marketing decisions, operation of a company and its success.

然而，当你慢慢学习"营销"这门学科，你会发现，我们肉眼所见的广告等营销方式，只是市场营销的冰山一角，埋在下面的部分有时更加重要。事实上，随着营销观念的不断发展，现在的营销不能单纯地被理解为举办一场营销活动或者打个广告。如何理解"营销"的概念，会影响到如何做营销决策、如何运营一家企业，甚至影响企业的成败。

Therefore, what is marketing? In this book, we will follow the views of Philip Kotler who's the father of modern marketing. He defined the field of social marketing that focuses on the value-oriented marketing which helps people modify their behavior toward healthier and safer living styles. He said that, "Marketing is a societal process by which individuals and groups obtain what they need and want through creating, offering, and exchanging products and services of value freely with others." Some important elements are summarized as follows.

因此，什么是营销？本书将使用现代营销学之父菲利普·科特勒的观点。他创造了营销的社会学定义，强调了营销的价值导向，即帮助人们修正他们的行为以获取更健康和安全的生活方式。他提出："营销是个人和团体通过创造有价值的产品和服务，并同别人进行交换，以获得其所需所欲之物的一种社会和管理过程。"营销的要素可以总结为以下几点。

（1）Marketing falls into management area. It is the process of analyzing, planning, executing and controlling the conception, pricing, promotion and distribution of ideas, goods, and services. Marketing is the management of demands as well as customer relationships.

营销是一个管理学概念。它是各种分析、计划、实施和控制，以及一系列定价、促销和分销理念、产品和服务的活动过程。营销管理涉及需求和顾客关系的管理。

（2）Marketing is a process. It is not a simple thing. It is a way that everything is done, so the word is not "marketing", but "marketingly".

营销是一个过程。它不是一件简单的事，它是如何将一件事情做好的完整过程，所以确切的用词，不是"营销"，而是"（如何）营销出去"。

（3）Marketing is all about exchange. It helps the customers to buy some products or personal service from producers, whereas producers get payments from consumers, along with their purchase information.

营销是关于"交换"的概念。它帮助顾客从生产者那里购买产品或私人服务，同时，生产者也能从这个过程中获得报酬，连同顾客的购买信息。

（4）The ultimate goal of marketing is to help individuals and groups obtain what they need and want. The way of reaching the goal is to create, communicate, and exchange value.

营销的最终目的是满足人类的各种需要和欲望。达到目的的方式是创造、传播和交换价值。

These elements will be detailed in the following chapters. Besides, there is also a management definition which describes marketing as "the art of selling products", and other academic and non-academic definition will be good to learn, as long as they help you understand the nature of marketing.

关于营销的特征，本书会在以下的章节中详细地描述。除此之外，管理学把营销定义为"销售的艺术"，还有其他学术或非学术的定义，都是值得学习的。这些定义能够帮助你理解营销的本质。

1.3　The Value of Marketing 营销的价值

Successful marketers communicate with their customers everyday. They talk to the customers, ask questions, and try their best to get a deeper understanding of what the customers desire by analyzing their behavior. This is how excellent marketers do to create and capture customer value, communicate and deliver value to customers. As a matter of fact, market value takes everyone involved in the marketing process into consideration. Benefit is the outcome sought by a customer that motivates buying behavior that satisfies a need or want. It is a desirable attribute that consumers can get from purchasing goods or services. Stakeholders—buyers, sellers, investors in a company, community residents, and even citizens of the nations where goods and services are made or sold, all have their needs to be satisfied. A Consumer is the ultimate user of a good, idea or a service. All the customers and potential customers, who share a common need that can be satisfied by a specific product, who have the resources to exchange for it, who are willing to make the exchange, and who have the authority to make the exchange, make up a market. Any location or medium used to conduct an exchange is a marketplace. Today, a marketplace is not necessarily a place where two parties meet and make transactions face to face. It can be a virtual venue on the internet. It is clear that consumers have a variety of needs, and sellers have their needs too. They expect to make profits from marketing, to maintain customer and partner relationships, and to be proud of selling the highest-quality products .

　　成功的营销人员每天和他们的顾客打交道，和他们聊天，问他们问题，试图通过分析他们的行为来更深刻地理解消费者的需求所在。这就是优秀的营销人员如何创造和抓住消费者价值，并为他们传播和传递价值的。实际上市场价值关乎所有参与到营销过程中的人。利益是驱使消费者做出购买行为来满足需要和欲望的动力。它是消费者购买感到满意的商品或服务即可获得的一种属性。利益相关者，包括买家、卖家、企业的投资者、社区居民甚至参与生产和销售商品和服务的国民，都有他们的需求。消费者是商品、理念和服务的最终使用者。所有消费者和潜在消费者，如果他们拥有同样能够被某样商品满足的需求，有可供交换的资源，有意愿去交换及有权交换，就组成了一个（消费者）市场。

任何进行交易的场所和中介都叫市场。现在的市场并不一定是一个实际场所，z 在那里买卖双方进行面对面交易。它可以是虚拟的网络市场。我们都知道消费者有五花八门的需求，而卖家也有他们的需求，他们期望从营销中获取利润，维护客户和合作伙伴的关系，为他们所售卖的高质量商品感到自豪。

The value of marketing lies in three aspects.

营销的价值体现在以下 3 个方面。

（1）Marketing is about meeting needs. The most basic concept in marketing is human needs. Needs are the recognition of any difference between a consumer's actual state and some ideal or desired state. There are psychological needs as food, warmth, air, water, and shelter; social needs as entertainment, education, sense of belonging, esteem and affection; personal needs as self-expression and self-realization.

营销满足需求。人类的需求是营销的最基本概念。当消费者的实际状况和想要的状况之间有差距，需求就产生了。需求有对食物、温度、空气、水、住所之类的生理需要；有对娱乐、教育、归属感、受尊重与爱之类的社会需要；还有对自我表达和自我实现之类的个人需要。

When needs refer to specific objects, they are wants. For example, two students feel hungry during lunch time class, they need food. The student from northern China wants to have a dish of dumplings, whereas the other student brought up in a western culture wants a pizza, cola, and French fries. Needs are basic human requirements that everybody may have, while wants are affected by social cultural environment. Therefore, wants are changing as the economy develops.

当需要被具体化为某一样物品的时候，欲望便产生了。比如，两位同学在中午的课上肚子饿了，他们需要食物。其中一位来自中国北方，他想吃一碗饺子，而另一位在西方家庭长大的孩子想要吃比萨、可乐和薯条。因此，需求是人类最基本的要求，每个人都有、但是欲望受到社会文化环境的影响，会随着经济发展而变化。

People have unlimited want even sometimes they do not admit, but they have limited ability of payment. Customers choose products which bring the greatest benefit, at a reasonable price within their paying ability. Many people want a big property, a luxury limo or a high-end jewelry, but not everyone can afford them. When wants are backed by an ability to pay, they are demands. Marketers should not only see how many people want their products, but more importantly, how many people are willing to pay for them, because they are the true source of profit.

虽然人们常常不承认他们有无限的欲望，但他们的支付能力却是有限的。消费者选择那些能给他们带来最大利益、定价合理且在自身支付能力内的产品。许多人想要大别墅、豪华轿车、高级首饰，但不是所有人都能负担得起。当想要的物品能够被支付时，欲望变成了需求。营销人员不能只看到有多少人想要他们的产品，更重要的是有多少人愿意掏钱购买产品，因为他们才是利润的真正来源。

It is noted that, marketers do not create needs. Needs are already there. What do marketers do if needs already exist? Marketers create wants, exert influence by persuading people to buy all those specific products or services that may meet their needs. Marketers promote famous-brand cosmetics for women which can make them look more elegant and beautiful, but marketers do not create needs for being beautiful.

需要注意的是，营销人员不创造需求。需求本就存在。如果需求已经存在，那么营销人员要做什么呢？营销人员创造欲望，他们通过劝说人们购买那些能够满足需求的具体商品或服务，来对消费者施加影响。营销人员给女性推销名牌化妆品，号称能够让她们更优雅、更美丽，但是营销人员没有创造消费者对美的需求。

（2）Marketing is about creating utility. Utility is the usefulness or benefit that consumers receive from buying, owning or consuming a product. There are four types of utility putting together to meet customers' needs: form utility, place utility, time utility, and possession utility.

营销创造效用。效用是消费者在购买、拥有和消费商品时所获得的利益。

营销创造了 4 个类型的效用，来满足消费者的需求：形态效用、地点效用、时间效用、占有效用。

Form utility refers to the benefits provided by marketing that turn raw materials into finished products. For example, woods, steel, and oil paint are put together to make desks; raw cow milk are sterilized, packed into milk boxes, and shipped to market for sale. Marketers create utility by transforming customers' basic needs into the products and services that deliver added value.

形态效用指把原材料转化成成品后所能够提供的效用。比如，把木头、钢筋、油漆组合在一起做成桌子；将生牛奶杀菌、包装、运输到市场卖。营销人员通过把客户最基本的需求变成有价值的产品和服务来创造效益。

Place utility refers to the convenience that marketers provide by making products available where wanted. For example, providing good-quality imported goods and services for domestic consumers; providing official website for customers to order online.

地点效用指把产品放在消费者需要并且容易购买的地方所提供的便利性。比如，为国内的消费者提供高质量的进口商品和服务；在官网提供线上购买途径。

Time utility means the ability of storing products until they are needed. Logistics plays an important role as it ensures customers receive products and services on time. For example, building vending machines where the physical stores are closed early; providing phone service and support 7/24.

时间效用指在消费者需要的时候出售商品的效用。物流的发展起到很大的作用，它能够保证消费者按时收到产品和服务。比如，在实体店关门的时候提供自动售货机；每周 7 天每天 24 小时提供商品的电话服务和支持。

在美国，"黑色星期五"之后的"网络星期一"（Cyber Monday），商家把大量储存的商品打折出售，通常能创造巨大销量

Possession utility allows the consumer to own, use, and enjoy the product. For example, an expensive piece of furniture might be made more easily available through a low interest financing deal. Or a bank may simplify the steps needed to obtain a loan. In both cases, the firm makes it easier for the consumer to possess the product.

所有权效用让消费者可以拥有、使用和享受产品。比如，一件贵重的家具可以通过低息借款方式来购买，或者银行为贷款交易简化办理手续。在这两种情况下，企业都为消费者提供了拥有商品的便利条件。

（3）Marketing is about exchange relationships. Another core concept under marketing transaction is exchange. Exchange is the act of obtaining a desired object from someone by offering something in return. People exchange currency to get the goods or ideas or services they want, or exchange new behavior for the item of value. For example, no drunk driving won't be fined by the policeman. There must be two parties in an exchange activity, both of whom agree with the terms of the exchange, and they are able to make delivery of the products of value.

营销是交换关系。营销交易的另一个核心概念是交换。交换是为了从某人那里获得想要的物品而做出的提供另外的物品的行为。人们用货币交换他们想要的商品、理念或服务，或用新的行为习惯交换同等价值的待遇，比如不酒驾就不会被罚款。交换必须有交易双方、有经同意的条款，并且双方有能力交付这些包含价值的产品。

Suppose you are in a restaurant and order your favorite meal. You eat the food and then you pay by cash. You have gone through and completed an exchange process. Or you use your Android or iPhone to download an App and you pay for it by your credit card.

假设你在一家餐厅点了最喜欢的菜，用完餐后，你用现金买单，这就完成了一个交换过程。或者，你用安卓或苹果手机下载一个应用软件，然后用信用卡为此付钱。

1.4　The Evolution of a Concept 营销的演化

The marketing discipline has developed just at the beginning of the 20th century in America, but the marketing concept preexisted the discipline. Marketing concept is a way of thinking, a philosophy, and an attitude or an idea that guides an organization's overall marketing activities. With the development of the productivity, human needs and wants evolve all the time. As we already know that marketing is there for meeting needs profitably, it has to keep up with the time or even walk ahead of the time. Thus, marketing concept is an ever-changing but relatively stable philosophy over a period of time that represents business thinking. Knowing how it develops over time and different marketing ideas help understand how marketing becomes what it is today and where its future may lie. In history, marketing goes through five stages: the production era, the selling era, the marketing era, the relationship era, and the triple bottom line orientation.

市场营销这门学科发展于 20 世纪初的美国，但是营销的观念远在它之前就存在了。营销观念是能够引导整个组织进行营销活动的思维方式、哲学或者理念。随着生产力的发展，人类的需要和欲望也不断演变。我们已经知道，营销是为了满足需求、获得利润，那么它必定要跟上时代甚至超越时代。因此，营销观念是一种不断变化的但在一段时期内相对稳定的哲学，它体现了商业思维。了解营销观念的发展过程和不同的营销观念之间的区别，能帮助理解当今营销的现状，以及它的未来所向。历史上，市场营销经历了五个阶段：生产时代、销售时代、市场营销时代、关系时代和三重底线导向。

1.4.1　The Production Era (1860s—1920s) 生产时代（19 世纪 60 年代—20 世纪 20 年代）

This was the period of industrial revolution in the United States. At this period, the country witnessed growth in electricity generation, rail transportation, division of labor, assembly lines, and mass production. These made it possible to produce goods more efficiently with new technology and new ways of using labor. Despite the increase in production of goods with these emerging ways of production, there was heavy demand for manufactured goods.

这是美国的工业革命时期。在这段时期里，美国经历了电力生产、铁路交通、劳动分工、流水线和大规模生产的发展。新科技的使用及新的用工方式提高了生产效率。尽管新生产方式的出现加速了工业生产，但对工业成品的需求依然强劲。

Under the production orientation, the market was seller-dominated because the demand greatly exceeds supply. Thus the management philosophy emphasized the efficiency of producing and distributing products. As long as a company had the resources to produce products, the ability to lower the costs, then set them at a reasonable price, it could easily take over the market. Marketing back then was not important at all because the goods literally sold themselves as long as people had no other choices. People had to take whatever the company produced. Their needs were extremely limited and were not considered important.

在生产导向下，由于需求远远大于供给，市场处于卖方市场。因此这种管理理念强调产品的生产效率和分配效率。一家企业只要有资源去生产产品，有能力降低成本，定一个相对合理的价格，这家企业就能轻松占领市场。那时候营销概念根本不重要，因为商品自己就能卖出去，人们没有选择，只能购买那些被生产出来的东西。他们的需求受到了极大的限制，也没有被重视。

Unfortunately, in some part of the world, this still exists as their economic situation is far from better off.

不幸的是，如今在世界某些地区，这种观念仍然存在，这些地区的经济远不够富足。

1.4.2　The Selling Era (1920s—1940s) 销售时代（20 世纪 20 年代—20 世纪 40 年代）

As the technology developed and the view of scientific management was proposed, some economies quickly moved forward into the selling era when supply exceeded demand in buyer's market. Selling orientation was a managerial view of marketing as a sales function, or a way to move products out of warehouses to reduce inventory. This selling orientation began to dominate around 1930s when the Americans were experiencing the Great Depression. People lacked purchasing power while the factories were able to produce greater amount of goods than those consumers needed. In order to survive, companies began to compete for obtaining customers and the era of pushy salespeople started.

随着科技发展，科学管理的观念被提出，一些经济体迅速地进入了销售时代，供给大于需求，变为买方市场。销售导向观念是一种把营销看成一种销售职能，或者一种为了减少库存而努力把产品从仓库里搬出来的方法。销售导向观念在 20 世纪 30 年代开始占有支配地位，那时候美国人正在经历"大萧条"。工厂可以生产比实际需要更多数量的商品，人们却缺乏购买力。为了生存下去，企业为获取顾客而相互竞争，咄咄逼人的促销员时代诞生了。

In this era, the greatest responsibility of most marketers was selling. All they had to care about was selling as many products as possible. The concept assumed that "consumers are unlikely to buy the product unless they are aggressively persuaded to do so-mostly that 'hard sell' approach". On the other hand, this is also the time when new advertising ideas and marketing techniques emerge, pushing marketing a step forward.

在这个时代，营销人员最大的责任就是"卖货"。他们只需要关心怎么卖出更多的产品。这种观念假设"消费者不可能去购买产品，除非促销员使用'强行推销'的办法，积极地说服他们去购买"。另一方面，这个时代同样催生了很多新的广告点子及营销技巧，将营销向前推动了一步。

The downside of selling orientation is that it focuses on the company side, but the consumer needs are still ignored. Sadly, a sales department was three to four times bigger than the marketing department. These companies soon died with their customers.

销售导向观念的不足在于，它只关注企业方面，而消费者的需要依然被忽略。可悲的是，当时的销售部门比营销部门要大三四倍。这类企业很快就随着他们的消费者一起陨落了。

1.4.3　The Marketing Era (1940s—1990s) 营销时代（20 世纪 40 年代—20 世纪 90 年代）

As the market became saturate, a fundamental shift happened in around 1950s, when more salespeople, who tried to sell their products by persuading customers to buy, were out of business. Business realized that customers had their own preferences, so they had to study what the customers need, want and their behaviors as to get a profound knowledge on them. Factories focused on manufacturing products which tailored customers' needs. All marketing efforts such as product, pricing, promotion, and distribution were integrated in accordance with customers.

大约在 20 世纪 50 年代，由于市场饱和，一项重大的改变发生了，那些试图通过强行推销劝说消费者购买产品的促销员失业了。企业发现消费者有自己的喜好，因此必须研究消费者需要什么、想要什么，并研究他们的消费行为，来获得更深刻的理解。工厂努力生产符合消费者需求的产品。所有的营销策略，比如产品、定价、促销、分销等都被整合在一起，与消费者保持一致。

The marketing orientation is not as prevalent as its prime time, but it is still in play.

现在的营销导向观念虽然没有它的黄金时期那么盛行，但在当今社会仍然有其影响力。

1.4.4 The Relationship Era (1990s—2010) 关系时代（20世纪90年代—2010年）

In this era, business adopted the consumer orientation which focused on ways to satisfy customers' needs and wants. The focus of companies shifted from single transaction towards building customer loyalty and developing lifetime relationship with clients. Business paid attention to the importance of creating bonds, considering that "the cost of attracting a new customer is estimated to be five times the cost of keeping a current customer happy". Therefore, dedication to providing higher customer service and establishing closer customer contact worked best in this era.

在关系时代，企业采取了消费者导向的理念，着力满足消费者的需要和欲望。企业的重心从完成单项交易转向建立消费者忠诚度，以及和客户建立终身的关系。考虑到"吸引一个新客户的成本是维护好一个老客户的5倍"，企业注意到了建立纽带的重要性。因此，在这个时代最好的做法是，致力于为消费者提供更高质量的服务，建立更密切的客户联系。

Companies and customers tended to coordinate with each other to create products. For example, Nike custom shoes were made to customers' exact specifications. On its official website, a customer was free to choose a material, a color, and an innovation according to his own preference. Once they finished design, the shoes would be delivered to the customer within 3–5 weeks and during the process the customer is informed of the updates. Customers were no longer mere buyers, they became designers even producers. More companies are now following this practice as in the context of Internet, making loyal consumers become marketers themselves by communicating values of the products and the company.

企业和顾客倾向于互相协作，一起来开发产品。比如，耐克为了满足顾客的确切需要推出了定制运动鞋。在耐克官网上，顾客可以根据自己的喜好自由选择鞋子的材料、颜色及创新点。设计完之后，鞋子会在3~5周之内送到顾客手中。在这期间，鞋子的最新制作情况和物流信息都会被发送给顾客。顾客不再是单纯的买家，他们变成了设计师，甚至是生产者。在互联网的背景下，更多企业采取了这样的做法，使忠实的消费者自己变成了营销人员，向外界传播该产品和该企业的价值。

1.4.5 The Triple Bottom Line Orientation (2010—) 三重底线导向（2010年至今）

This term "triple bottom line" (TBL or 3BL) is an accounting framework, which borrowed by professor Philip Kotler and is used to illustrate a newest philosophy of looking at marketing today. The triple bottom line orientation seeks to broaden the focus on the financial bottom line as it used to be, to include social responsibility and environmental responsibilities. It has three components:

三重底线是一个会计学术语，被菲利普·科特勒教授借用来描述当今最新的营销哲学。之前人们只关注财务底线，而三重底线导向扩大了其内涵，把社会责任和环境责任也包含进来。它有三个要素。

（1）The financial bottom line: Financial profits to stakeholders.

（2）The social bottom line: Contributing to the communities in which the company operates.

（3）The environmental bottom line: Creating sustainable business practices that minimize damage to the environment or that even improve it.

（1）财务底线：给利益相关者提供的利润。

（2）社会底线：为企业运营所在的社区做贡献。

（3）环境底线：进行可持续的商业活动，使对环境的损害最小化，甚至改善环境。

Before, people think a company that do not harm the environment is a good one, but nowadays it is obviously not enough. The Alibaba Group offers an opportunity by inviting organizations to grow trees in the dessert regions for consumers who use Alipay. It also requires a company to take social responsibility. A Nielsen report released in October 2015 found 56% of consumers were willing to pay more for products offered by companies committed to social values. For example, Alibaba enables Alipay for the payment of public transportations, hospitals, gas fees, etc.

在这之前，人们认为，只要不损害环境的企业就是一家好企业，但是现在这么做显然不够。阿里巴巴集团邀请一些组织与之合作，为使用支付宝的消费者提供在沙漠地区种树的机会。这就要求企业担负起社会责任。尼尔森 2015 年 10 月的一份报告中的数据显示，56% 的消费者更愿意购买努力实现社会价值的企业产品。比如，阿里巴巴集团的支付宝能够为公共交通、医疗、煤气等缴费。

1.5　The Scope of Marketing 市场营销的范围

There are 10 types of offerings that can be marketed:

有 10 种产品能够被营销。

Goods. Physical goods are the most commonly seen products that marketers are involved in. Food, drinks, clothes, stationary, house appliances, etc. are consumer goods that support an economy to grow.

商品。有形实物商品是营销人员参与最多的产品。食物、饮料、衣物、文具、家庭用品等，都是维持经济增长的消费品。

Services. Services are called the third industry following agriculture and industrial industries, yet it takes greater importance as economy advances. Restaurants, hotels, airlines, hair salons, law firms, accounting firms, etc. are parts of service industry. Many market offerings consist of a variable mix of goods and services.

服务。服务业是农业和工业之后的第三产业，它随着经济发展变得越来越重要。餐厅、酒店、航空公司、美发店、律师事务所、会计师事务所等都属于服务业。市场上众多的供应物是由不同比例的商品和服务混合而成的。

Experiences. Visiting a museum, an old country villa tour, a cruise trip, are experiences that people create and market. It brings people feelings that different from their day-to-day life. The Wizarding World of Harry Potter and Disneyland are of this sort.

体验。参观博物馆、参观乡村别墅、乘坐游轮旅行，都是人们在创造和营销的"体验"。它能带给人们和日常生活不一样的感觉。哈利·波特魔法世界、迪士尼乐园都属于这一类。

Events. The Olympics, Spring Festival Gala, Super Bowl are big events that marketers can reap some profit from. So they make efforts in promoting these great events to attract the attention of the whole world. Others like the Double-Eleven Day, which is a famous Chinese shopping day similar to the Black Friday of America, all kinds of performances and trade shows fall into this category.

事件。奥林匹克运动会、春节联欢晚会、超级碗橄榄球赛都是营销人员能从中赢利的大事件。所以他们努力营销这些大事件来吸引全世界的注意。其他如"双十一"购物节（与美国黑色星期五相近的中国最著名的购物节），还有各类表演、商业展示会都属于此类产品。

Persons. Pop stars, writers, musicians, and celebrities in all walks of life can be a great business in the marketing world. When singers release new songs, artists hold exhibitions, film directors make their new movies, marketers are expected to help them do the business.

人。流行明星、作家、音乐家，以及各行各业的名人都会成为营销的一大笔生意。当歌手发行新唱片、艺术家办展览、电影导演拍新片的时候，他们希望营销人员能帮助他们做好经营工作。

Places. Nations, cities, regions and destinations are places which attract people to either travel, make an investment, or purchase local special products to create revenue for the local governments. Place marketers are commercial banks, local business associations, and advertising and public relations agencies.

场所。国家、城市、地区和旅游胜地希望吸引人们去旅游、投资、购买特产，来提高当地政府的收入。场所营销者可以是商业银行、当地商业协会和广告公关企业。

Properties. Properties include a piece of land or real estate, and a financial property. Property marketers are most likely to be real estate agents and share dealers.

财产。财产包括房产和金融财产。财产营销者大多是房地产企业和股票经纪人等。

Organizations. Organizations as companies and non-for-profit institutions are competing to attract eyeballs nowadays. They are establishing images to either get profits or donations by claiming themselves to be socially responsible and environmentally friendly. As Holiday Inn puts "Pleasing people the world over", an organization builds up an image to let itself stand out of the crowd.

组织。企业或者非营利机构正在竞相吸引眼球。为了获取利润和捐款，他们打造自身形象，声称自己具有社会责任感、对环境友好。正如假日酒店号称要"让全世界的人感到满意"，组织都在为自己树立形象，以期脱颖而出。

Information. The production, packaging, and distribution of information is one of society's major industries. Information marketers include schools and universities, encyclopedia publishers, public libraries, etc.

信息。信息的生产、包装和分发是一个社会的主要产业之一。信息营销者包括学校和大学、百科全书出版商、公共图书馆等。

Ideas. Every society owns a series of core values that need to be marketed to the public. Idea marketing is most commonly found in public service advertising. The government tries to cultivate better social mood by telling people to stop spitting, stop littering, helping the eldly, and loving family.

理念。每个社会都有自己的一套核心价值观需要推销给公众。理念营销在公益广告中最常见，政府努力培养更好的社会风气，告诉人们不要随地吐痰、不要随地乱扔垃圾、帮助老人、关爱家人。

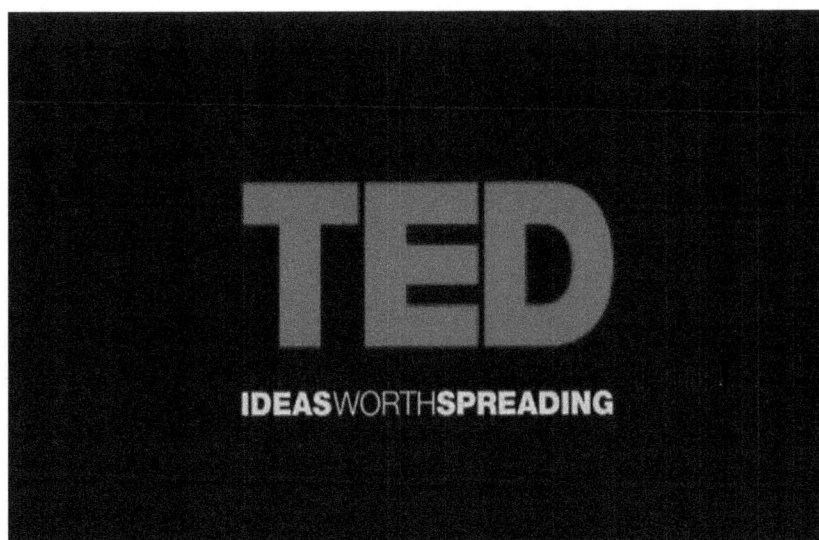

TED 向人们传播关于科技、娱乐和设计的具有价值的理念

◎ **阅读推荐**

郭国庆，贾淼磊 . 营销思想史 [M]. 北京：中国人民大学出版社，2012.

李飞 . 中国营销学史 [M]. 北京：经济科学出版社，2013.

菲利普·科特勒，加里·阿姆斯特朗 . 市场营销：原理与实践 [M]. 楼尊，译 . 北京：中国人民大学出版社，2015.

菲利普·科特勒 . 营销革命 3.0：从产品到顾客，再到人文精神 [M]. 毕崇毅，译 . 北京：机械工业出版社，2011.

菲利普·科特勒 . 营销十宗罪——如何避免企业营销的致命错误 [M]. 李桂华，译 . 北京：机械工业出版社，2014.

威廉·科恩 . 跟德鲁克学营销 [M]. 蒋宗福，译 . 北京：中信出版社，2014.

2

Market Planning

营销策划

2.1　Three Levels of Business Planning 商业计划的三个层面

Some companies are running without a formal plan. In other companies, managers may find it so time-consuming to carry out a plan that they would rather give it a go when ideas come up. Some managers believe they do not need a plan to get business done. There are others who consider that the ever-changing market will make all the plans laid aside and neglected in the end.

一些企业在经营的过程中没有正式的计划。另一些企业的管理者则认为拟订计划太耗时，因此有好点子出现的时候，他们宁可直接付诸实践而非做计划。

23

一些管理者认为他们不需要计划就能做成生意。还有一些人认为瞬息变换的市场会让计划搁置一旁，最终被遗忘。

As a matter of fact, there are so many good reasons to create a formal business plan that managers do not know about. A good business plan benefits all no matter it is big or small, a start-up or a well-established business. It urges managers to think from the whole picture of a company, to better implement and control. An updated business plan is useful for forecasting or raising additional capital for expansion, and if you decide to sell or close the business, the business plan can include strategies and timelines for the transfer to new ownership or dissolution of the company.

事实上，管理者并不了解做一项正式的商业计划是有充足的理由的。一个优秀的商业计划可使企业受益，不论它规模的大小，是初创企业或者是健全的大公司。计划能督促管理者对整个公司进行全盘考虑，更好地实践和控制。一个实时更新的商业计划有利于预测未来、增加资产以扩大规模。另外，如果你决定卖掉或者关闭公司，商业计划可以包含转型为新企业或解散公司的战略和时间线。

Business planning occurs in three levels: strategic level, functional level, and operational level.

商业计划从三个层面着手：战略层面、职能层面、业务层面。

2.1.1 Strategic Planning 战略规划

Strategic planning is the organizational management activity that matches the company's resources (such as its financial assets and workforce) and capabilities (the things it is able to do well because of its expertise and experience) to its market opportunities for long-term growth. It is set by top-level corporate management such as the CEO, chairman, and senior executives, to determine the company where to go for the next couple of years, how it will spend money and time, allocate human resources to achieve the goals, and how it will know whether the mission has been accomplished yet.

战略规划是为了企业长期发展而进行的将企业的资源（如金融资产和劳动力）和能力（能利用专业知识和经验办事的素质）与市场机会进行匹配的组织管理活动。战略规划由首席执行官、主席、高级主管等高层管理人员制定，目标是确定企业未来几年的发展方向、如何花费资金和时间、分配人力资源，以及如何衡量目标是否达成。

Strategic planning should be conducted when the organization is just started, or in the preparation of a new department or a product, and should be adjusted at least once on a yearly basis for the coming fiscal year.

战略规划应该在组织刚起步的时候就制定，或者出现在新部门或新产品的准备阶段，同时为下一财年的到来，至少需要一年调整一次。

2.1.2 Functional Planning 职能计划

A functional area refers to a strategic business unit (SBU) within an organization undertaking a distinguished external market task. Many companies based their structure on functional areas, where they build departments around those functions and assign employees according to their expertise. Companies with this structure are often deemed to have greater efficiency. Human resources department, financial department, marketing department, and customer service department are the functional areas most commonly seen in the business environment. Therefore, the planning made by marketing professionals in the functional area of marketing is called market planning.

职能区域是指组织内承担重要外部市场任务的战略业务单元（SBU）。许多公司的结构基于职能区域，他们围绕这些职能建立部门，并根据他们的专业知识分配员工。采用这种结构的公司通常效率较高。人力资源部、财务部、市场部、客服部是企业中最常见的职能部门。因此，由市场营销专业人员在市场营销的职能领域所做的计划就称为市场营销计划。

While strategic planning only lays out the guidelines and makes visionary decisions for an organization, functional planning turns it into more tangible, specific and practical tasks. A successful functional planning is indispensable that not a single business can be done without it, as it is a detailed plan for specific activities.

Information in each functional plan can contribute to the overall decision-making process. Financial plans indicate the quantity, type and timing of the inputs, which provides a reference for the company's cash flow budget. Human resource planning offers the data of how many labors are available throughout the year, helping the company manage the human capital in advance.

战略规划只是为组织制定指导方针并做出有远见的决定，而职能计划将其转化为更触手可及、更具体、更实际的任务。一个成功的职能计划是不可缺少的，因为它是针对特定活动的详细计划，没有它一个业务也做不成。每一个功能计划中的信息都可以对整个决策过程做出贡献。财务计划列明投入的数量、类型和时机，为公司的现金流预算提供参考。人力资源计划提供了全年可用劳动力的数据，帮助公司提前管理人力资本。

Functional planning is a mid-term planning carried out by middle management with the assistant of top management. Plans in each functional area are made to determine their goals and strategies respectively. Managers in a functional area must be informed what they should be doing at the functional level. Objectives should not be too big or too small, and the assessment is to be made to measure the goal setting and its achievement, assuring each functional planning serves the corporation's top mission.

职能计划是中层管理者在高层管理者的协助下进行的中期规划。每个职能区域的计划都是为了确定各自的目标和战略而制订的。职能部门的经理必须被告知他们在该岗位级别上应该做什么。另外，制定的目标不应该太大或太小，并且需要相应的评估机制，确保每个职能计划都服务于公司的最高使命。

2.1.3 Operational Planning 业务计划

Operational planning is created by low-level first-line management, such as sales managers, marketing communication managers, marketing research managers. It presents highly-detailed information to direct people to accomplish day-to-day activities. The operational plan provides what tasks must be undertaken, who are responsible of each task, when the task must be completed, and how much resources to be allocated for the task. For example, the strategic plan for a convenient store company may require longer working hours in the next month for an expected sales growth, the operational plan tells which particular shop assistant will be responsible for which branch on each different day, how much longer they will be working additionally and how much more will they be paid. To sum up, it is the implementation and control of strategies that developed in the higher level plans.

业务计划是由底层的一线管理人员制订的，如销售经理、市场传播经理、市场调研经理等。业务计划会提供非常详细的信息来指导人们完成日常活动。这种可操作计划提出必须执行的任务、每个任务的负责人、必须完成任务的时间及为任务分配多少资源。例如，在便利店的战略规划中，可能要求员工延长工作时间，来实现下个月的销售增长预期，而业务计划则要告诉具体的店员，他将在哪一天负责哪一个分店，将额外工作多长时间、会多收到多少工资。综上所述，业务计划是为了具体执行和控制那些更高层计划中所布置的战略任务。

Just like the functional planning provides data information for the strategic planning, operational planning track and collect data such as number of new customers, sales calls per month, customer turnover and customer loyalty, for the use of planning at higher levels. Although all the operational plans are developed under the instruction of the strategic and functional planning, and managers know what to achieve in the operational level, each separate part of the company creates its own operational plans for its own purpose. Operational planning covers a shorter period, and measurement of its success is a regular work for employees. Management and staff from a certain single area of the business refer to operational planning in carrying out their daily work.

就像职能计划为战略规划提供数据信息一样，业务计划跟踪和收集新客户数量、每月销售电话数、客户流失率、客户忠诚度等数据，供更高层次的规划使用。虽然所有的业务计划都是在战略规划和职能计划的指导下制订的——这样管理者就知道在业务层面上要达到什么目标——但是公司的每个独立部门都为各自的目标制订了自己的业务计划。业务计划在较短的时间内执行，衡量业务计划的目标是否达成是员工的一项常规工作。某一业务领域的管理人员和工作人员在开展日常工作时，通常以业务计划为指导。

The complete operational planning contains the follows:

完整的业务计划包括以下方面：

- Clear purpose 清晰的目标
- Activities to be delivered 要执行的活动
- Desired outcomes 预期成果
- Staffing and resources requirements 所需人手及资源
- Timeline for implementation 计划执行的时间表
- Quality and quantity standards 质量和数量标准
- Measurement and control process 测控过程

Operational planning can be divided into two forms, single-use planning and standing planning. As the name suggests, single-use planning is carried out a course of action that is expected to appear only once. For example, when a company decide to serve as sponsor in a particular event, it needs single-use planning to make sure the promotion activity goes well. Standing planning is adopted repeatedly for the recurring problems within a company. The policies for employee interaction and procedures of reporting internal issues are typically of this type.

业务计划可以分为两种形式，即单一目标计划和长设计划。顾名思义，单一目标计划是指执行预期只出现一次的操作。例如，当一家公司决定作为某一特定活动的赞助商时，它需要一个单一目标计划来确保促销活动顺利进行。而对于公司内部反复出现的问题，要反复采用长设计划。员工之间互动交流的政策、公司内部问题的汇报流程通常是这种类型的。

2.2 The Complete Marketing Planning 完整的营销计划

Marketing planning is vital to business success as it is at the core among the overall company. It helps focus the mind of a company on what is going to attain and how to achieve the goal. The steps of a making a marketing plan are logically similar to the steps at strategic level. Marketing plan derives from strategic plan, so they share the same sense of value in running the business. The greatest difference between them lies in that marketing professionals only focus on the issues in relation to a company's marketing mix-marketing tools with a combination of product, price, promotion, and place (physical distribution), to influence consumers to purchase. Marketing planning explains how to achieve goals with a series of marketing efforts. It considers the value creation as a priority, so all the productions and activities should be designed to assure that marketing elements are working together so that customers can identify the value in purchasing the product and service.

营销计划对商业成功来说至关重要，因为它是整个公司的核心。它帮助公司将注意力集中在将要实现的目标及如何实现目标上。制订营销计划的步骤在逻辑上与战略层面的规划步骤相似。营销计划来源于战略规划，所以它们在经营企业的过程中有着共同的价值观。两者最大的区别在于，营销专业人士只关注与公司营销组合相关的问题，即结合产品、价格、促销和地点（实物分销）的营销手段，来影响消费者购买。营销计划解释了如何通过一系列的市场努力来达成目标。它将价值创造作为优先项，因此所有的生产和活动都应该做好相应的设计，确保营销元素协同工作，以便客户在购买产品和服务时能够识别这些价值。

When we write a formal market planning report, we include the introduction, the research methods, and the outcome in the content, such as executive summary, market analysis, SWOT analysis, objectives, marketing research, strategies, implementation, budget and control, to make it readable. No matter how we classify and present everything in the end, the process contains the following work to accomplish in order to carry out a complete report.

在撰写正式的营销计划报告时，我们会在内容中加入引言、研究方法和结果，如执行摘要、市场分析、SWOT 分析、目标、市场调研、战略、执行、预算和控制等，使其具有可读性。无论我们最终如何分类和呈现每项内容，完成一份完整的报告的过程都包含了以下工作。

2.2.1 Situational Analysis 环境分析

First and foremost, before marketers know which direction to go next, they must get a full understanding of the current macro- and micro-environment in which the planning will take place, so that the planning will be in consistent with the real-time market condition. We apply SWOT analysis and PEST analysis to perform the internal and external environment analysis.

首先，在营销人员知道下一步的发展方向之前，他们必须充分了解当前的宏观和微观环境，这样计划才会符合实时的市场情况。在这个部分，我们运用 SWOT 分析和 PEST 分析进行内外部环境分析。

1. The Internal Environment 内部环境

The internal environment consists of elements that are within a company's control, such as the quality of products and services, physical facilities, technologies, people, financial stability, and corporate culture. There are a number of strengths and weaknesses lie in the internal business environment, and it is marketers' responsibility to take them objectively. When we discuss all the factors within a company that govern the way the employees think, feel, and behave so as to influence a company's transactions and performances—a set of implicit values, codes, spirits, beliefs, and practices passed down to staff at each level—they constitute a company's corporate culture.

内部环境由公司可控范围内的元素组成，如产品和服务的质量、物理设施、技术、人员、财务稳定性和企业文化。企业内部的商业环境有很多优势和劣势，营销人员有责任客观地看待它们。当提到公司里主导员工的思维方式、感觉和行为，从而影响公司的交易和业绩的所有因素——这一系列隐含的价值观、准则、精神、信仰和实践能够传达到每个级别的员工，它们就是一家公司的企业文化。

A fine corporate culture is not some standards determined by a particular powerful person as a senior manager, although they often try to, or some sentences written in the mission statement, it is developed by the interaction between top management and the unseen rules and custom arising from the working groups.

优良的企业文化不是由像高级经理这样强势的人物独自制定的（虽然他们经常做这种尝试），也不是一些写在使命宣言里的句子，而是在工作中，由高层管理人员从工作群中与看不见的规则和惯例之间的相互作用而逐渐演化成型的。

Strong and vigorous corporate culture where employees have quick responses to stimulus and high motivation, is vital enough to influence a company's productivity, profitability, and growth rates. It forms a company's differential strengths among competitors and creates its long-term survival. Amazon's corporate culture pushes employees to go beyond traditional limits and conventions to develop bright ideas and solutions. With an intense cutthroat workplace culture, Amazon's senior managers encourage their reports to attack one another's ideas in meetings; workers suffering from cancer or miscarriages are pushed out and many employees resort to crying at their desks. The best performer in 2016 amongst Apple, Google/Alphabet, Facebook, Netflix, and Amazon has been Amazon with an outstanding yearly return of 13.2%.

强大而充满活力的企业文化——员工对激励措施反应迅速、积极性高——对企业的生产率、盈利能力和增长率至关重要。它形成了企业在竞争对手之间的差异化优势，造就了企业的长期生存能力。亚马逊的企业文化促使员工超越传统的限制和惯例，开发出奇思妙想和解决方案。在竞争激烈的职场中，亚马逊的高级经理们鼓励他们的下属在会议上互相攻击对方的想法，患有癌症或经历流产的员工被淘汰，许多员工可能坐在办公桌前哭泣。2016年，在苹果、谷歌、脸书、网飞和亚马逊这五家公司中，亚马逊的业绩一直遥遥领先，年回报率高达 13.2%。

This type of risk-taking culture is important to marketing function for a company constantly needs to take some risks for improving the quality of their products and services. What marketers do is never the same every day, the consumers they are contacting, the partners they are working with, and the activities they are conducting can alter greatly from day to day. Unlike the jobs that require rigorous and disciplined workers, marketing departments are full of opportunities and challenges, thus a broader culture that encourages an open-minded, creative thinking, and rich imagination is always inspiring to marketers.

这种冒险文化对于营销工作是很重要的，因为一个公司为了提高产品和服务的质量，需要不断地承担一些风险。营销人员每天的工作绝不是一成不变的，他们所接触的消费者、合作伙伴及他们所进行的活动每天都在发生着巨大的变化。与要求员工严格自律的工作不同，营销部门充满了机遇和挑战，因此，一种鼓励开放思维、创造性想法和丰富想象力的更开放的文化，总是能够激励营销人员。

2. The External Environment 外部环境

The external environment consists of a set of more indirect uncontrollable factors that have impact on the company's position and its performances. PEST analysis is a commonly used tool for mapping the external environment.

外部环境由一系列间接的不可控因素组成，这些不可控因素影响着公司的定位和市场表现。PEST 分析是描绘外部环境的常用工具。

The political and legal environment. The political framework comprises the overall government policy system created in relation to business, whereas the legal framework refers to all laws and legal regulations, such as commercial law regime of taxes, labor law, environmental law.

政治和法律环境。政治框架包括与商业相关的整体政府政策体系，而法律框架则是指一切法律法规，如税法、劳动法、环境法等。

Political and legal issues are the macro environment that need to be stable, for they affect a company's ability to be profitable and successful. Political instability can be disastrous, yet it is complicated as well as unpredictable. For example, some Chinese factories in Africa are built for the aid program, however, the workers are from time to time risking their lives in being harmed or even killed by the armed conflicts, and the factories are on a high risk of destruction. Subsidies in this case can be a good decision for the employees working overseas. In addition, companies should also consider their local power structure, and discuss how anticipated shifts in power could affect their business.

政治和法律问题是需要稳定的宏观环境，因为它们影响公司的盈利和成功。政治不稳定可能是灾难性的，但它既复杂又不可预测。例如，中国在非洲援建的工厂的工人们无时无刻不冒着生命危险，可能在武装冲突中受到伤害甚至死亡，工厂也面临着巨大的被毁坏的风险。在这种情况下，发放补贴对于在海外工作的员工来说是一个好政策。此外，企业还应考虑当地的权力结构，并讨论预期的权力转移将如何影响其业务。

Legal issues that must be considered include tax guidelines, copyright and property law enforcement, political stability, trade regulations, social and environmental policy, employment laws and safety regulations. Marketers in food or finance industry may face severe regulations, for food and finance are two critical aspects for people's livelihood. The exporters may pay particular attention on International Trade Laws and the interim rules aiming at some special industries. On the other hand, nowadays, with the strengthening of consumers' right-protection awareness, marketers can no longer ignore the law issues. Consumer Protection Laws ensures consumers rights and grants them with fair trade, and empowers consumers to fight against business fraud and unfair practices. Other legislations that apply to all industries is the unfair competition law and the antitrust law. Companies have to abide by the legal system, otherwise they will be punished for breaking the law.

必须考虑的法律问题包括税务准则、版权和财产执法、政治稳定、贸易法规、社会和环境政策、就业法律和安全法规。比如食品和金融行业的营销人员可能会面临严厉的监管，因为这是关乎民生的两个关键领域。出口商可能会特别注意针对某些特殊行业的国际贸易法和暂行规则。如今，随着消费者维权意识的增强，营销人员也不能再忽视法律问题。消费者权益保护法保障了消费者的权利，赋予了他们公平贸易的权利，使消费者能够打击商业欺诈和不公平行为。其他适用于所有行业的法律还有反不正当竞争法及反垄断类的法规。公司必须遵守法律制度，否则就会因违法受到惩罚。

The economic environment. There is an overall patter of change in the economy, which is called the business cycle, including periods of prosperity, recession, depression, and recovery, that affect consumer and business purchasing power. The economic environment examines how the economy affects a business in terms of taxation, government spending, general demands, interest rates, exchange rates, and global economic factors. In the condition of depression, which sees price of goods falls sharply, there is little demand because people literally have no money to spend, exporters face stagnation or severe decline in output. The most recent example is the situation in 2008 financial crisis. During the recovery when the prices for goods and services rise again, inflation occurs. The purchasing power of currency is falling, because the goods require more amount of money to purchase. The more money floods into the economy, the less the worth of bills is.

经济环境。 经济有一个整体的变化模式，称为商业周期，包括繁荣、衰退、萧条和复苏的时期，它影响消费者和企业的购买力。经济环境从税收、政府支出、社会总需求、利率、汇率和全球经济因素等方面考察经济对企业的影响。在商品价格大幅下跌的萧条时期，需求很少，因为人们实际上没有钱可花，出口商面临停滞或产出严重下降。最近的一个例子是 2008 年的金融危机。而在经济复苏期间，当商品和服务价格再次上涨时，就会发生通货膨胀。此时货币的购买力在下降，因为商品需要更多的钱来购买。流入经济体的资金越多，票据的价值就越低。

2020 年，新冠肺炎疫情暴发，旅游、餐饮、娱乐等行业遭到重创，全球正经历 90 年来最严重经济衰退

Marketers especially need to be careful about the business cycle, because it affects how much and what consumers purchase. During times of prosperity, people buy a good deal of commodities with great confidence, and suppliers maintain a high productivity. Due to the fast-growing economy, marketers are spending efforts in creating and promoting new products, to meet the consumers' booming demands. In times of recession, people simply buy less things, especially those products have price elastic demand. Companies who sell the type of product which has alternative inexpensive varieties, will soon be out of business. Those in the industry whose product demands barely fluctuate as the prices rise or fall, will survive better. People who sell diamonds and Apple iPhones can even grow their sales. Marketers who sell salt, tap water, bread, and rice may only see a slight reduction of the profit.

营销人员尤其需要小心商业周期，因为它会影响消费者购买的产品和数量。在繁荣时期，人们满怀信心地购买大量商品，供应商保持高生产率。由于经济的快速增长，营销人员正在努力创造和推广新产品，以满足消费者日益增长的需求。在经济衰退时期，人们就会少买东西，尤其是那些有价格弹性需求的产品。如果一个公司的产品有价格低廉的替代产品，那它很快就会倒闭。产品需求几乎不会随着价格的涨跌而波动的企业将生存得更好。销售钻石、苹果手机的人甚至可以增加销量。销售食盐、自来水、面包和大米的商人可能只会看到利润略有下降。

The sociocultural environment. Sociocultural environment refers to the dynamics of people's lifestyle, characteristics of individuals and groups and their behaviors, believes, values. It is the artificial structure formed by long-term human activities that can be contrasted with the natural environment. It analyzes the demographic and cultural aspects of the market. We will discuss the culture factors in later chapters on consumer behavior. Demographics provides the statistical study of the populations, such as the size, gender, age, marital status, religion, occupation, disposable income, educational background. The raw data cannot tell a story, so marketers should integrate all the data over a period to see the changes of potential customers' family structure, preferences, income levels, so as to figure out the future trends in the marketing area. Analyzing sociocultural environment helps marketers examine the consumers' needs and their motivations of buying, and more importantly, the attitude towards the products and the market trends.

社会文化环境。 社会文化环境是指人的生活方式、个体和群体的特征及其行为、信仰、价值观的动态变化，是人类长期活动形成的与自然环境相对照的人工结构。它从市场的人口和文化方面分析问题。我们将在后面关于消费者行为的章节中讨论文化因素。人口统计学提供人口的统计研究，如人口规模、性别、年龄、婚姻状况、宗教、职业、可支配收入、教育背景等。原始数据并不能说明问题，所以营销者应该整合一段时间内的所有数据，看一看潜在客户的家庭结构、偏好、收入水平的变化，从而判断出营销领域的未来趋势。分析社会文化环境有助于营销者了解消费者的需求和购买动机，更重要的是，了解他们对产品和市场趋势的态度。

The technological environment. It refers to the fast developing and advancing world of technology. A technological product is just something that man created using the application of knowledge to improve a person's life, environment or society. New technologies not only create new processes and procedures but also spur new industries. Equipments and ways of production that were not possible a couple of years back are the main stream now. The advanced technology, online shopping, bar coding and computer aided design are all improvements to the way companies do business and the customers facilitate their own life. The rising of artificial intelligence technology will take the place of a large amount of jobs that involve repetitive work in the late future. These developments can benefit customers as well as organizations manufacturing the products.

技术环境。 这是指快速发展和进步的技术世界。科技产品是人类利用知识的应用来改善个人生活、环境或社会而创造出来的东西。新技术不仅创造了新的生产过程和程序，还激发出了新的产业。几年前不可能的设备和生产方式现在已成为主流。先进的技术、网上购物、条码和计算机辅助设计都有助于企业经营方式的改进，也使客户方便了自己的生活。人工智能技术的兴起将会在不久的将来取代大量的重复性工作。这些发展可以使客户和生产产品的公司受益。

Unfortunately, sometimes organizations examine the external environment for the sake of it, not because they really understand how importance of bringing it to the strategic thinking. The external analysis does have some shortcomings. It only looks for what we know about the PEST and SWOT factors. Moreover, planners have to consider all the factors even if some of them are of little relevance. It is also hard to predict the future if the influencing factors are dynamic and shift abruptly. There are limitations in PEST and SWOT analyses, so experienced managers also analyze market competition, consumers, suppliers, employee unions, public opinions or demographic features, as long as they matter to the profitability.

遗憾的是，有时公司分析外部环境是为了分析而分析，而不是因为它们真正理解将外部环境分析引入战略思维中的重要性。外部分析确实存在一些不足。它只对 PEST 和 SWOT 里提到的因素进行考察。此外，规划人员必须一一考虑所有的因素，即使其中一些因素看似无关紧要。如果影响因素是动态的、突变的，则很难预测未来。PEST 和 SWOT 分析是有局限性的，所以经验丰富的管理者还会分析市场竞争、消费者、供应商、员工工会、舆论或人口特征，只要与盈利能力有关。

2.2.2 Setting Objectives 设定目标

Marketing objectives support the overall company's goals. Objectives establish priorities for marketing resources and efforts, provide incentives for marketing team and a measure of success or failure. Marketing objectives deal with all the market-related elements, including increasing sales, building brand awareness, growing market share, launching new products or services, targeting new customers, entering new markets internationally or locally, improving shareholder relations, and enhancing customer relationships, according to the position a company is currently in.

营销目标支持整个公司的目标。营销目标为营销资源和活动确定优先顺序，激励营销团队，并提供衡量成功或失败的标准。市场目标涉及所有与市场相关的元素，包括根据公司目前的定位来提升销量、建立品牌知名度、增加市场份额、发布新产品或服务、聚焦新客户、进入国际或本地的新市场、改善股东关系、增强客户关系。

Effective objectives meet the SMART criteria. Specific means objectives must be detailed exactly what needs to be done. Measurable requires achievement and progress can be quantified. Achievable means objectives should not be too high or too low, and is accepted by those responsible for achieving it. Realistic means there are sufficient human, physical, and financial resources. Time-bounded requires time period for each task is clearly stated. Any objective that is inconsistent with the criteria may lead to failure and is to be revised.

有效的目标符合 SMART 准则。具体的意思是必须详细说明目标，以及需要做什么。可以衡量的标准要求成就和进步是可以量化的。可以达到的意思是目标不应该太高或太低，并被那些负责实现它的人所接受。相关的意味着有足够的人力、物力和财力。截止期限要求对每个任务的时间段进行明确说明。任何与 SMART 准则不符的目标都可能导致失败，必须加以修订。

2.2.3 Marketing Strategies 营销策略

Marketing is all about creating value and building profitable customer relationship. Thus, marketing strategies are brought out to solve two key questions: Which customers will we serve (segmentation and targeting)? How will we create value for them (positioning)? To answer the two questions, marketers carefully develop the 4Ps marketing mix (product, price, promotion, and place).

营销就是创造价值，建立有利可图的客户关系。因此，人们提出营销策略是为了解决两个关键问题：我们将服务哪些客户（细分和聚焦）？我们将如何为他们创造价值（定位）？为了回答这两个问题，营销人员精心制定了 4Ps 营销组合（产品、价格、促销、地点）。

1. Market Segmentation 市场细分

Marketing segmentation is dividing a broad market into subgroups of customers according to some shared characteristics, in terms of geographic, demographic, psychographic, and behavioral factors. Customers in each subgroup have similar types of preferences, common needs and wants, shared lifestyles or the same demographic profiles. In doing so, marketers can evaluate and select the most potentially profitable segments to be their target audience, so as to concentrate their efforts on the marketing mix that designed for each particular group, instead of putting all their energy in the boundless market.

市场细分是根据一些共同的特征，如地理、人口、心理和行为因素，将一个广阔的市场划分为若干消费者群。每个消费者群中的客户具有类似的偏好类型、共同的需求和渴望、共享的生活方式或相同的人口统计特征。这样做，营销人员可以评估和选择最有潜在利润的细分市场作为他们的目标，从而将他们的精力集中在为每个特定群体设计的营销组合上，而不是将他们的全部精力投入无限的市场中。

How to segment the market depends on the business a company is doing. One basis of segmentation may be suitable for a certain type of business but is useless for another. Juice company may segment market into fashionable young women who pursue personality, health, and energy, plus others who do not appear these characteristics. McDonald segments market according to local people's lifestyle, and determines that leisure type and convenient type persons to be its potential customers. Miller brewing company divides the customers into light beer drinkers and heavy beer drinkers, and creates marketing strategies to attract the latter who consume the amount of beer eight times of the former. Cosmetic company L'Oreal creates its products of high-end and low-end based on customers' skin colors, incomes, and ages. However, if a company producing milk divides consumers by their income or gender, it usually makes little difference. All in all, segmentation requires a deep study of the market.

如何细分市场取决于公司所做的业务。细分的标准可能适用于某一类型的业务，但对另一种业务则毫无用处。果汁公司可能会将市场细分为追求个性、健康和活力的时尚年轻女性和不具备这些特征的人。麦当劳根据当地人的生活方式细分市场，确定将休闲型和追求方便型人群列为其潜在客户。米勒酿酒公司将顾客分为轻度啤酒饮用者和重度啤酒饮用者，并制定营销策略来吸引后者，后者的啤酒消费量是前者的 8 倍。欧莱雅化妆品公司根据顾客的肤色、收入和年龄，分别推出了高端和低端的产品。然而，如果一家生产牛奶的公司用收入或性别来划分消费者，通常不会产生什么差别。总之，细分需要对市场进行深入的研究。

2. Market Targeting 目标市场选择

Targeting refers to the process of evaluating the segments' attractiveness and choosing the best one or more as the target. The target market consists of consumers a company wants to satisfy, or for whom the marketing strategies are designed.

目标市场选择是指对细分市场的吸引力进行评估，并从中选择最优的一个或多个作为目标的过程。目标市场包括公司想要满足的消费者，或者说是公司设计的营销策略所针对的对象。

A company with a single product may see the market as a whole, or choose a small segment to serve. If a company provides drinks or basic foods, it may place its products wherever customers can reach. Coca-Cola has been producing coke in one flavor and one package with its only secret formula for almost 100 years, meeting the needs of 156 nations and regions worldwide. To make a universally recognized product with the lowest cost, it has to be unique in some of its features, otherwise it will be substituted easily.

拥有单一产品的公司可以将市场视为一个整体，或者选择服务于一小部分细分市场。如果一个公司的产品是饮料或主食，它可以把产品放在顾客触手可及的任何地方。近 100 年来，可口可乐一直在用其唯一的秘方生产同一种口味、同一种包装的可口可乐，满足了全球 156 个国家和地区的需求。如果要以最低的成本制造出举世公认的产品，它必须在某些方面具有独特性，否则就很容易被替代。

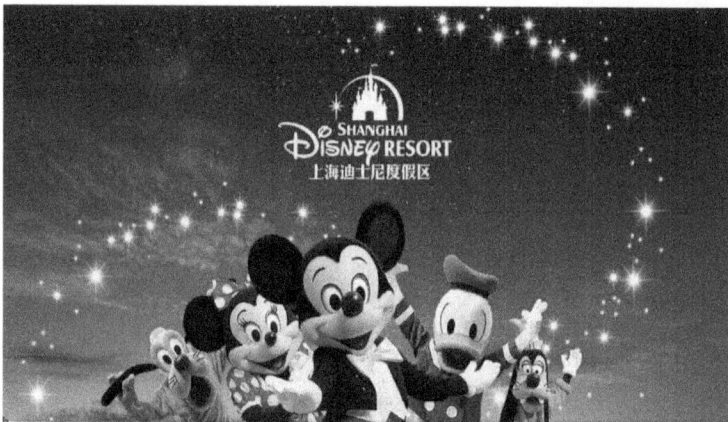

半个世纪以来，迪士尼走出美国本土，走向东京、巴黎、香港、上海

More ambitious companies select several similar segments to enter. Ningbo PeaceBird Fashion Co., Ltd is a clothing retailer. It implements a multi-brand portfolio strategy with many brands, including PeaceBird Women, PeaceBird Men, LED'IN, Material Girl, Amazing Peace, and Mini Peace. These brands are tailored for differentiated market segments and complementing each other in terms of target customers, brand positioning, and style, satisfying customers' increasingly diversified needs.

更有野心的公司会选择进军几个类似的细分市场。宁波太平鸟服饰有限公司是一家服装零售企业。公司实施梯度品牌发展战略，拥有太平鸟女装、太平鸟男装、乐町女装、"物质女孩"女装、Amazing Peace 男装、Mini Peace 童装等多个品牌。各品牌针对差异化的细分市场，在目标消费群、品牌定位及产品设计等方面相互补充，满足日益细分的消费群体日益变化的多元需求。

Other small start-ups only pick a small section to give it a try. Once it proves successful, the company seeks to enter more segments. Procter & Gamble Co. was a manufacturer specialized in making soaps. Later on, due to its excellent management it developed into producing personal care and hygienic products, and even snacks and beverages.

其他小型初创公司只挑选一小部分市场进行尝试。一旦成功，公司就会寻求进入更多的细分市场。宝洁公司以前是一家专业生产肥皂的生产商。后来，由于其优秀的管理，它将生产领域扩展到个人护理和卫生用品，甚至零食和饮料。

3. Market Positioning 市场定位

Positioning is a strategy that makes a product or brand occupy a distinctive place, relative to competing brands, in target consumers' minds. In a word, positioning is how people think of you. It is the image a company wants to portray to the public. The impression of a product or a brand in one's mind is hard to create, and it is so stable that it can hardly be changed as well. As one positioning expert says, positioning is "why a shopper will pay a little more for your brand". Positioning creates a reason for customers to purchase from you, not competitors.

定位是一种使产品或品牌相对于竞争品牌在目标消费者心目中占有独特地位的策略。总之，定位就是人们对你的看法，是一家公司希望向公众展示的形象。一个产品或一个品牌在一个人的脑海里的印象是很难塑造的，它会很稳定，很难改变。正如一位定位专家所说，定位就是"为什么消费者会为你的品牌多花点钱"。定位为客户提供了一个购买你的产品的理由，而不是竞争对手的。

Either the way the product designed or the way how marketers communicate value to consumers is of equal importance. Marketers must find or create distinguished characteristics in the product, then find a proper way to express so that the target audience can accept and remember. It is challenging for marketers to differentiate their products, which means to make it special and more valuable in some ways than others. Wal-mart says it saves your money, MasterCard promises "priceless" experiences, Subway offers fresh food, and Pepsi claims to be the choice of a new generation. A company may face hardship in establishing successful positioning, because how people think of you is not simply decided by you. Moreover, a company may have several different types of users for its product. In that case, marketers need to vary the messaging channels accordingly based on the audience. In positioning, each marketing project and activity must support the image the company intends to set up.

无论是产品设计的方式，还是营销人员向消费者传达价值的方式，都同样重要。营销人员必须在产品中找到或创造出与众不同的特点，然后找到合适的表达方式，使目标受众能够接受和记住。对营销人员来说，使其产品区别于其他竞品是一项艰巨的任务，这意味着要使自己的产品在某些方面比其他产品更特别、更有价值。沃尔玛说它可以为消费者省钱，万事达卡承诺"无价"的体验，赛百味提供新鲜食品，百事可乐声称它是新一代的选择。一个公司在建立成功的定位时可能会遇到困难，因为人们对你的看法不是简单地由你决定的。此外，一个公司的产品可能有几种不同类型的用户。在这种情况下，营销人员需要根据受众相应地改变消息传递的渠道。在定位上，每一个营销项目和活动都必须支撑公司想要树立的形象。

4. Developing Marketing Mix 制定有效的营销策略

All the four strategies of the marketing mix interact with each other. If they are handled right, they can lead to a great success. The marketing mix needs a lot of marketing research and consultation with several people, from users to trade to manufacturing and several others.

营销组合的四种策略都是相互作用的。如果处理得当，它们可以带来巨大的成功。这个营销组合需要很多的市场调研和咨询，从用户到经销商、制造商，以及其他方面。

Product strategies. Marketing activities cannot keep going without something to sell. A product can be either a tangible good or an intangible service or a mix of good and service, that fulfills a need or want of consumers. For product strategies, marketers ask what needs does the product satisfy? What features does it have to meet those needs? What size, color, should it be? What is it called? How is it branded? How is it different from competition? It is imperative to have a clear grasp of these questions and make a full understanding of what your product is, before successful marketing.

产品策略。没有产品可卖，营销活动就无法执行。产品可以是有形的商品，可以是无形的服务，也可以是商品和服务的组合，来满足消费者的需要。对于产品策略，营销者会问：产品满足了消费者的什么需求？它具备什么功能来满足这些需求？它应该是什么尺寸、什么颜色？它叫什么？它会贴上怎样的标签？它和竞品有什么不同？在成功营销之前，必须清楚地把握这些问题，充分了解你的产品是什么。

Price strategies. Price is the money a customer pays in order to obtain a product. In the 4Ps, pricing determination is the critical factor that affects supplies, demands, and profits. Price should not be set too low or too high, even though marketers try to sell their products at the highest price possible. A fair price reflects the true value in the product that can be delivered. As the value perceived by consumers not only comes from product function, but also the energy saved, personal feeling etc., which is impossible to measure precisely, so even the same product may be priced differently to different types of consumers. All the cost will be charged to wholesalers and retailers and finally to consumers through price.

价格策略。价格是顾客为了得到某种产品而支付的钱。在 4Ps 中，定价是影响供给、需求和利润的关键因素。价格不应该定得太低或太高，即使营销人员会试图以尽可能高的价格销售他们的产品。公平的价格反映了可交付的产品的真实价值。由于消费者感知到的价值不仅来自产品的功能，还来自方便地购买该产品所节约的精力及个人的感受等，这些都是无法精确衡量的。所以即使是同一种产品，针对不同类型的消费者也可能会采取不同的定价策略。所有的成本都将通过价格由批发商和零售商承担，最终转嫁给消费者。

Promotion strategies. Promotion is how marketers effectively send the product messages such as its features and benefits to the target market. There are lots of promotion tools can be used. Whether marketers use online advertising, TV ads, direct marketing mailshots, personal selling or establish public relations through press reports, depends on the type of audience they are targeting. Marketers also consider the best season and timing to ensure the greatest efficiency of the promotions.

促销策略。促销是营销者如何有效地向目标市场传递产品信息，如产品的特点和好处。有很多促销工具可以使用。市场营销人员是使用网络广告、电视广告、直接营销邮件、个人销售，还是通过媒体报道建立公共关系，这取决于他们的目标受众类型。营销人员还会考虑最佳的季节和时间，以确保最高的促销效率。

Place strategies. Place strategies are the activities of putting the product when and where is available for consumers. Place strategies aim at making the product or service in the right location for consumers to find and purchase easily. In developing place strategies, marketers need to know where exactly their target audiences are looking for the products, from a convenient store or in a supermarket, through online or offline, from wholesalers or retailers. Concentrated industry also affects where marketers place the product or service, for it attracts the same types of consumers and allows them to shop around and compare.

渠道策略。渠道策略是指将产品放置在消费者可以使用的时间和地点的活动。渠道策略的目标是将产品或服务放在合适的位置，让消费者更容易找到和购买。在制定渠道策略时，营销人员需要准确地知道他们的目标受众在哪里寻找产品，是去便利店还是去超市，在线上还是在线下，是找批发商还是零售商。产业聚集也会影响到营销人员将产品或服务放置在哪里，因为它会吸引相同类型的消费者，并让他们就近购物和货比三家。

2.2.4　Administrator 执行和控制

Once a thorough and comprehensive marketing plan is done, it is time to bring it into action. Implementation means execution, or the actual steps the company will take to promote its business. These steps may include running ads, launching a website or sending direct mails. If the implementation isn't completed according to plan, the company won't achieve its strategic objectives. It is said that marketing without implementation is like trying to score profits without taking the necessary shots. Marketers should remember a fact that most of brilliant plans fail without full implementation.

一旦一个周密的、全面的营销计划制定好了，就是时候将它付诸行动了。执行意味着贯彻实施，即公司将采取的实际步骤来推进其业务。这些步骤可能包括投放广告、建立网站或发送直接邮寄广告。如果营销方案没有按计划完成，公司就无法实现战略目标。有人说，没有执行的营销计划如同企图不劳而获。营销人员应该记住这样一个事实：大多数出色的计划都因为没有充分执行而失败了。

The process of implementation has to be controlled. The annual plan, profitability, and efficiency are under monitoring for the effective control can lower the cost of implementation. Benchmarks of sales volume, market share, stock rotation etc. are set to evaluate how well the marketing group accomplish their goals. Gaps between the planned and the actual results are constantly tracked. Marketers usually set an accountability system, to monitor the specific responsibilities for the specific tasks related to each and every marketing plan component. For example, who updates the website, who contacts with the consumers, and when will each stage complete?

This kind of following up and checking completion and due dates is a daily business routine if marketers want the marketing efforts to be effective.

执行的过程必须加以控制。年度计划、盈利能力、效率都应该被监控，因为有效控制可以降低执行成本。设定销量、市场占有率、股票周转率等指标，可以用来评估营销团队完成目标的情况。有效控制还应不断地跟踪记录计划和实际结果之间的差距。营销者通常会设立一个问责制，对与每个营销计划组成部分相关的具体任务的具体职责进行监控。例如，谁更新网站，谁与消费者联系，每个阶段什么时候完成。如果营销人员希望营销工作有效，这种跟踪检查完成情况和到期日的做法是一种常规工作。

◎ **阅读推荐**

吴晓波. 激荡三十年：中国企业 1978—2008（上）[M]. 北京：中信出版社，2014.

科特勒. 国家营销——创造国家财富的战略方法 [M]. 俞利军，译. 北京：华夏出版社，2001.

唐兴通. 引爆社群——移动互联网时代的新 4C 法则 [M]. 北京：机械工业出版社，2017.

埃尔文·E. 罗斯. 共享经济——市场设计及其应用 [M]. 傅帅雄，译. 北京：机械工业出版社，2015.

板砖大余，姜亚东. O2O 进化论——数据商业时代全景图 [M]. 北京：中信出版社，2014.

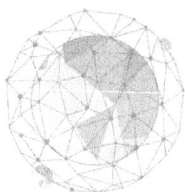

3

Marketing Research

营销调研

知识解锁 Knowledge Unlocked

以下问题的答案，可在本章寻找：

1. 理解营销信息系统在营销决策中所扮演的角色。
2. 描述营销调研的过程，以及数据搜集方法和抽样方法。
3. 了解问卷设计的注意事项。
4. 理解在线调研的广泛应用。

3.1 Marketing Information System 营销信息系统

Now we have talked about marketing is a management process that managers make important marketing decisions for a company to meet its long-term objectives. The marketing plan is developed for mapping and supporting those marketing decisions. Yet, how do marketers know what to analyze, which objectives to aim at, what strategies to take? Just as what we need to know for making decisions from which restaurant should be chosen for entertaining our friends, what to be given as a birthday gift to parents, which college to enter, which company to serve, in every process, we need information to back up our rational decisions. In fact, information comes from data. Data is the facts or statistics gathered by researchers. When the unorganized data is processed, transformed, and refined in a way that researchers can use, concerning a particular event or subject, it becomes information.

现在我们已经讨论了市场营销是一个管理过程，管理者为了实现公司的长期目标而做出重要的市场营销决策。制订营销计划是为了绘制和支持这些营销决策。然而，营销人员如何知道要分析什么内容、针对什么目标、采取什么策略？正如我们在做以下决策时所需要知道的一样——应该选择哪家餐馆招待朋友、选什么作为生日礼物送给父母、去哪所大学就读、服务于哪家公司——在营销的每一个过程中，我们需要信息来支持我们的理性决策。事实上，信息来源于数据，而数据是研究人员收集的事实或统计资料。当研究人员用相应的方式处理、转换和细化原本无序的数据（涉及特定事件或主题），这些数据就变成了信息。

Marketers do not make decisions off the top of their head, they have to integrate the information from various reliable sources, make sense of it, to deal with customer needs. Sometimes, information is available in public, but under more circumstances, marketers need to collect information by conducting researches. Accurate, up-to-date and relevant information is collected for their own particular use.

营销人员不会拍脑袋凭空做出决定，他们必须整合来自各种可靠来源的信息，弄明白这些信息的含义，以满足客户的需求。有时候，信息是公开的，但是在更多的情况下，营销者需要通过调研来收集信息。他们为了特定的目标来收集准确的、最新的和与研究问题相关的信息。

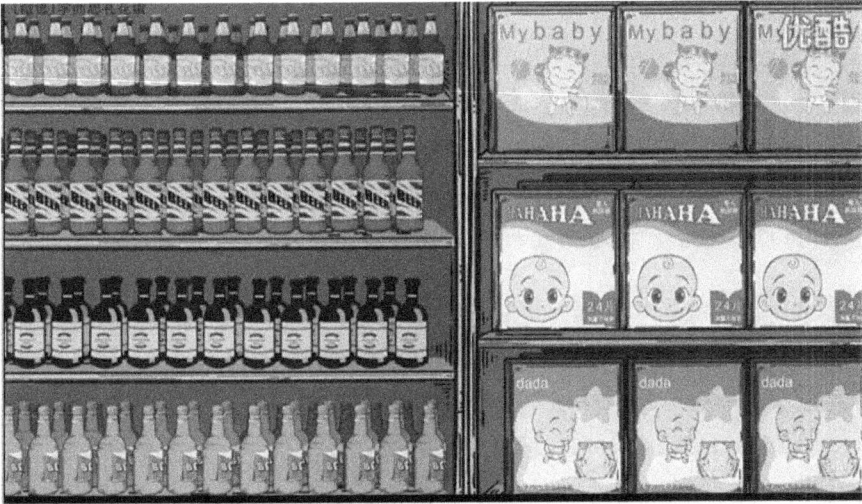

沃尔玛超市发现，年轻的父亲在购买尿布的同时，往往会顺便为自己购买啤酒，这样就会出现啤酒与尿布这两件看上去不相干的商品经常会出现在相邻货架上的现象

Marketing research can produce tons of information that has to be managed to ensures it has value to decision makers. To marketing professionals, marketing information system (MIS) is a significant tool to solve this problem. To Kotler, a marketing information system is a continuing and interacting structure that consists of people, equipment, and procedures to gather, sort, analyze, evaluate, and distribute needed, timely, and accurate information to marketing decision makers.

市场调查可以产生海量的信息，必须对这些信息加以管理，以确保它对决策者有价值。对于营销专家来说，营销信息系统（MIS）是解决这一问题的重要工具。科特勒认为，营销信息系统是一个持续的、相互作用的结构，它由人员、设备和流程组成，用于收集、分类、分析、评估并向营销决策者分发他们所需的及时的、准确的信息。

MIS is a software program that provides information about marketing research. The main functions of MIS lies in four aspects: (1) identify the type of information that marketing and advertising decision makers need; (2) collect data, and sort it for future access; (3) interpret the data and store the information; (4) distribute relevant data to managers who will use it for product or service promotion. It provides a company with rapid and incredible detail about buyer wants, preferences and behavior, allows users to process data in a very easy and organized approach, thus greatly improving the efficiency at work. A marketing information system includes three components: (1) the computer hardware and software needed to analyze data and generate reports; (2) the people who use it; (3) four types of data—identity data, descriptive data, quantitative data, and qualitative data.

营销信息系统是一个提供市场调研信息的软件程序。管理信息系统的主要功能有4个：（1）确定市场营销和广告决策者需要的信息类型；（2）收集数据并对其进行整理，以便将来访问；（3）解读数据并存储信息；（4）将相关数据分发给管理者，管理者将使用这些数据进行产品或服务推广。它为公司提供了关于买方需求、偏好和行为的快速和难以置信的细节，让用户以非常简单和有组织的方式处理数据，从而大大提高了工作效率。营销信息系统包括3个组成部分：（1）分析数据、生成报告所需的计算机软硬件；（2）使用数据的用户；（3）4类数据：身份数据、描述性数据、定量数据和定性数据。

Marketers collect data using different means. For example, when you scan your consumer loyalty card in a supermarket, or when a company rewards you with a gift for completing its questionnaire, you are leaving your personal data. They are used for analyzing your and other consumers' behavior and help companies with marketing promotion. As a matter of fact, for a company, customer information is as equal important as the money they pay for the product. The latter is for the current revenue, and the former is for expecting future profits.

营销人员使用不同的方法收集数据。例如，当你在超市扫描消费者会员卡时，或者当一家公司因为你完成问卷调查而奖励你一份礼物时，你的个人数据就被保存下来了。这些数据会用于分析包括你和其他消费者在内的消费者行为，并帮助企业进行市场推广。事实上，对于一个公司来说，客户的信息和他们为产品支付的钱一样重要。后者代表了当前的收入，前者则用于预计未来利润。

Sources for data are classified into four main categories: internal company data, marketing intelligence, marketing research, and acquired database.

数据来源主要分为四大类：公司内部数据、营销情报、营销调研和现有数据库。

1. Internal Company Data 公司内部数据

Internal company data is the information produced by the operation inside a company. It comes from any department within the company that carries information on customer transactions, demographics, psychographics, and buying behavior, to solve problems. For example, customer service department records customer satisfaction and service problems, accounting department prepares financial data on sales, costs, and cash flows, human resources department reviews workforce data to determine if the employee retention, tardiness and absentee rates signal that you are not keeping your workers happy. Internal data helps determine whether the strategies the company is currently using are successful or if shifts should be made.

公司内部数据是指公司内部的经营活动所产生的信息。它来自公司内部的任何一个部门，包含关于客户交易、人口统计、心理统计特征和购买行为的信息，可用以解决问题。例如，客户服务部记录客户满意度和服务问题，财务部准备有关销售、成本和现金流的财务数据，人力资源部审查员工数据，从员工留存率、迟到率和缺勤率等指标来查看员工是否满意。内部数据有助于判断公司目前使用的战略是否成功，或者是否应该进行调整。

By using the internal company data system, marketers know a customer's buying history, the shipping dates, inventory levels, production schedules, and they can easily access to exactly which customer buys what kind of products in what quantities and at what intervals. For example, Zara, the Spanish clothing and accessories retailer, gives each of its sales associates a customized personal digital assistant (PDA device) connected to the head office. As customers try on clothes, the Zara's staff asks them ongoing questions. Would you prefer this skirt in blue? What if the length was shorter? Immediately, the staff inputs the customer information into his PDAs. This data are collected from every Zara store, and are sent to the head office timely. The customers feedback helps determine what Zara's designers will create next. The easy-to-use device facilitates the internal communication on sales.

通过使用公司内部数据系统，营销人员可以了解客户的购买历史、发货日期、库存水平、生产计划，并且很容易查看到到底是哪个客户在什么时间、购买了什么产品、购买了多少。例如，西班牙的服装和配饰零售商 Zara 为每位销售伙伴提供了一款与总部相连的定制化个人数字助理（PDA）。顾客在试穿衣服时，Zara 的员工会不断地问他们问题：你喜欢这条蓝色的裙子吗？长度更短的话会喜欢吗？员工立即将客户反馈的信息输入他的 PDA。每一家 Zara 店铺都在收集这些数据，并及时发送到总部。顾客的反馈决定了 Zara 的设计师下一步要做什么。该设备使用方便，便于内部销售沟通。

As the concept of Web 2.0 was popularized in 2004, it represented a huge shift in the way digital information was managed. With more companies and workforces going global and the rise of social technology, people are working remotely more than ever before. Employees want access to information fast and they need it to accomplish tasks. Since then, intranets have become a valuable tool for employees and organizations. An intranet is a private network accessible only to an organization's staff that helps employees get stuff done and work better. It can be a website, communication channel or a collaboration platform. Sensitive internal business information, such as sales data, cost data, strategies, change of personnel, research results, is all confidential and for internal-use-only, and is restricted to be sent by internal devices such as USB flash disks, cell phones or laptops that are only accessible to the internal network. Today, organizations, no matter big or small, are using intranets to send internal emails, manage supply chain, manage purchase and storage, and maintain customer relationships.

2004 年，Web 2.0 概念的普及，标志着数字信息管理方式的巨大转变。随着越来越多的公司和劳动力在全球范围流动，以及社交技术的兴起，人们远程办公的情况比以往任何时候都要多。员工希望快速获取信息，因为他们需要信息来完成任务。从那时起，内网成了对员工和组织有利的工具。内网是只有组织的员工才能访问的私有网络，它帮助员工更好地完成工作。它可以是网站、沟通渠道或协作平台。敏感的内部业务信息，如销售数据、成本数据、策略、人员变动、研究成果等，均为机密，仅供内部使用，仅限于通过内网访问的优盘、手机或笔记本等内部设备发送。今天的组织，无论大小，都在使用内网发送内电子邮件、管理供应链、管理采购和库存、维护客户关系。

2. Marketing Intelligence 营销情报

Marketing intelligence is the everyday information relevant to a company's markets, gathered and analyzed specially for the purpose of accurate and confident decision-making in determining market opportunity, market penetration strategy, and market development metrics. This information can be external or internal. At its core, market intelligence uses multiple sources of information to create a broad picture of the company's existing market, customers, problems, competition, and growth potential for new products and services. Sources of raw data for that analysis include newspapers, trade publications, social media and surveys, among many others.

营销情报是与公司的市场相关的日常发展情况的信息，是为了准确、自信地做出决策而专门收集和分析的。这些决策包括确定市场机会、市场渗透策略和市场发展指标等。这些信息可以是外部的，也可以是内部的。营销情报的核心是利用多种信息来源，对公司现有的市场、客户、问题、竞争及新产品和服务的增长潜力进行全面了解。这种分析的原始数据来源包括报纸、贸易出版物、社交媒体和调查等。

Managers usually collect marketing intelligence data either by themselves or through various research or government agencies. If a company is small, it is easy to get started with a common-sense approach. For companies who want to determine how they are faring in certain markets, they may order secondary market research reports from companies like Nielsen or Forrester Research, who is professional in carrying out a research report in a relatively short time, and usually costs more. Government data is also easy to obtain. The population census is considered crucial through which population density, trends, demographic characteristics, etc. is determined, and the same can be used to make judicious market plans. Also, the data about the literacy level, agricultural production, inflation and recession, is provided by the government that acts as an important tool for information, and they can be useful to gather relevant information about the prevailing market trends.

　　管理者通常自己或通过各种研究或政府机构收集营销情报数据。如果公司规模很小，那么从常识性的方法入手营销情报数据会比较容易。对于那些想要确定自己在某些市场上表现如何的公司，他们可能会从尼尔森或弗雷斯特研究公司等调研公司订购二级市场研究报告，这些公司擅长在相对较短的时间内完成一份研究报告，通常成本更高。政府数据也很容易获得。人口普查被认为是描述人口密度、趋势、人口特征等指标的关键，它可以用来制订明智的市场计划。此外，关于识字率、农业生产、通货膨胀和经济衰退的数据是由政府提供的，这些数据是重要的信息工具，可以用来收集有关当前市场趋势的有关信息。

Marketing intelligence information can be gathered from customers as well. The most common and easy way to gain marketing intelligence is through the use of customer feedback system. Generally, it is online, where the customer is required to give his valuable feedback or suggestion on company's website about the product or service consumed by him. Also, the feedback can be taken in person by asking the customers to fill up a form after they have availed the services. This is a more reliable form of information since it is directly provided by the customer himself. In addition, it includes finding published information about the number and type of potential customers, and keeping up to date with developments in the particular area from magazines, journals or business associations, and checking for customer comments and feedback online that will help the business improve its offer or service.

　　营销情报信息也可以从客户那里收集。获取市场情报最常见、最简单的方法是使用客户反馈系统。一般来说，它是个在线系统，顾客需要在公司的网站上对自己所消费的产品或服务给出有价值的反馈或建议。此外，公司可以要求顾客在使用服务后当面填写一份表格，以获取反馈。这种信息更可靠，因为它是由客户自己直接提供的。此外，它还包括从已发布的信息中查找潜在客户数量和类型，并从杂志、期刊或商业协会了解特定领域的最新进展，查看客户的评论和在线反馈，以帮助企业改进其提供的产品及服务。

Some marketers gain intelligence from competitors and competitor's customers. By observing competitors, it can be as simple as visiting their competitors' websites or store, or buy and analyze competitor's products to study features, monitor their sales, check for new patents, and examine various types of physical evidence. For example, a company regularly checks out competitors' parking lots. Full lots indicates plenty of work and prosperity, and half-full lots might suggest hard times.

一些营销人员从竞争对手和竞争对手的客户那里获取情报。通过观察竞争对手——可以简单到访问竞争对手的网站或商店，或者购买和分析竞争对手的产品，研究其特点，监测其销售，查阅新专利，检验各种实物证据。例如，一家公司定期检查竞争对手的停车场。停车场满场意味着对手有大量的业务、经营繁荣，而停车场半满则意味着公司正遭遇艰难时期。

Nowadays, Internet is serving as a new source of intelligence information. Most companies now place their description of products and services in detail on their websites, to attract customers, investors, suppliers, and partners. On the other hand, this may attract competitors who may have greater power of producing and more extensive base of selling, thus exposing the company to a greater risk. For example, the ingenious design Stikbox is a smart phone case that has a built-in selfie stick, so that people can use it to easily take pictures without carrying around a separate selfie stick. The Stikbox selfie stick phone case was originally funded by a successful Kickstarter campaign where they raised over 50 thousand dollars for the case back in January of 2016. What's surprising is they are already for sale on Amazon, presumably someone has stolen their idea and came to market faster than them.

如今，互联网正成为一种新的情报信息来源。大多数公司现在都在网站上详细描述产品和服务，以吸引客户、投资者、供应商和合作伙伴。这可能会吸引生产能力更强、销售基础更广泛的竞争对手，从而使公司面临更大的风险。例如，设计巧妙的 Stikbox 是一款内置自拍杆的智能手机保护套，人们可以在不随身携带自拍杆的情况下轻松拍照。这款名为 Stikbox 的自拍杆手机保护套最初是由一个成功的 Kickstarter 创业者峰会赞助的，他们在 2016 年 1 月为这款保护套募集了 5 万多美元资金。令人惊讶的是，当时它们已经在亚马逊上有售了，想必是有人盗用了它们的创意，以比它们更快的速度进入市场。

Sometimes, companies engage in special activities for intelligence. They hire a specialist who visits several stores and showrooms to check the customer experience with the product or service. For example, retailer or a service provider send its own person as a "mystery guest" who acts as a customer himself and check the quality of a product to see how customers are treated by their employees. Usually, companies in fast-moving consumer goods industries use this approach for collecting information and assessing staff.

有时，公司会从事特殊的情报活动。他们会雇用一位专家，让他探访几家门店和展示厅，去观察顾客对产品或服务的体验。例如，零售商或服务提供商派出雇员作为"神秘客户"扮演消费者，来检查产品和服务的质量，了解员工如何对待客户。通常，快速消费品行业的公司使用这种方法来收集信息和评估员工工作。

By keeping marketers more focused, centering business goals on consumers, collecting relevant, real information about what works and what does not to pursue growth opportunities, just like other information, marketing intelligence reduces risk. Although marketing intelligence is an extremely important aspect of business success, it is just a beginning. The data has to be translated properly with other data in the MIS to create a complete and useful report for marketing managers.

营销情报让营销人员更加专注，将业务目标集中在消费者身上，收集相关的真实信息，了解哪些信息有效，哪些信息无法用于寻求增长机会，和其他信息一样，营销情报可以降低风险。尽管营销情报是商业成功的一个极其重要的方面，但它只是一个开始。营销情报数据必须与营销信息系统中的其他数据一起被正确地解读，才能为营销经理创建一个完整而有用的报告。

3. Marketing Research 营销调研

Marketing research refers to the systematic design, collection, analysis, and reporting of relevant data to specific marketing situation. Marketing research help marketers assess the market potential and market share, understand customer satisfaction and purchase behavior, and measure the effectiveness of marketing mix in pricing, product, distribution, and promotion activities. While marketing intelligence keeps alert of what happens every day in the marketplace, marketing research is conducted when unique information is needed to answers specific questions. Whether should we target older generations or the younger for a health care product? Should the product be promoted through online advertisement or join a sponsorship program? What is our competitors are doing about the new trend? Why our loyal customers are reducing in recent months? The more a company knows the exact answers for very specific questions, the bigger chance for it to succeed. There are mainly two types of marketing research reports included in the MIS that companies will read: syndicated research reports and custom research reports.

营销调研是指对具体的市场情况进行系统的数据设计、收集、分析和报告。营销调研帮助市场营销者评估市场潜力和市场份额，了解客户满意度和购买行为，并衡量市场营销组合在定价、产品、分销和促销活动中的有效性。营销情报对市场每天发生的事情保持警醒，而营销调研则需要提供特殊的信息来回答特定的问题。我们应该针对老年人还是年轻人来开发保健产品？产品应该通过网络广告推广还是加入赞助计划？面对这一新趋势我们的竞争对手做了什么？为什么我们的忠实客户在最近几个月减少了？一个公司对非常具体的问题知道的准确答案越多，它成功的机会就越大。企业将在 MIS 中阅读的营销研究报告主要有两种类型：联合研究报告和定制研究报告。

Syndicate means trade union formed by a group of large companies for shared common interests to strengthen their position in the market. The members of Syndicate enjoy special treatment, for Syndicate has the power of lowering the purchasing price of raw materials and raising the selling price, promoting unified operation. As the names suggests, Syndicated research is the research by firms that collect data on a regular basis and sell the reports to multiple companies to make a profit. Well-known syndicate research companies are Nielsen, Kantar, IMS Health, etc. They collect information in different industries covering housing, beverages, electronic appliances, medical industry, technology industry and so on, offering valuable insights in the field.

辛迪加是指由一群拥有共同利益的大公司组成的工会，以加强其在市场上的地位。辛迪加的成员享受特殊待遇，因为辛迪加具有降低原材料采购价格、提高销售价格、促进统一经营的能力。顾名思义，联合研究报告是指公司定期收集数据，并将报告出售给多家公司以获取利润的研究。著名的联合研究公司有尼尔森、康度、艾美仕等，它们收集了不同行业的信息，涵盖了住房、饮料、电器、医疗、科技等行业，在该领域提供了有价值的见解。

A syndicated research provider focuses solely on specific types of data such as scan data, surveys or product launch analysis and provides bigger picture and long-term strategic insights. A firm can specialize in research for one industry or may cover multiple industries. Many companies use syndicated information as a cost-effective way to gain a broad view of their product or service environment.

联合研究提供商只关注特定类型的数据，如扫描数据、调查或产品发布分析，并提供更大的图景和长期战略意见。一个公司可以专门研究一个行业，也可以研究多个行业。许多公司使用联合研究信息，作为获取产品或服务环境的广泛视角的一种高性价比的方式。

Benefits to working with a syndicated market research firm include: providing overview of the market, identifying general market trends, offering competitive intelligence, and measuring brand awareness. Syndicated research provides context on macro-level analysis which is broad but shallow. It gives a good description such as who is using the gymnasium this year, and gives prediction for how the future of the high-end liquor market lies.

与联合市场研究公司合作的好处包括：提供市场概况、识别一般市场趋势、提供竞争情报和衡量品牌知名度。联合研究提供了宏观层面分析的背景，这是广泛而浅显的。比如，它很好地描述了今年谁在使用这个体育馆，并预测了高端白酒市场的未来。

For example, Euromonitor International's Passport database provides syndicated research for 27 different industries in more than 80 countries globally. A soft drink company could purchase such a subscription report that covers all areas where their business may overlap, such as soft drinks, hot drinks, retailing and consumer foodservice, to see how well their competitors are doing and gain ideas on the most recent trends within the 80 countries researched. This information may help them develop a viable market entry strategy or decide which type of new products to introduce to a new market. It is very useful to this soft drink company, but because a syndicated research report is also available to all other buyers of the Passport database, it offers no more solution for any single company that needs deeper insights.

例如，欧睿信息咨询公司的 Passport 数据库为全球 80 多个国家的 27 个不同行业提供研究报告。一家软饮料公司可以购买这样一份涵盖可能有交集的所有领域的订阅报告，如软饮料、热饮、零售和消费食品服务，以了解所调查的80 个国家的竞争对手的经营情况，并了解在这些领域的最新趋势。这些信息可以帮助他们制定一个可行的市场进入策略，或者决定将哪种类型的新产品投入一个新的市场。这些信息对这家软饮料公司非常有用，但由于联合研究报告也可用于 Passport 数据库的所有其他买家，因此它无法为任何需要更深入了解的单个公司提供更多解决方案。

So if the information a business requires is unique to its own or is never asked before, when syndicated research is unable to provide the best insights, businesses may resort to custom research.

因此，如果企业所需要的信息是非常独特的，或者以前从未有公司要求过，当联合研究无法提供最佳的见解时，企业可能会求助于定制研究。

Custom research refers to customized research designed for a single company to provide tailored information its managers require. It is particularly helpful for companies who want to know why certain trends are unfolding. For example, a travel service company wants to obtain information about its competitors, particularly CITS (China International Travel Service) and CYTS (China Youth Travel Service), and the business also wants to look at their cooperation with the emerging market—homestay, to see if it is possible to attract young customers and increase sales for its brand. This type of information calls for a custom research. A benefit to working with a custom research firm is that a company can control the requirements for a project, ensuring that all results, data, and analysis fit its specific needs.

定制研究是指为单个公司设计的专项研究，以提供经理们所需要的特定信息。对于那些想知道目前市场趋势发展的公司来说，它尤其有帮助。例如，如果一家旅行社想要获得有关竞争对手的信息，特别是国旅（中国国际旅行社）和中青旅（中国青年旅行社）的信息，也想知道他们和"民宿"这一新兴市场能否进行合作，是否可以吸引年轻的顾客、增加销售自己的产品。这类信息需要从定制研究中获取。与定制研究公司合作的好处是，企业可以控制项目的需求，确保所有结果、数据和分析都符合其特定需求。

As the company develops, their strategies advance along with the way to obtain information. In more cases, they rely on both the syndicated research and custom research to address major hurdles within their strategies. Some companies even have their own in-house research department which conduct studies on its own behalf.

随着公司的发展，他们的策略随着获取信息的方式而不断更新。在更多的案例中，他们依靠联合研究和定制研究来解决他们的策略中的主要障碍。有些公司甚至有自己的内部研究部门，为本公司开展研究。

4. Acquired Database 现成数据库

A truly large amount of information is available in the form of database. Yearbooks, state statistics bureau database, and government database contain economic and demographic information on individuals, groups, and companies. Most of them provide data with no or little cost. Recently, some research companies begin to sell their social network information on social networks such as Facebook and MicroBlog, which can be expensive.

数据库的形式提供了大量的信息。像年鉴、国家统计局数据、政府部门的数据库，都包含了个人、群体和企业的经济和人口统计信息。其中的大多数数据在获取时没有成本或成本很低。最近，一些研究公司开始在脸书和微博等社交网络上销售他们的社交网络信息，这些信息一般价格较高。

Some companies are selling their customer database to non-competing companies. But improper use of acquired database can cause a series of problems.

Under normal circumstances, companies use the data for analyzing consumer market trends and product planning. Others use the data for outbound mailing and unsolicited phone calls, which has caused alarm in government. The American and Australia governments have introduced stricter policies such as anti-spam laws, and the Chinese government has organized an anti-spam association, in preventing and the abuse of customer information for marketing purpose. To protect our own privacy and to be free from sales calls and junk mails, now people have the choice of whether to give their personal information or not.

一些公司正在把他们的客户数据库卖给非竞争对手公司。但是，不恰当使用现成数据库会导致一系列的问题。在正常情况下，公司使用这些数据来分析消费者市场趋势和产品规划。然而有些人会将这些数据用于发送垃圾邮件、给客户拨打来路不明的电话等，这些行为已经引起了政府的警觉。美国和澳大利亚政府已经出台了愈发严格的政策法规，如反垃圾邮件法；中国政府成立了一个反垃圾邮件协会，从营销角度考虑，防止滥用客户信息。为了保护我们自己的隐私，远离电话推销和垃圾邮件，现在人们可以选择是否提供自己的个人信息。

3.2　Steps in the Marketing Research Process 营销调研步骤

Modern marketing research involves going outdoor being together with the consumers, or inviting clients to company to attend a survey, then collecting data, identifying problems. Marketing research is problem-solving oriented. It aims at identifying problems quickly and providing valuable advices for the company to carry out strategies to maintain or gain its market position. The market research process is a systematic methodology for informing business decisions. Whether hiring an outside research company for the research or conducting the research on its own, the process is the same as follows.

现代营销调研包括与消费者一起外出，或邀请客户到公司参加调查，然后收集数据，发现问题。营销调研是以解决问题为导向的。它的目的是快速发现问题，并为公司实施战略以保持现有市场或获得更大市场提供有价值的建议。营销调研过程是为商业决策提供信息的系统方法。无论是聘请外部研究公司进行研究，还是自己进行研究，过程都是一样的。营销调研步骤如下。

3.2.1　Define the Research Problem 定义研究问题

Defining the research problem is the most important step as it lays a foundation for the rest of the marketing research. It is why you want to do the research, what problems you are trying to figure out. Here, the problem does not necessarily mean something wrong, and it is simply the difficulty that is to be overcome, or the question relating to marketing that is waiting for an answer. Problem definition involves discussion with decision makers, interviews with industry experts, analyses of secondary data, and some qualitative research, such as focus groups interview.

确定研究问题是最重要的一步，因为它是开展营销调研的前提。研究问题包括：为什么你要做这项研究，你想发现什么问题。在这里，"问题"并不一定意味着出错，它单纯是指需要克服的困难，或者是与营销有关的有待解决的事项。这里所说的"问题"包括与决策者的讨论、与行业专家的访谈、对二手数据的分析，以及一些定性研究，如焦点小组访谈。

At this stage, researchers have three critical issues to determine:

在这个阶段，研究人员有 3 个关键问题需要确定：

（1）Specify the research objectives;

明确研究目标；

（2）Identify the consumer population of interest;

确定感兴趣的消费者群体；

（3）Place the problem in an environmental context.

在环境的背景下考虑问题。

3.2.2　Determine the Research Design 确定研究设计

1.Three Types of Research Method 3 种研究类型

（1）Exploratory research is a technique that marketers use to gather preliminary information that will help define the problem and suggest hypotheses. For example, a marketer has heard about social media marketing techniques which are employed by their competitors with great success, but he is not familiar with using these for his own products or services. Under this situation, exploratory research is the right tool employed to gain insights about the application of social media in marketing.

探索性研究是营销人员用来收集初步信息的一种技术，它将有助于发现问题并提出假设。例如，一个营销人员听说过他们的竞争对手成功使用的社交媒体营销技术，但是他不熟悉如何将这些技术用于自己的产品或服务。在这种情况下，探索性研究是洞察社会化媒体在营销中的应用的正确工具。

（2）Descriptive research describes marketing problems, situations, or markets, such as the market potential for a product or the demographics and attitudes of consumers. Sometimes people ask the question why. For example, why should I change the package of our product? The answer may be a new package appeals to more young customers who generate more revenue. But how do you know this is correct or not? Descriptive research only provides the description of the market phenomenon, and causal research sheds lights on cause-and-effect relationships between market variables.

描述性研究描述营销问题、情况或市场，如产品的市场潜力或消费者的人口统计特征和态度。有时人们会问"为什么"这类问题。例如，我为什么要改变我们产品的包装？答案可能是一个新的包装吸引了更多的年轻客户，他们创造了更多的收入。但是你怎么知道这是对的还是错的呢？描述性研究只提供对市场现象的描述，而因果关系研究则揭示了市场变量之间的因果关系。

（3）A causal research is more like a scientific experiment which test the relationships between different independent variables and the dependent variable—the outcome. Although it seems to be a technical job accomplished in the lab, it can be applied to the business setting. The process of doing causal research involves several controlled variables which are considered to be possible factors influencing the outcome. For example, when the manager of a call center asks the question "Why is the user satisfaction declining?", he thinks of some likely reasons, such as the poor quality of the new product, the longtime of response, the unpleasant attitude of the staff, the average improvement of the service in the industry. The aim of the causal research in this case is to test each of the variables to determine which one or ones contribute to the declining user satisfaction.

因果研究更像是一种科学实验，它检验了不同的自变量和"结果"这一因变量之间的关系。虽然它似乎是在实验室中完成的一项技术工作，但它可以应用于实际业务场景。因果研究的过程，由几个被认为可能影响结果的控制变量组成。例如，当呼叫中心的经理在寻找"为什么用户满意度在下降"这一现象可能的原因时，他认为，新产品的质量差、对客户的回应时间过长、员工态度差、服务行业整体水平等可能是其影响因素。在此例中，因果研究的目的是找出哪个或哪些变量是造成用户满意度下降的原因。

2. Secondary Data 二手数据

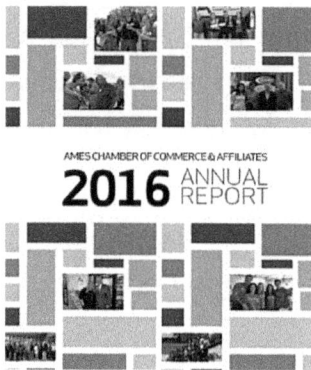

Chamber of Commerce 商会

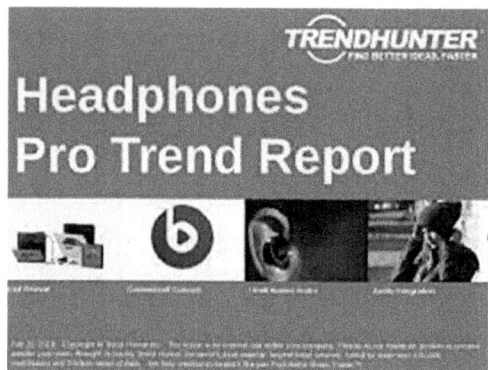

Research firms 调查公司

There are two types of data that we are gathering. First, we take a look at secondary data. Secondary data is the data that has been collected and interpreted by someone other than the users, for some other purposes. Common sources of secondary data for social science include censuses, information collected by government departments, reference books, accounting documents, articles, and other publications. For example, a hotel who needs to know about its customers can simply check its guest history system, which is a database for secondary information. Investigators first ask whether there is data that already available to answer the question they asked, for it saves a great amount of time and energy.

我们通常收集两种类型的数据。首先，我们看一看二手数据。二手数据是由数据使用者以外的其他人出于其他目的收集和解释的统计资料。社会科学的二手数据一般来自人口普查、政府部门收集的信息、参考书、会计文件、文章和其他出版物。例如，酒店要了解客户，可以简单地查找客户历史记录系统，该系统就是一个二手信息的数据库。在发现问题时，营销调研人员首先会找寻是否有现成的数据来回答他们的问题，因为这样可以节省大量的时间和精力。

3. Primary Data 原始数据

Primary data is the data gathered directly from respondents to specifically address the question at hand. It is the basic and original material of secondary data that provides raw evidence of the researcher. It is collected when the researchers have specific questions that tailored their own objectives. Researchers use surveys, interviews, and direct observations to obtain primary data.

原始数据是直接从受访者那里收集的数据，以明确地解决手头的问题。它是二手数据的基础和原始资料，为研究者提供了未经加工的证据。当研究人员针对自己的目标对象提出特定的问题时，就会收集这些信息。研究人员使用调查、访谈和直接观察来获得原始数据。

Focus group 焦点小组

Customer Surveys 消费者调查

The advantages of primary data are that it addresses the specific issues the researcher has a high level of control over what sort of data is collected, how data is collected, from whom, the size of the project, time frame and goal. It is completely designed by the researchers. Primary data can be accurate and timely. Unlike the secondary data, that can directly solve the problem needed. However, the process usually takes long time, comparing to the rapid change of marketplace. Moreover, other than the questionnaire papers and equipment for experiment of some sort, it takes professional marketing researchers skills and knowledge to compile and interpret the findings, and it is usually expensive.

原始数据的优点是它解决了特定的问题，研究人员对收集什么类型的数据、如何收集数据、从谁那里收集数据、项目的规模、时间框架和目标有高度的控制权。它完全是由研究人员设计的。原始数据是准确、及时的。与二手数据不同，它可以直接解决所关注的问题。然而，与市场的快速变化相比，这个过程通常需要较长时间。此外，除了问卷调查和某种实验设备外，还需要专业的市场研究人员的技能和知识来编写和解读研究结果，通常价格不菲。

In practice, secondary data is combined with primary data to support as evidence for a complete marketing research report.

在实践中，二手数据与原始数据通常结合使用，作为完整的市场调研报告的依据。

3.2.3　The Contact Method 收集数据的方式

Collecting secondary data is relatively simple. All you have to do is to find the resourceful publications such as government reports, technical and trade journals, public records, statistical and history documents, or even unpublished work. Before using secondary data, keep in mind that it must be checked for three important elements—reliability, suitability and adequacy. Researchers usually look into the authors of the material, the publisher, the methods employed, as well as the objective, scope of the studies to examine whether it has the value in use.

收集二手数据相对简单。你所要做的就是找到资源丰富的出版物，如政府工作报告、技术和贸易期刊、公开数据、统计和历史文件，甚至是未出版的作品。在使用二手数据之前，请记住必须检查三个重要元素——可靠性、适用性和充分性。研究人员通常会调查材料的作者、出版社、所采用的研究方法，以及研究的目标和范围，以检验它是否有使用价值。

By comparison, primary data can be collected by various means, and each has its advantages and limitations.

相比之下，原始数据可以通过各种方式收集，每种方式都有其优点和局限性。

1. Questionnaires 问卷调查

It is true that survey questionnaire is the most commonly used technique for collecting data. It takes forms of mail questionnaire and online questionnaire.

调查问卷是收集数据最常用的方法。它一般有邮件问卷和线上问卷两种形式。

Mailing the designed questionnaire has a low cost, and it offers a highly degree of freedom to respondents. It depends on the mail receivers' interests to answer it, which may lead to a low rate of responses. It takes researchers a bit long for getting back all the questionnaires. There is also a potential risk that the selected respondents cannot receive the mail if it directly goes to the spam mail box, or if the receiver simply ignores them. Once the mails are sent, researchers hardly have control over the other end of the computer.

以邮件形式发送已设计好的调查问卷成本低，给被调查者提供了较高的自由度。但它取决于邮件接收者是否有兴趣来回答，这可能导致较低的回复率，并且研究人员要花很长时间才能回收所有的问卷。还有一种潜在的风险是，如果邮件直接进入垃圾邮箱，或者收件人忽略了它们，那么被选中的受访者将无法接收邮件。一旦邮件发送出去，研究人员几乎无法控制计算机的另一端。

Nowadays, online questionnaires have gained popularity. Without geographic restrictions, online questionnaires can have a large sample which makes the data more reliable. Although giving out questionnaires on the internet costs little, providing respondents with great convenience and adequate time, researchers are concerned about the quality of the answers, for no one is sure about who is typing in front of a computer. However, companies develop more ways of eliminating these concerns. They conduct researches either through companies' official websites or official accounts on social media such as Facebook and WeChat. For getting quality answers, companies select diverse respondents, present surveys in different forms, and the respondents are rewarded with coupons, discounts, or invitation to the special activities.

如今，线上调查问卷越来越流行。在没有地域限制的情况下，在线问卷可以拥有大规模样本，这使数据更加可靠。虽然在互联网上发放调查问卷的成本微乎其微，为受访者提供了极大的便利和足够的时间，但研究人员担心的是答案的质量，因为没有人知道到底是谁在电脑前打字。尽管如此，一些公司开发了更多消除这些担忧的方法。他们通过公司官方网站或脸书、微信等社交媒体上的官方账号进行调查研究。为了获得高质量的答案，公司会选择不同的受访者，以不同的形式进行调研，并奖励受访者优惠券、折扣优惠或邀请他们参加特别的活动。

2. Interviews 访谈

Interviews involve presentation of oral verbal stimuli. It can be achieved by two ways: telephone interviews and personal interviews.

访谈涉及口头语言刺激的表达方式，可以通过电话访谈和私人访谈两种方式实现。

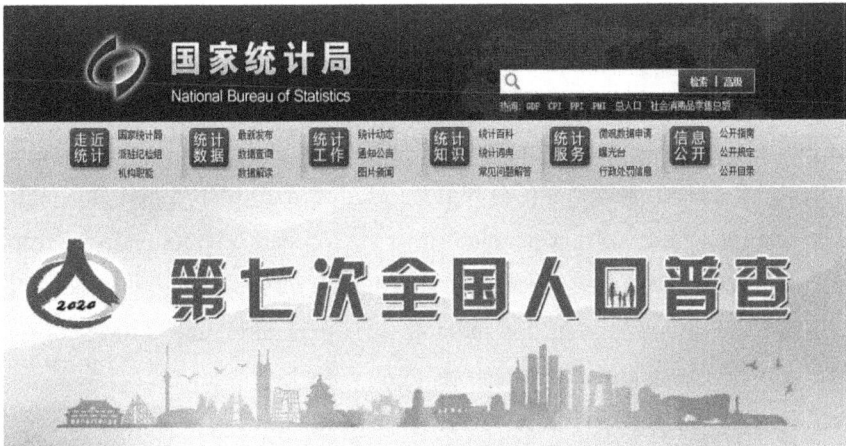

中国的人口普查，被誉为全球规模最大的调查项目，涉及 14 亿人口，通过面对面访谈、电话访谈等方式进行

Telephone interviews require the interviewer to collect information by contacting respondents on telephone and asking questions orally. It is flexible, cheaper and faster, the rate of response can be raised by recalling, and the interviewer staff can come from any field. Telephone interview is still in use but has been strongly opposed by many. Telephone calls made in anytime has caused some extra bother, making some company phone numbers end up being added to the do-not-call list. The questions designed should be short and right to the point, for any interview that exceeding five minutes can be annoying. Because of the time limitation, less information is collected. On the phones, people may lie either for not understanding the questions or for wishing to end the call as soon as possible.

电话访谈要求访谈者电话联系被受访者并通过口头提问来收集信息。它很灵活，也更便宜、快捷，通过回忆可以提高回复率，被访谈对象可以来自任何领域。如今电话访谈方式仍在使用，但遭到了许多人的强烈反对。无时无刻不在拨打的电话带来一些额外的麻烦，使一些公司的电话号码最终被列入了黑名单。设计的问题应该简短，切中要害，任何超过 5 分钟的访谈都是令人厌烦的。由于时间的限制，收集的信息较少。在电话中，人们可能会因为不理解问题或希望尽快结束通话而撒谎。

Personal interviews even send message by facial expressions, posture and eye contact. It requires the interviewer ask questions face-to-face to the respondents. It can be direct personal investigation, structured or unstructured interview, focus group etc. By interviewing, the two parts have a thorough communication in understanding survey questions, misinterpretation can be avoided especially by unstructured interview, so that personal information can be obtained, the response rate almost reaches a hundred percent, all making the responses in high quality. There are still some shortcomings in this method. It is expensive, more time-consuming comparing to questionnaires. Furthermore, high-skilled interviewers are necessary for controlling the procedure. However, with other people around, the interviewees may have imaginary information or less frank answers to hide their true feelings, and the interviewer who records the answer may have bias problems.

个人访谈更能通过面部表情、手势和眼神交流来传递信息。它要求访谈者面对面地提问。可以是直接的个人调查，结构化或非结构化的面试，焦点小组等。通过访谈，双方在对调查问题的理解上进行了深入沟通，尤其是非结构化访谈可以避免误解，从而获得个人化的信息，回复率几乎达到100%，所有的回答都是高质量的。这种方法仍有一些缺点。它较为昂贵，比问卷调查更耗时。此外，高技能的访谈者是控制过程所必需的。然而，在周围有其他人的情况下，受访者可能给出有虚构的信息或不太坦率的答案来隐藏他们的真实感受，而记录答案的访谈者也可能存在偏见。

3. Observation 观察

Observation is using a passive instrument to record customers' behavior, often without his or her knowledge. This can be done through personal observation, unobtrusive measures, and mechanical observation.

观察是用一种被动的工具来记录顾客的行为，通常是在顾客不知情的情况下进行的。这可以通过个人观察、无干扰测量和仪器观察来实现。

Researchers use personal observation technique to understand how consumers act in response to marketing activities by watching them in action. For example, researchers are sent to stand nearby a supermarket, watching and recording how many consumers during what time are buying how many products. They often use a video camera to take down the details for further strategies.

研究人员利用个人观察的方法，通过观察消费者的行为，来了解他们对营销活动的反应。例如，研究人员被派到一家超市附近，观察并记录有多少消费者在什么时候购买了多少商品。他们经常用摄像机记录下细节以便今后制定改进策略。

Unobtrusive measures are taken to avoid the circumstances that people change their answers or behavior once they know they are being observed. When being observed, people want their answers to be recorded, so many of them intend to provide answers that conform to cultural norms, match the experimenter's expectations, or for political reasons. In unobtrusive research, researchers do not directly contact with the research participants. Therefore, subjects' behavior are not affected by the research itself. For example, the data of students satisfaction with the new lecturer can be collected by recording the attendance at classes, whether students pay highly attention in class, or their interaction with the lecturer rather than directly asking them by interview or questionnaire.

无干扰测量是为了避免人们在知道自己被观察后改变答案或行为的情况。当（意识到）被观察时，人们希望他们的回答被记录下来，所以他们中的许多人倾向于提供符合文化规范、符合实验者预期或政治正确的答案。在无干扰测量中，研究人员不直接与研究参与者接触。因此，研究对象的行为不受研究本身的影响。例如，学生对新讲师的满意度的数据可以通过记录上课的出勤率、学生是否在课堂上聚精会神或他们与讲师的互动来收集，而不是直接通过访谈或问卷的方式来询问。

Mechanical observation is a data collection method that relies on instruments or devices to record consumers' behavior. Various types of mechanical devices include motion-picture or video camera, the audiometer, the psycho galvanometer, the eye-tracking monitor, and the pupilometer. Some of them have to be applied with

23

334

33

observers' permission and their knowledge to use it, while others do not. For example, the X-ray machine used by immigration officer inspecting the contents of a suitcase, turnstiles recording the number of people entering or leaving the building, optical scanners in the supermarket scanning the goods sold. More techniques are developed to measure consumers' behavior. The virtual sites you visit may be consistently being monitored without your knowledge, so, be careful when you think you are anonymously browsing the web.

仪器观察是一种依靠仪器或设备记录消费者行为的数据收集方法。各种类型的机械设备包括活动摄影或摄像机、听力计、精神电流计、眼球跟踪监视器和瞳孔仪。其中一些应用程序必须获得被调查者的知晓和同意才能使用，而另一些则不需要。例如，入境安检人员使用 X 光机检查手提箱内的物品，旋转门记录进出大楼的人数，超市的扫描枪扫描售出的商品。如今，人们开发出了更多的技术来衡量消费者的行为。你所访问的虚拟站点可能在您不知情的情况下一直受到监视，因此，当你认为你正在匿名浏览网页时，请小心。

3.2.4 Design The Sample 设计样本

Now it is time to decide the sample, that is, which group of people are to be studied. The population of interest is the sampling unit, the number of the people surveyed is the sample size, and the way that people in the sample are chosen is called the sampling procedure. Sometimes, the population is small so that researchers include every member into the study. Usually, the population is too large for the researchers to survey all its members. A small, carefully selected number of group are included in the research, to represent the entire population. In other words, how to choose the sampling procedure depends on whether it reflects the characteristics of the population from which it is drawn. There are generally two types of sampling methods: probability and non-probability sampling.

现在是确定样本的时候了，即研究哪一组人。研究所感兴趣的总体被称为抽样单元，被调查的人数被称为样本量，在样本中选择样本的方式被称为抽样方法。有时，总体很小，所以研究人员把每个成员都包括在研究中。通常，样本总体都太多，研究人员无法调查所有的成员。这种情况下，研究中会用一小部分经过精心挑选的群体，来代表整个样本。换句话说，如何选择抽样过程，取决于抽样过程是否反映了抽样总体的特征。一般有两种抽样方法：概率抽样和非概率抽样。

1. Probability Sampling 概率抽样

With a probability sample, each member of the population has a known non-zero chance of being selected. Probability sampling methods include random sampling, systematic sampling, stratified sampling, and cluster sampling.

对于概率样本，总体中的每个单位被抽中的概率都是非零的。概率抽样方法包括随机抽样、系统抽样、分层抽样和整群抽样。

In random sampling, every member of the population has a known and equal chance of selection. If there is a large population, it is heavy work to identify every member of it, so the subject becomes unbiased. The procedure of defining a random sample is just like a lottery method, it is usually generated by computers. Systematic sampling is often used instead of random sampling. After the sample size is confirmed, researchers choose the Nth member from the list which contains no hidden order, to form a desired sample. Both of these two methods can be conducted through a very simple operation.

在随机抽样中，总体中的每个样本都有一个已知的相等的抽样率。如果有个很大的总体样本量，要区分其中每一个单位都很费功夫，所以这个主体是无偏的。定义随机样本的过程就像抽奖一样，通常是由计算机生成的。研究人员通常用系统抽样代替随机抽样。在确定了样本规模后，研究人员从不包含隐藏顺序的列表中选择第 N 个成员，形成所需的样本。这两种方法都可以通过非常简单的操作来实现。

Stratified sampling is more advanced because it reduces sampling error. It works best when a heterogeneous population is split into fairly homogeneous groups, which means the subgroups are mutually exclusive. Researchers then randomly draw a sample from each of the groups. For example, assume there is a research studying which age group like the TV show most. With the people who watch the TV show, the population is divided into four age groups: below 20, 20-40, 40-60, and above 60. From each subgroup, researchers randomly choose 50 people to participate in the study. The sample size is 50*4=200. Or the researchers can choose respondents in portion to their percentage of the population.

分层抽样更先进，因为它减少了抽样误差。当一个异类总体被划分为相当同质的多个分层时这意味着这些分层是互斥的，它的效果最好。然后研究人员从各层随机抽取一个样本。例如，假设有一个项目正在研究哪个年龄段的人最喜欢看电视。根据看电视的人，调查对象被分为 4 个年龄段：20 岁以下、20~40 岁、40~60 岁和 60 岁以上。研究人员从每个分层中随机选择 50 人参与研究。样本容量为 50×4=200 人。或者研究人员可以根据他们在总体中所占的比例来选择受访者。

Unlikely, cluster sampling requires division the population into groups (clusters) with each group containing characteristics that are similar to the population. Researchers obtain a simple random sample from so many clusters. Data is originated from all the members from the randomly selected clusters. For example, assume the population is all the college students in a local college district. There are 20 different colleges in total, where 4 of them are randomly selected as the clusters. Researchers then select every student from each of these 4 colleges, creating a sample.

不同的是，整群抽样要求将总体划分为多个组（群集），每个组都包含与总体相似的特征。研究人员从这么多的群集中获得一个简单的随机样本。数据来自随机选择的群集中的所有成员。例如，假设总体是本地大学城的所有大学生。总共有 20 所不同的学院，随机选择其中 4 所作为群集。然后研究人员从这 4 所学院中选中每一个学生，组成一个样本。

英国林肯大学与兰卡斯特大学联合调查显示，苹果用户不如安卓用户诚实、谦虚，却比安卓用户感情更丰富

2. Non-Probability Sampling 非概率抽样

Sometimes researchers need an answer quickly, just want to form a general picture of the problem, or they do not have enough time to form a probability sample, then they may choose a non-probability sampling method. Non-probability sampling methods are based on human choice rather than random selection. They can be suggestive of what is generally going on, but there is no way to ensure the sample is representative of the population, so they are called "sampling disaster".

有时研究人员想要快速得到答案，只需大概了解某问题，或者他们没有足够的时间做概率抽样，那么他们可能会选择非概率抽样方法。非概率抽样方法是基于人的主观选择而不是随机选择。它们可以作为总体情况的参考，但无法保证样本一定能代表总体，因此也被称为"抽样灾难"。

The meaning of the non-probability sampling can be inferred from their names. The sample in a convenience sampling is selected because it is convenient to obtain. It is often used in the preliminary research for getting an approximation of the truth. Likewise, judgment sampling is based on researchers' judgment. For example, a researcher decides to draw an entire sample from 10 "representative" colleges among all the colleges nationwide. The researcher must have the confidence of the chosen ones are truly "representative" of the population. Quota sampling is the non-probability sampling equals to stratified sampling. The difference lies in quota sampling relies on convenience sampling or judgment sampling rather than random sampling in choosing sample members in the subgroups.

非概率抽样的含义可以从它们的名字中推断出来。之所以选择方便抽样中的样本，正是因为它便于获得。它常用于初步研究，以获得接近事实的结果。同样，判断抽样是基于研究人员的判断。例如，一位研究人员决定从全国所有大学中的 10 所"有代表性"的学院中抽取整个样本。研究人员必须有足够的信心，使其选择真正能够"代表"总体。配额抽样是一种非概率抽样，相当于分层抽样。不同之处在于，配额抽样在选择子群中的样本成员时是基于方便或判断，而不是随机抽样。

3.2.5　Analyze the Data 分析数据

After getting raw data, researchers begin the data cleaning, by removing data that have accidentally been duplicated or by correcting data that have obviously been recorded wrong. The answers to the open-ended questions are pasted together, so that researchers can compare and summarize the information.

在获得原始数据后，研究人员通过删除意外重复的数据或纠正明显记录错误的数据来开始数据清理。开放式问题的答案被粘贴在一起，这样研究人员可以比较和总结信息。

Analyzing the data to ensure it is as accurate as possible. If the research is collected by hand using a pen and pencil, it is better to computerize the information. If respondents have already entered the answers directly into a computer in an online research, companies may begin to process the results with software. A program such as Microsoft Excel or a statistical program such as Predictive Analytics Software (PASW, which was formerly known as SPSS) is used to tabulate or calculate the basic results of the research, such as the total number of participants and how collectively they answered various questions. The programs can also be used to calculate averages, percentages, standard deviations, means, medians, and so forth.

分析数据，确保数据尽可能准确。如果研究是用钢笔和铅笔手工收集的，最好将信息电脑化。如果受访者已经在网上的调研中直接将答案输入电脑，公司可能会开始用软件处理结果。可使用 Microsoft Excel 之类的程序或预测分析软件之类的统计程序如 PASW（以前称为 SPSS）来制表或计算研究的基本结果，比如参与者的总数及他们如何共同回答各种问题。这些程序还可以用来计算平均值、百分比、标准差、平均值、中位数等。

3.2.6　Write the Research Report 撰写调研报告

With all the above work done, it is time to present all the work in a brief and easy-to-understand way for the readers. A well-organized research report will include six basic sections.

完成以上所有工作后，是时候以一种简单易懂的方式向读者呈现所有的工作了。一份优质的研究报告将包括 6 个基本部分。

（1）Title page. This explains what the report is about, when it is conducted, it is produced and requested by whom.

标题页。它包括了报告的内容、何时执行、由谁编撰。

（2）Executive summary. It is the condensed version of the report, listing the main points and summarizing the details. Who do not have time to read through the report will read this part to get a general idea and results of the work.

摘要。它是完整报告的压缩版本，列出了要点并总结了细节。没有时间通读报告的人会通读这一部分，以了解工作的总体思路和结果。

（3）Methodology. It explains how the research was designed and conducted. The size of the sample, the description of its characteristics, and the statistical technique that was employed to analyze the data, have to be explicated.

研究方法。它解释了这项研究是如何设计和实施的。这部分必须说明样本的大小、特征的描述及用于分析数据的统计技术。

（4）Discussion and conclusion. This section includes a complete discussion of the study results. The results is presented in tabulations, cross-tabulations, and detailed statistical findings uncovered by researchers, as well as the secondary data at hand that back up the findings.

讨论和结论。该部分包括对研究结果的完整讨论。结果以表格、交叉表格和研究人员的详细统计发现，以及支持这些结果的现成二手数据的形式呈现。

（5）Recommendations. Researchers also act as advisers for outlining the course of managerial action based on the findings.

建议。研究人员还充当顾问，提炼出基于这些发现的管理行动。

（6）Limitations. Errors, such as sampling errors, interviewer errors, should be stated in detail, so that decision makers have the idea of its overall impacts.

局限性。如抽样误差、访谈者误差等各类误差，应该加以详细说明，以便决策者了解其对总体的影响。

Other additional sections such as market competition and supply chain options can be involved in the report if necessary. While writing the report, it is important to note that there should not be many buzz words as the report will be read not only by marketing managers, but also by clients who are not in the area. Therefore, a standard for a well-presented report is that it is understood by people without marketing knowledge.

如有需要，报告还可加入其他部分，如市场竞争和供应链选择。在撰写报告时，重要的是要注意不要使用太多华丽的辞藻，因为不仅营销经理会阅读报告，对该领域不熟悉的客户也会阅读报告。因此，一篇优秀调研报告的标准是，不懂营销知识的人也能够理解它。

3.3　Questionnaire Design 问卷设计

Most of us are familiar with questionnaires. We all have filled out some questionnaires more or less for others, and they look similar. When asked to design a questionnaire, people just randomly raise some questions about personal information and those related to the research goals. There are other rules and instructions that make your questionnaire a professional one.

我们大多数人都熟悉问卷调查。我们都或多或少地为别人填写过一些问卷，它们看起来很相似。当设计问卷时，大家通常只是随意地提出一些关于个人信息和与研究目的相关的问题。这里有一些规则，能让你的问卷看起来更专业。

An important aspect of questionnaire design is the types of questions. Survey questions can be classified into closed-end questions and open-end questions. Closed-end questions include all the possible answers, and subjects make choices among them. Questions of this kind may offer simple alternatives such as "Yes" or "No", or ask the respondents to choose one or more from several categories. Closed-end questions also ask scale questions in forms of importance scale or agreement scale. This type of questions requires the designer to write appropriate and mutually exclusive categories. The closed-end questions are easy to answer, and finite set of responses makes the survey more manageable. However, it does not allow respondents to develop ideas by forcing them to choose between given alternatives.

问卷设计的重点之一是问题的类型。调查问题可以分为封闭式问题和开放式问题。封闭式问题包括所有可能的答案，受访者在这些答案中做出选择。这类问题可以提供简单的选项，如"是"或"否"，或者让受访者从几个类别中选择一个或多个答案。封闭式问题还可以以重要性量表或一致性量表的形式提出量表问题。这类问题要求设计人员编写恰当且互斥的选项。封闭式的问题很容易回答，有限的答案使调查更易于管理。然而，封闭式问题强迫受访者在给定的选择中做出选择，不允许受访者开拓自己的思路。

Open-end questions do not provide any choices, in contrast, they allow respondents to answer in their own words, so answers may be unanticipated and new ideas may emerge when there is little existing information about a subject. Therefore, open-end questions are useful in exploratory research. The disadvantages lie in time-consuming for respondents, and difficult to recognize the hand writings and analyze the answers.

开放式问题不提供任何选择，相反，他们让受访者用自己的话来回答，所以答案可能是意料之外的，在研究主体的现有信息相当贫乏的情况下，开放式问题的答案中可能会出现新思路。因此，开放性问题在探索性研究中用处较大。它的缺点是答卷耗时长，对于手写的答案很难识别并进行分析。

3.4　Online Research 在线调研

Researchers gather data from online by two ways: one is online tracking; the other is by online survey such as online interview, online focus group, bulletin boards, mobile search, and communities.

研究人员通过两种方式从网上收集数据：一种是在线跟踪；另一种是通过在线调查达成，如在线访谈、在线焦点小组、论坛、移动搜索和社区。

3.4.1　Online Tracking 在线跟踪

Marketers keep track on consumers' online behavior. Online tracking is enabled by cookies. Cookies are not the dessert, they are small files inserted by a website sponsor in a user's hard drive to store the user's information when they connect the web. The website you visit sends cookies to your computer. Computer stores the cookies in a file located inside your web browser. The design of cookies is to track consumers' online activity. For example, online retailers use cookies to keep track of the items in a user's shopping cart as they explore the site. Without cookies, your shopping cart would reset to zero every time you clicked a new link on the site. That would make it impossible to buy anything online. Cookies enable customized services. E-commercial platforms such as Amazon.com and Taobao.com recommends items to their consumers according to what they have bought in the past.

营销人员跟踪消费者的在线行为。在线跟踪是由 cookie 支持的。cookie 不是甜点，它们是网站赞助商插入用户硬盘驱动器的小文件，用于在用户连接网站时存储的用户信息。你访问的网站会向你的电脑发送 cookie。计算机将

cookie 存储在位于 web 浏览器内的文件中。cookie 的设计是为了跟踪消费者的在线活动。例如，在线零售商在用户浏览网站时使用 cookie 跟踪用户购物车中的商品。如果没有 cookie，每次点击站点上的新链接时，您的购物车都将被清空，这将使人们不可能在网上买到任何东西。cookie 支持定制服务。亚马逊和淘宝网等电子商务平台会根据消费者过去的购买情况向他们推荐商品。

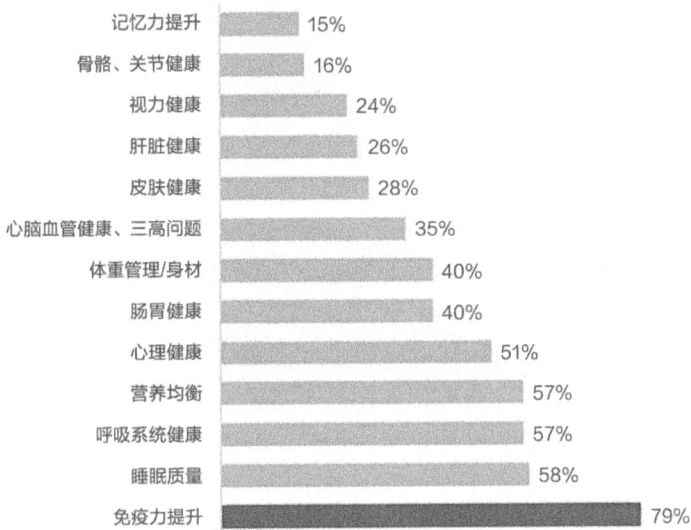

新冠肺炎疫防控情期间，人们最关注"免疫力的提升"这一健康问题

Still, as more marketers are using cookies for commercial purpose, there raises a lot concern about the privacy and security. Under normal circumstances, the data in a cookie will not affect how computer runs. However, there is a chance that viruses and malware may be disguised as cookies. It can be managed by changing protection levels in the browser, or deleting cookie files, or installing an anti-cookie software.

尽管如此，随着越来越多的营销人员将 cookie 用于商业目的，人们对其隐私和安全性的担忧也越来越多。在正常情况下，cookie 中的数据不会影响计算机的运行方式。但是，病毒和恶意软件有可能伪装成 cookie。它可以通过改变浏览器中的保护级别、删除 cookie 文件或安装反 cookie 软件来管理。

3.4.2 Online Survey 在线调查

Online surveys take many forms. Interviews, questionnaires, focus groups, video diaries, blogging, journaling or communities can all be realized on the Internet. Marketers use online surveys to get feedback from consumers.

网上调查有多种形式。访谈、问卷调查、焦点小组、视频日记、博客、日志或社区都可以在互联网上实现。营销人员利用在线调查来获得消费者的反馈。

New product release. Companies put a new product survey on its website to see how consumers like them. Some companies allow consumers to upload audio and video review on their websites or directly to the social media, which helps a company understand what is working and what is not working. Other companies provide co-creation service with consumers, so as to keep up with the latest trends.

新产品发布。公司在其网站上发布了一项新产品调查，以了解消费者对它们的喜爱程度。一些公司允许消费者在其网站上或直接向社交媒体上传音频和视频评论，这有助于公司了解什么是可行的，什么是不可行的。其他公司提供与消费者共同创作的服务，以跟上最新的潮流。

Predicting market reaction. Companies make use of the internet to test consumers' response to their brands. For example, if you type "Maotai" on Taobao. com, JD. com, you can see the sales volume and reviews, at least "likes" and "dislikes". Companies choose the best strategy for precise marketing based on these data.

预测市场的反应。公司利用互联网来测试消费者对其品牌的反应。例如，如果你在淘宝、京东上输入"茅台"，你可以看到销量和评论，至少可以看到"喜欢"和"不喜欢"。公司根据这些数据选择最佳的精确营销策略。

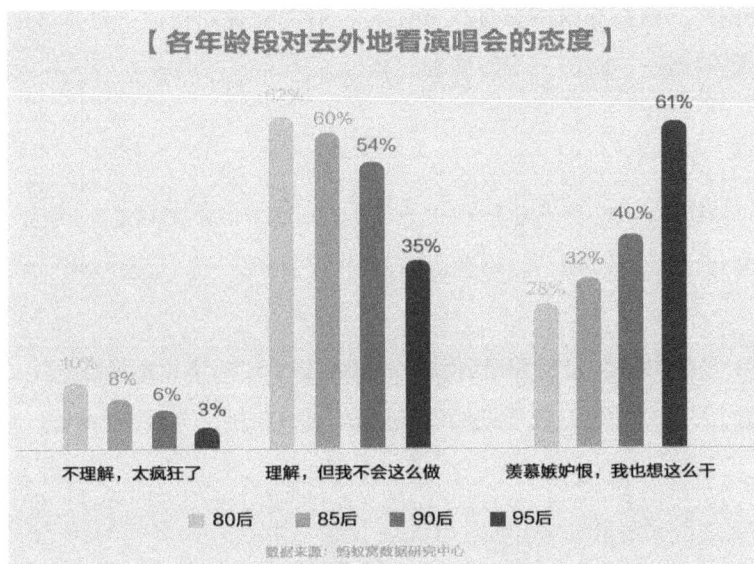

【各年龄段对去外地看演唱会的态度】

各年龄段对去外地看演唱会的态度调查，80后最宽容，95后最跟风

Exploratory research. Before the products go to massive production, some companies use focus group to conduct exploratory research. Jewelry industry has long been practiced of letting online shoppers try fine jewelry by established and emerging designers for a short period, allowing a client to take merchandise home prior to making a purchase. Consumers are required to attend a virtual focus group for a discussion.

探索性研究。在产品大规模生产之前，一些公司会利用焦点小组进行探索性研究。珠宝行业长期以来的做法是，请网上购物者短期试用老牌和新设计师设计的高级珠宝，让客户在购买之前把商品带回家。之后，消费者需要参加一个虚拟的焦点小组，对使用的产品进行讨论。

Marketers favor online surveys for they are much cheaper and take much shorter time. Other advantages include consumers appeared to be more honest than they are interviewed face-to-face, and multinational corporations can easily conduct research online as long as there is connection to the Internet.

市场营销人员喜欢在线调查，因为它们便宜得多，耗时也短得多。与面对面的访谈相比，在线测试的其他优势还有，消费者表现得似乎更加诚实；另外，只需与互联网相连，跨国公司便能够轻松地在网上进行调查。

◎ **推荐**

麦克·丹尼尔，盖茨 . 当代市场调研 [M]. 李桂华，译 . 北京：机械工业出版社，2012.

阿尔文·伯恩斯，罗纳德·布什 . 营销调研 [M]. 于洪彦等，译 . 北京：中国人民大学出版社，2017.

纳雷希·马尔霍特拉 . 营销调研精要 [M]. 张婧，译 . 北京：人民大学出版社，2016.

郑宗成，陈进，张文双 . 市场研究实务与方法 [M]. 广州：广东经济出版社，2011.

4

Consumer Behavior

消费者行为

知识解锁 Knowledge Unlocked

以下问题的答案，可在本章寻找：

1. 谁是消费者？

2. 消费者会做什么样的决策？

3. 消费者如何做出购买决策？

4. 是什么在影响消费者的行为？

4.1 Consumer and Consumer Behavior 消费者和消费者行为

We have learned how marketers obtain data, analyze and make use of information to understand the marketplace in the previous chapter, now we move on to a more important element: consumer. The aim of marketing is to satisfy consumer needs and wants profitably, and the study of consumer behavior is to analyze how consumers think and act in the process of selecting, purchasing, using, and disposing of goods and services, to satisfy their own needs and wants. In a word, consumer behavior tries to figure out five "W"s and one "H", that is, what, when, who, where, how much customers buy, and more importantly, why they buy. It also examines how internal, social, and environmental factors affect the behavior of consumers. It is called the "lifeblood" of any business.

上一章，我们学习了营销者如何获取数据、分析和利用信息来了解市场，现在我们来看看一个更重要的元素：消费者。营销的目的是满足消费者的需求和欲望并获得回报，而消费者行为研究是分析消费者在选择、购买、使用和处置商品和服务的过程中是如何思考和行动的，以满足自己的需求和欲望。总之，消费者行为研究试图找出 5 个 "W" 和一个 "H"，即什么时候、谁、在哪里、买了什么、买了多少，更重要的是，他们为什么买。除此之外，它还考察内部、社会和环境因素如何影响消费者的行为，也因此被称为企业的 "生命线"。

Consumers are never easy to understand or serve. They change their minds at the last minute. Despite that marketers can easily obtain the information of the five "W"s, they are not likely to know exactly why customers buy through simple observation. As we are all consumers, we can use our own examples as illustration of the theories in this chapter. Before we go into any detail about the tough task, let's take a look at three basic concepts.

理解和服务消费者从来都不是一件简单的事，他们会在购买的最后一刻改变主意。尽管营销人员可以很容易地获得 5W 信息，但他们不太可能通过简单的观察就知道客户购买的确切原因。作为消费者，我们可以用自己的经历作为例子来学习本章的理论。在详细介绍这项艰巨的任务之前，让我们先来看看 3 个基本概念。

4.1.1 Consumer 消费者

Consumer is the buyer, decision-maker, or the ultimate consumer of goods, services and ideas. The three roles of consumer can be played by only one person, or three different persons. A lady who buys a birthday cake for her child is a buyer, her family is the ultimate consumer, and the decision-maker may be her husband. They are all called "consumers".

消费者是商品、服务和理念的购买者、决策者或最终消费者。消费者的三个角色可以仅由一个人或者三个不同的人扮演。给孩子买生日蛋糕的女士是"购买者"，她的家庭是"最终消费者"，而"决策者"可能是她的丈夫。他们都被称为"消费者"。

4.1.2 Consumer Market 消费市场

Consumer market consists of all the individuals and households who buy or acquire goods and services for personal consumption. In consumer market, people make their own decisions about how to spend money and what products to buy. The more purchases are made frequently in a market, the more active is the consumer market. The US is made up of more than 300 million population, yet it owns the largest consumer market.

消费市场是指为个人消费而购买或获得商品和服务的所有个人和家庭。在消费市场上，人们自己决定如何花钱，买什么产品。市场上频繁交易的商品越多，消费市场就越活跃。美国人口仅3亿多人，但它拥有全世界最大消费市场。

4.1.3 Consumer Behavior 消费者行为

Consumer behavior is the dynamic interaction of the affect and cognition, behavior and the environment in the process of select, use and dispose of products and services, that is, the observable behavior of a consumer. It is the psychology of marketing. It consists of the buying decision-making process and the action a customer takes, which influenced by both internal and external factors. We will address this topic over the coming pages.

消费者行为是消费者在选择、使用和处置产品和服务过程中，情感与认知、行为与环境的动态交互，即消费者的可观察行为。这是营销心理学。它包括购买决策的过程和顾客所采取的行动，这些都受到内部和外部因素的影响。我们将在接下来的篇章中讨论这个话题。

4.2　Consumer Decision-Making Model 消费者决策模型

4.2.1　Consumer Involvement 消费者参与

People do not go through every step of the decision-making process every time they purchase. You can think of many circumstances when you grab something from the shelf of a store without consideration. At other times, you look at a collection of goods, compare them, and finally pick one of them. Basically, consumers spend more time, energy, and money on the purchases when they think is "risky". Perceived risk is the belief consumers hold that choice of a product will produce negative financial (high-priced items), physical (whether functions satisfy needs), psychological (no experience that may cause anxiety) or social (products that are important to peer group) consequences. Especially, when customers buy expensive, new or complex products and services such as houses, cars, new electronic products, signing up an insurance contract, they may face a set of uncertainties about the products or services. For example, when you book a hotel online for a trip, you worry about if it will charge extra fees or offer free cancellation. In this case, the perceived risk of booking the hotel is high.

人们不会在每次消费时都把决策过程的每一步完整地经历一遍。在很多情况下，你会不加思考地从商店的货架上拿东西。另一些时候，你会仔细查看一组商品，相互比较，最后选择其中一个。大致来说，当消费者认为存在"风险"时，他们会在购买上花费更多的时间、精力和金钱。感知风险是指消费者认为，选择一种产品会产生负面的财务（高价商品）、身体（功能是否满足需求）、心理（是否会导致焦虑的体验）或社会（对同频群体很重要的产品）后果。特别是当消费者购买昂贵的、新颖的或复杂的产品和服务，如房屋、汽车、新电子产品及签订保险合同时，他们可能会面临一系列关于产品或服务的不确定性。例如，当你在网上预订旅行的酒店时，你担心它是否会收取额外费用及是否提供免费取消服务。在这种情况下，预订酒店的感知风险很高。

High perceived risk products require high involvement of a consumer. Consumers are highly involved when they think the product is expensive, purchased infrequently, and highly self-expressive. For example, when you buy a gift for your boss's wife for her birthday party for the first time, you are concerned about what to buy, how much to spend, how to package it, and so on. You may ask for your colleague's advice, search extensively for more information online. If the gift that may suit her is not what you are familiar with, you may become very careful about the price and the image the brand represents, to avoid embarrassment. Consumers with high involvement engage in extended problem solving.

高感知风险的产品需要消费者的高度参与。当消费者认为产品昂贵、购买频率低、表达自我意识的能力强时，他们就会高度投入。例如，当你第一次为老板的妻子买生日礼物时，你会考虑买什么、花多少钱、如何包装等。你可以询问同事的建议，在网上广泛搜索更多信息。如果适合她的礼物不是你所熟悉的，你可能会对礼物的价格和它的品牌形象非常谨慎，以避免尴尬。高参与度的消费者参与的复杂决策被称为深入型问题解决决策。

By contrast, when the perceived risk is low, consumers make low involvement decisions. These decisions are more straightforward and repetitive. The products in this case are not important enough to worth the consumer's time, exhaustive information search. They require little time, money, and energy. For example, when you buy a bottle of drink after tiring workout, you probably step into the convenient store, open the fridge, and take whatever you feel comfortable with. The whole procedure will take less than three minutes, and you feel alright even if the drink does not fit your taste, because it costs so little that you can easily change to another. Purchase behavior without much to consider is called habitual decision making.

相比之下，当感知风险较低时，消费者的参与度较低。这样的购买决策更加直截了当、重复性高。在这种情况下，产品还没有重要到值得消费者花时间、详尽地搜索信息的地步。它们只需要很少的时间、金钱和精力。例如，当你辛苦地健身完之后，去买一瓶饮料，你可能会走进便利店，打开冰柜，随手拿走任何你觉得喝着会舒服的东西。整个过程只需要不到 3 分钟，即使你喝的饮料不合你的口味，你也会感觉还好，因为它的成本很低，你可以轻松地换一种。不经过太多考虑的购买行为称为习惯性决策。

Consumers with low involvement usually passively receive information as they watch television or read magazines. This explains why sometimes marketers would rather invest more on the store display fee rather than engaging in improving its quality, in order to attract the consumers' attention at first sight.

低参与度的消费者通常在看电视或杂志时被动地接收信息。这就解释了为什么有的时候为了第一时间吸引消费者注意，营销人员更愿意在陈列费上投入更多，而非提高质量。

Limited problem solving falls in the middle, where consumers already have some information but they need more to make a proper decision. Buying a movie ticket is an example. You are going to spend some time on looking for a movie that is worth watching, because you do not want to waste 2 hours sitting in the cinema which is supposed to be fun. You may log on to the web reading introduction of the movie, browsing comments from the previous audiences, or rely on your friend's recommendation, all to simplify the decision-making procedure.

有限的问题解决型决策介于深入型问题解决决策和习惯性决策中间。在这种情况下，消费者已经掌握了一些信息，但他们需要更多的信息来做出恰当的决定。买电影票就是一个例子。你要花一些时间去找一部值得看的电影，因为你不想浪费 2 个小时坐在电影院里，看电影这件事本应该很有趣才对。为此，你可能上网阅读电影介绍，浏览之前观众的评论，或者听从朋友的推荐，这些都是为了简化决策过程。

4.2.2　Types of Buying Decision Behavior 购买决策行为的类型

There are four types of consumer buying behavior, based on both consumer involvement and differences between brands while purchasing any product.

根据消费者在购买产品时的参与程度和品牌间的差异，消费者购买行为可分为 4 个类型。

（1）**Complex buying behavior.** When the consumer is highly involved in the purchasing, and at the same time there are significant differences between alternative brands that present different values, the consumer is tend to exhibit complex buying behavior. In such cases, the product searched for buying is relatively expensive and risky. It is also more self-expressive and the frequency of purchase is occasionally. The consumer makes efforts in gathering the information in regards to the product, to fully understand its benefit that meets his own requirements. For example, consumer shows complex buying behavior when buying a personal laptop. He may choose between brands, develop beliefs and attitudes about them, get a clear idea of the technical parameters, and make a final decision after this learning process.

复杂的购买行为。当消费者在购买时高度参与，且替代品牌之间存在价值的显著差异时，消费者倾向于表现出复杂的购买行为。在这种情况下，搜索购买的产品是相对昂贵和有风险的。这种商品更具有自我表现性，购买的频率也比较低。在这个过程中，消费者努力收集与产品相关的信息，充分了解其是否符合自身需求。例如，消费者在购买个人笔记本电脑时表现出复杂的购买行为。他可能会在品牌之间进行选择，形成对品牌的信念和态度，对技术参数形成清晰的认识，并在这个学习过程之后做出最终的决定。

（2）**Dissonance-reducing buying behavior.** Dissonance buying behavior represents the case when consumer involvement is high but sees little difference between brands. The purchase is expensive, risky, and infrequent, but making a final decision would be fairly quickly for there is not much to choose from brands. The consumer may respond to a good price or quality service.

减少失调感的购买行为。失调的购买行为下，消费者的参与度很高，但品牌之间的差异很小。商品购买价格高昂，风险较大，购买频率较低，但消费者做出最终决定是相当快的，因为没有太多的品牌可供选择。这时，消费者可能会对优惠的价格或优质的服务做出反应，决定购买。

After the purchase, the consumer may experience dissonance that comes from dissatisfying features of the product or hearing favorable things about other brands. The consumer will respond to these kinds of information and establish a set of new beliefs. Marketing communications here should provide after-sale service and support to help customers reducing doubts about the products he or she has chosen.

购买之后，消费者可能会感到某种"失衡"，这是由于消费者发现产品不令人满意或者听到了对其他品牌的好评。消费者会对这些信息做出反应，并建立一套新的观念。在这里，营销传播应该提供售后服务和支持，帮助客户减少对他们所选择的产品的疑虑。

（3）**Variety seeking behavior.** Sometimes the consumer involvement is low but differences between brands are extraordinary. Here the consumer is observed to do a lot of brands switching, not due to dissatisfaction from earlier products but due to testing the variety. For example, each time you buy snacks such as crisps or cookies you just want to try more different flavors for an evaluation. Fast food restaurants like KFC and Pizza Hut introduce new dishes in a high frequency, to satisfy customers' needs for various tastes. Companies in this case should adopt the strategy of offering special deals, free samples, coupons, and discounts, providing reasons to test something new.

寻求变化的购买行为。有时，消费者的参与度很低，但品牌之间的差异非常大。在这种情况下，研究人员观察到消费者会多次更换品牌，不是由于对之前购买产品不满意，而是由于想尝试不同品牌。例如，每次你买薯片或饼干这种零食，你只是想尝试更多新的口味。肯德基、必胜客等快餐店会频繁推出新菜品，满足顾客对不同口味的需求。在这种情况下，公司应该采取提供特别菜品、免费样品、优惠券和折扣的策略，为消费者提供尝鲜的理由。

Habitual buying behavior. Habitual buying behavior is the type in which the involvement of consumers in the purchase is low along with the few differences among the alternative brands. The products are often cheap and purchased frequently. For example, if a consumer buys salt or pepper from the supermarket, he or she may exhibit habitual buying behavior. In habitual buying, the consumer does not learn much about the product features, nor they develop attitudes towards the products. They passively receive information from magazines, TV commercials etc. The consumer does not form post purchase evaluation because they involve so little. Companies producing this kind of products often use symbols and images to create the brand awareness, or show repeating short duration advertising messages to strengthen memory of the consumers.

（4）**习惯性的购买行为**。习惯性购买行为是指消费者对购买行为的参与度较低，并且不同品牌之间的差异较小。这些产品通常很便宜且经常购买。例如，如果一个消费者从超市购买盐或胡椒，他或她可能表现出习惯性的购买行为。在习惯性的购买中，消费者对产品的特点了解不多，也没有形成对产品的态度，他们从杂志、电视广告等中被动地接受信息。消费者不会形成购后评价，因为他们的参与度很低。生产这类产品的公司经常使用符号和图像来建立品牌知名度，或者通过展示重复的短时间广告信息来增强消费者的记忆。

4.3　Consumer Decision-Making Process 消费者决策过程

Consumer decision-making process is the mental activity and the action that a consumer goes through in regards to market transactions before, during and after the purchase of a good or a service. Although decision-making cannot be seen, we can infer from the behavior that a decision has been made.

消费者决策过程是指消费者在购买某种商品或服务之前、当中和之后所经历的心理活动和行为。虽然决策过程不可见，但我们可以从行为推断出决策已经做出了。

Note that consumers do not always move in the exact order through the process, they may skip or reverse some of these stages. It can depend on the type of product, the buying stage of the consumer, and even financial status. However, we use the following model for it shows all the considerations that a consumer may face in a complex buying situation. A marketer has to understand these steps in order to effectively communicate to consumers, so as to properly lead the consumers to complete their purchases.

请注意，在整个流程中，消费者并不总是按照确切的顺序移动，他们可能跳过或反转其中一些阶段。它可以取决于产品的类型、消费者的购买阶段甚至是财务状况。但是，我们使用下面的模型显示了消费者在复杂的购买情况下可能面临的所有考虑过程。营销者必须了解这些步骤，以便有效地与消费者沟通，从而正确地引导消费者完成购买。

4.3.1 Need Recognition 需要认知

The first step in the process is the consumers find that they have a need for something. Need recognition occurs whenever the consumer sees a significant difference between his or her current state and some desired or ideal state. Need can be triggered by some very basic impulses that you experience, such as when you are hungry during a midday class, you feel cold under the sudden low temperature. All these are called internal stimuli. A need can also occur when you are affected by the outside influences, which are called external stimuli. For example, an advertisement or a discussion with friends may drive you to buy a new mobile phone.

这个过程的第一步是消费者发现他们对某样东西有需求。当消费者看到他或她的当前状态与某些期望或理想状态之间的显著差异时，就会产生需求。需求可以由你所经历的一些非常基本的冲动所触发。例如，当你在中午上课时感到饥饿，突然的低温会让你感到寒冷。所有这些都被称为内部刺激。当你受到外界的影响，也就是所谓的外部刺激时，需求也会出现。例如，一条广告或与朋友的讨论可能会驱使你购买一部新手机。

Although most need recognition arises when there is a true need, marketers can still exert influence on potential audiences by creating advertising messages and sales components to help customers recognize their current problems, and create wants by telling them there is a product that can fulfill their needs.

虽然大多数的需求识别是在真正的需求出现的时候产生的，但是营销人员仍然可以通过创建广告信息和销售组合来影响潜在的受众，帮助客户认识到他们当前遇到的问题，再告诉他们有种新产品可以满足解决他们的问题，以此创造需求。

4.3.2 Information Search 信息搜索

After a customer develops a need or a want, he or she needs to search information to get a well understanding of the alternatives that can best satisfy their needs. Information can stem from both internal and external sources. Internal information search is utilizing information from memory, such as when you search your mind for past experiences of examining and using the product. External information search consists of searching information from the outside sources, such as personal sources (family members, friends, neighbors), commercial sources (packaging, advertising, dealer websites), and public sources (newspaper, customer reports, Internet). External information sources are what marketers can control.

在客户产生一种需求之后，需要搜索信息，以更好地了解最能满足他们需求的选择。信息可以来自内部和外部。内部信息搜索是利用来自记忆的信息，例如当你搜索时你的大脑寻找过去测试及使用产品的经验。外部信息搜索包括从外部来源搜索信息，如个人来源（家庭成员、朋友、邻居）、商业来源（包装、广告、经销商网站）和公共来源（报纸、消费者报告、互联网）。其中，外部信息来源是营销人员可以控制的。

By information search, the customer learns more about competing brands, some of which meet the initial criteria, some may be newly added to the list, others are dropped from consideration. Finally, there are a range of most favorable alternatives left. Marketing strategy at this stage is to provide information where and when the customers are likely to search.

通过信息搜索，客户可以了解到更多竞争品牌的信息，其中一些符合最初的标准，一些可能会被新加入列表中，另一些则会被踢出去。最后，产生一系列最有利的候选者。在这个阶段的营销策略是：提供一些信息，以保证客户在最可能的时间和地点搜索到这些信息。

4.3.3 Evaluation of Alternatives 评估候选产品

Here, customers carefully compare each attribute that a product possesses. For example, if Lisa wants to buy a digital camera, the attributes she cares about are processor, lens, and price. What she also has to know is how important she thinks these attributes are, and how relevant they are to her real needs. If there is a camera with all the attributes that dominate others, Lisa would probably buy it. But if the first has the best processor, the second has the best lens, and the third one has the most reasonable price, Lisa would add a particular weight to each of the attributes, give each camera feature a score, then do the calculation. The score winner would be the final choice for Lisa.

在这一过程中，客户会仔细比较产品的每项性能。例如，如果莉萨想买一台数码相机，她关心的属性是处理器、镜头和价格。她还需要知道的是，她认为这些性能有多重要，以及这些性能与她的实际需求有多大相关性。如果有一款相机与其他相机相比各项性能都更好，莉萨很可能会买它。但是如果第一款有最好的处理器，第二款有最好的镜头，第三款有最合理的价格，莉萨会给每个性能增加一个特定的权重，为每个相机的功能进行评分，然后计算结果。获胜者将是莉萨的最后选择。

In real life, it is easy for some customers to establish valuation criteria, but it is hard for others, especially when buying new products, to have a clear dimension for evaluation. A weapon for marketers at this stage is to educate customers which attributes to look for—usually those their products are good at. Marketing strategies are understanding consumer criteria, highlighting product features, and communicating their own superiorities to potential customers.

在现实生活中，有些客户很容易建立评估标准，但另一些客户，尤其是在购买新产品时，很难有一个明确的衡量标准。在这个阶段，营销人员的一个武器是教育客户，让他们懂得应该关注哪些性能——通常是他们自己产品所擅长的那些性能。这个过程中，营销策略是了解消费者的标准，突出产品的特点，向潜在客户传达自己的优势。

4.3.4 Purchase Decision 购买决策

After all the thinking and weighing the advantages and disadvantages of each product, a customer finally makes a decision on the purchase.

经过反复思考，权衡每一个产品的优点和缺点后，客户最终做出购买决定。

Note that the purchase intention does not equal to purchase decision. There are two influential factors sit between them, which are attitudes of others and the unexpected situational factors. Either a negative feedback from friends or a sudden price drop of the competing brands may falter your determination. Besides, there may be a lag between the purchase decision and the actual possession of the physical product. Even you have clicked the button of paying for the stuff from online shopping cart, it may take days for the product to get you. Consumers may change their minds during the waiting period. To reduce the uncertainty of making the final deal, smart marketers study the factors that provoke a feeling of risk in consumers and give their strongest support.

请注意，购买意向并不等于购买决定。他们之间还有两个影响因素，一个是他人的态度，另一个是意想不到的情境因素。无论是来自朋友的负面反馈，还是竞争品牌的突然降价，都可能动摇你的决心。此外，购买决定和实际拥有实物产品之间可能存在一定的时间差。即使你点击了网上购物车的付款按钮，也可能需要几天的时间才能收到商品。在等待收货期间，消费者可能会改变主意。为了减少最后交易的不确定性，聪明的营销者研究那些能激起消费者风险感的因素，并给予他们最有力的支持。

4.3.5　Post-Purchase Behavior 购后行为

The buying process does not stop yet, nor do the marketers' job. After purchase, the consumer evaluates the performance of the product and feels either satisfied or dissatisfied about it, then will engage in post-purchase behavior.

购买过程还没有停止，营销人员的工作也没有停止。消费者在购买后对产品的性能进行评价，对产品感到满意或不满意，就会做出购后行为。

How do consumers decide whether they are satisfied or not? Technically, other than just saying "good" or "bad", it is measured by the level of consumer satisfaction. Consumers compare their expectations with the product performance. When the performance falls short of expectations, the consumer is dissatisfied; if it meets expectations, the customer is satisfied; if the performance exceeds expectations, the consumer is delighted.

消费者如何确定他们是否满意？严格来讲，除了说"好"或"坏"之外，它是由消费者满意度来衡量的。消费者将他们的期望与产品性能进行比较。当产品性能低于预期时，消费者不满意；如果满足了期望，消费者就满意了；如果超出预期，消费者就会感到高兴。

After generating those feelings and attitudes about a product, the customer takes action. Satisfied customer may introduce the product to others and is more likely to buy it again. Dissatisfied customer may return the product, choose never to buy it, complain to the company, or even take legal actions. In the Internet era, customer satisfaction is proved to be double-edged. Warning from an irritated customer can be a disaster for a brand. Companies nowadays are more than careful in dealing with customer complaints. To reduce customer dissatisfaction, companies should regularly measure consumer satisfaction. Besides, it is better for them to encourage accurate customer expectations, provide honest advertising and sales presentation before the deal, then make follow-up feedback, ask customers for suggestions from time to time, control product quality, and build a fast-channel for settling complaints.

在产生了对产品的感觉和态度之后，消费者就会采取行动。满意的消费者可能会把产品介绍给其他人并且更有可能再次购买。不满意的消费者可以选择退货、不再购买、向公司投诉甚至采取法律行动。在互联网时代，消费者满意度被证明是一把双刃剑。一个恼怒的消费者的警告对一个品牌来说可能会是一场灾难。现在的公司在处理客户投诉时都非常小心。为了减少消费者的不满，公司应该定期测量消费者的满意度。此外，最好是在交易前就鼓励消费者建立准确的期望，提供真实的广告和销售演示，然后进行后续反馈，不时询问消费者的建议，控制产品质量，建立快速的投诉解决渠道。

Marketers study the overall consumer decision-making process to prepare strategies in advance, in order to efficiently market their products. For example, if customers have little knowledge or hold negative attitude towards the product, the marketer can encourage them to speak out the unfavorable details and try to help them change their perceptions, or make modification of the product.

营销者研究整个消费者决策过程，提前准备策略，以有效地营销自己的产品。例如，如果消费者对产品缺乏了解或持有负面的态度，营销人员可以鼓励他们说出不满意的细节，试图帮助他们改变对产品的看法，或者对产品进行改进。

4.4 Factors of Affecting Consumer Behavior 影响消费者行为的因素

Experienced marketers not only have to learn consumer buying process, but also try to understand all the factors that influence consumer behavior, which marketers believe will affect consumers' purchase decisions. These influencing factors help to answer questions such as why a particular customer choose to buy the specific cell phone. There are three categories: internal, social, and situational factors.

有经验的营销者不仅要学习消费者的购买过程，还要努力了解所有影响消费者行为的因素，营销者认为这些因素会影响消费者的购买决策。这些影响因素有助于回答一些问题，如为什么特定的客户选择购买某款特定的手机。这些因素可分为三类：内在因素、社会因素和情境因素。

4.4.1 Internal Influences 内在因素

Internal influences are those factors lying deeply within a human being that make every single person so different and unique. Even if a group of students with similar study in the same classroom for years, they can exhibit totally different preferences in their dresses and computer brands. They usually come from consumers' own lifestyle and way of thinking. It includes perception, motivation, learning, attitude, personality, family lifecycle, and lifestyle.

内在影响因素是那些深藏在个体内部的因素，它们使每个人都与众不同。即使是在同一间教室里学习多年的一群学生，他们对自己的服装、电脑品牌的偏好也会完全不同。这些偏好通常源于消费者自己的生活方式和思维方式。其中包括知觉、动机、学习、态度、个性、家庭生命周期和生活方式。

1. Perception 知觉

Perception is how we interpret the information received by sensory receptors like eyes, ears, nose, mouth, and fingers. Perception depends not only on physical stimuli but also on an individual's past experiences. Different people can form completely different perceptions of the same situation. For example, most people are terrified of snakes, but a zoologist shows nothing but interest and enthusiasm.

知觉是我们解读眼睛、耳朵、鼻子、嘴巴和手指等感官接收信息的方式。知觉不仅取决于物理刺激，也取决于个人过去的经历。不同的人对同一情况会有完全不同的看法。例如，大多数人都害怕蛇，但动物学家却对蛇表现出兴趣和热情。

对健怡可口可乐 (Diet Coke) 和健怡百事可乐 (Diet Pepsi) 的口味进行盲测，结果没有发现任何区别。但对品牌版本的测试显示，65% 的消费者更喜欢健怡可乐，只有 23% 的消费者更喜欢健怡百事

2. Motivation 动机

Motivation is probably the most substantial internal influence that affect purchase behavior. It refers to a person's internal drive to satisfy unfulfilled needs or direct goal-achieving behavior. We have mentioned that needs arise from the gap between the desired state and the actual state. For example, if you go to work by crowded bus every day, you may experience unpleasant feelings and thus there is a need to a more comfortable and personal transportation. You ask friends for advice and do some information search, and finally buy a car.

动机可能是影响购买行为的最重要的内在影响因素。它指的是一个人满足未被满足的需求或直接实现目标的内在驱动力。我们已经提到，需求产生于理想状态和实际状态之间的差距。例如，如果你每天乘坐拥挤的公共汽车去上班，你可能会感觉不愉快，因此有必要拥有一个更舒适和私人的交通工具。你向朋友寻求建议、进行信息搜索，最后买了一辆车。

Psychologists have developed motivation theories, among which American psychologist Abraham Maslow's Need Theory is the most influential. The theory states that there are five levels of human needs arranged in a hierarchy. In order of importance, these five categories are physiological, safety, social, esteem, and self-actualization needs. The lower level's needs should to be satisfied before a person has a higher level's needs. One wouldn't be able to meet the need of buying a new car if he or she is often short of money for foods.

心理学家提出了动机理论，其中以美国心理学家亚伯拉罕·马斯洛的需求理论影响最大。该理论认为，人类的需求有 5 个层次，按重要性排序，分别是生理需求、安全需求、社交需求、尊重需求和自我实现需求。在一个人有更高层次的需求之前，低层次的需求应该得到满足。如果一个人经常买不起食物，他就不可能满足买新车的需求。

However, Maslow's theory cannot explain a consumer's motivation for every purchase. There are a variety of motivations why consumers buy. Some people desire to buy something nobody else has, such as limited edition bags; some wish to buy something everybody else is buying, and their preference for buying increases with the popularity of the product, such as an iPhone; under other circumstances, people purchase products because they need them to survive, such as shoes and medicine. People want the product to save money, time, energy, and space, thus to reduce risks and troubles. Understanding customers' level of needs is very essential to direct customers towards purchase decisions. For example, some people go to a coffee shop for filling their bellies, whereas others may step into the cafe for initiating a discussion with business friends. There are still others have different needs going into a coffee shop. So, it is essential for marketers to distinguish those needs segmentations to better serve their customers.

然而，马斯洛的理论并不能解释消费者每次购买的动机。消费者购买的动机多种多样。有些人想买别人没有的东西，比如限量版手袋；有些人希望买其他人都在买的东西，而且产品越流行，他们越喜欢购买，比如苹果手机；在其他情况下，人们购买产品是因为生存所需，比如鞋子和药品。人们希望产品能够节省金钱、时间、精力和空间，从而减少风险和麻烦。了解客户的需求水平对于指导客户做出购买决策至关重要。例如，一些人去咖啡店是为了填饱肚子，而另一些人可能是为了和商务伙伴进行讨论。还有一些人对去咖啡店另有需求。因此，为了更好地服务客户，市场营销人员必须区分不同需求所形成的细分市场。

3. Learning 学习

Human behavior is mostly learnt. Learning describes the changes of behavior arising from experience of interaction with the environment. Learning can occur deliberately, when women consumers will collect information on purpose for getting more knowledge about an unfamiliar digital product. It also happens unintentionally, when consumer can recognize famous brands even they have never used them with companies' help. There are several theories describing how people learn.

人类的行为大多是后天习得的。学习描述了在与环境的互动中所产生的行为变化。学习可以是有意为之，比如，当女性消费者为了获取更多不熟悉的码字产品的知识而有意收集信息；它也会在无意中发生，你会发现有时候消费者可以认出著名的品牌，即使他们从来没有在公司宣传的影响下使用过它们。有几种理论描述了人们是如何学习的。

4. Attitude 态度

Attitude is often reflected in an individual's act and buying patterns. It puts people in a frame of liking or disliking things. Once formed, attitude is hard to change. People living a healthy lifestyle rarely have fizzy drinks that contains high sugar and calories, nor do they eat fast food such as McDonald's or KFC.

态度往往反映在一个人的行为和购买模式上。它将人们置于喜欢或不喜欢事物的框架中。态度一旦形成就很难改变。崇尚健康生活方式的人很少喝高糖高热量的碳酸饮料，也不吃麦当劳或肯德基等快餐。

For this reason, smart marketers do not try to change consumers' attitudes, however,they fit their products into the existing attitudes. For example, Coca Cola introduces diet coke, Oreo creates Oreo Thins, and yogurt brands claims to contain probiotics, all for nowadays' overwhelming attitude towards healthy living.

因此，聪明的营销者不会试图改变消费者的态度，然而他们会让自己的产品迎合现有的态度。例如，可口可乐推出了健怡可乐，奥利奥推出了奥利奥薄饼，酸奶品牌声称含有益生菌，所有这些都是为了迎合如今人们对健康生活的压倒性态度。

5. Personality 个性

Personality refers to a set of unique psychological characteristics that consistently influence how a person responds to the environment. The following are some specific personality traits correlated with consumer behavior that imply relevant marketing strategies.

个性是指一组独特的心理特征，这些特征持续地影响着一个人对环境的反应。以下是一些与消费者行为相关的特定人格特征，每种个性对应相关的营销战略。

（1）Innovativeness: Innovative consumers are always on the lookout for new products. Cutting-edge products such as new technology devices can easily catch their eyes, and some may appear as surprisingly fashion-conscious.

创新：具有创新精神的消费者总是在寻找新产品。像新技术产品这样的尖端产品很容易吸引他们的眼球，并且有些消费者可能表现出惊人的时尚品位。

（2）Frugality: Consumers with this personality often restrain themselves and think heavily about purchases. They are sensitive to the price, or rather, the cost performance. Marketing strategies focus on avoiding expensive and inefficient products, emphasizing reduction of waste and practical utility.

节俭：有这种性格的消费者经常会克制自己，对购买的事情会慎重考虑。他们对价格很敏感，或者更确切地说，对性价比很敏感。营销策略是应注重避免向他们推销昂贵和低效的产品，强调减少浪费和实用性。

（3）Self-confidence: It is the degree to which a person has the ability of making a positive evaluation and a good decision. Consumers with full self-confidence can search information by themselves and form their own attitudes, of whom the marketers should avoid excessive intervention. By contrast, being the best pick of implementing the marketing strategies, those with low self-confidence are more easily influenced by marketers.

自信：是一个人做出积极评价和正确决定的能力。充满自信的消费者可以自己搜索信息，形成自己的态度，营销人员应避免过度干预。相比之下，作为执行营销策略的最佳对象，自信心不足的人更容易受到营销人员的影响。

（4）Sociability: It is the ability to be fond of the company of others. Consumers who are sociable are inclined to seek out the opportunity of social contact with others. They may respond to products that can entertain people and bring people together.

社交能力：指的是与人交往的能力。社交型的消费者倾向于寻找与他人社交的机会。他们可能会对娱乐大众、让人们可以聚在一起的产品给出回应。

（5）Anxiety: Consumers with anxiety express fear and are lack of security in purchase. They have more post-purchase dissonance and often feel upset after getting the products home. Marketing strategies include asking questions regarding their feelings, providing them with information about their concern so they can make an informed decision. Learn to apologize for the situation even if you are not the cause of the problem.

焦虑：焦虑的消费者会表现出恐惧，在购买时缺乏安全感。他们更多地感到购后不协调，把产品买回家后经常会感到不安。这时的营销策略包括可以询问他们的感受，向他们提供有关他们所关心的问题的信息，以便他们能够更确信自己的选择。面对这样的消费者要学会为出现的任何问题道歉，即使不是你造成了这个问题。

6. Age Group 年龄层

Think about what you would buy when you were a little child, maybe you have found that the product you like is different according to the age group you belong to.

想想当你还是个小孩子的时候，你会买什么，也许你会发现你喜欢的产品根据你所属的年龄段不同而不同。

各年龄段消费者心理和消费行为特征

Besides age, scientists found that consumer behavior depends more on family life cycle—the stages through which family members pass through from childhood to your retirement years. Young singles between 18 and 24, are found to buy more snack foods and staples, among them there are far more motorcycle riders, magazine readers, Internet users and cell phone users. Married couples with children, have a need for day care, baby foods, sports equipment, skill lessons, youth-group activity support etc. Mature couples tend to invest more than the other groups in financial products and vacation or weekend homes.

除了年龄之外，科学家还发现，消费者的行为更多地取决于家庭生命周期——家庭成员从童年到退休的各个阶段。18~24 岁的年轻单身人士会购买更多的零食和生活必需品，其中骑摩托车的人、杂志读者、互联网用户和手机用户占比更高。已婚夫妇且有孩子，他们会对对日托、婴儿食品、运动器材、技能课程、青少年活动支持等有需求。成熟的夫妇往往比其他群体更倾向于购买投资理财产品、度假产品或周末度假屋。

7. Lifestyle 生活方式

A lifestyle is a pattern of living that determines how people choose to spend their time, money, and energy, and that reflects their preferences and opinions. It is a more comprehensive concept that profiles a person's whole pattern of acting and interacting in the world. Studies show that consumers choose to buy products in order to define or actualize their lifestyles. Lifestyle includes things like bowling, cooking, car racing, attending charity events, having pets, interest in politics, watching sporting events and so on.

生活方式是一种生活的模式，它决定了人们如何选择花费他们的时间、金钱和精力，并反映了他们的喜好和观点。它是一个更综合的概念，概括了一个人在世界上的整体行为和互动模式。研究表明，消费者选择购买产品是为了定义或实现他的生活方式。生活方式包括打保龄球、做饭、赛车、参加慈善活动、养宠物、对政治感兴趣、观看体育赛事等。

Putting together psychology and demographics, psychographics or lifestyle refers to consumers' AIO, that is, activities (work, hobbies, shopping, sports, social events), interests (food, fashion, family, recreation) and opinion (about themselves, social issues, business, products). It is a dimension for measuring consumers' lifestyle, so that the marketer will better understand the wants and needs of the consumers.

结合心理学和人口统计学，消费心态学（生活方式）指的是消费者的 AIO，即活动（工作、爱好、购物、体育、社交活动）、兴趣（食物、时尚、家庭、娱乐）和意见（关于他们自己、社会问题、商业，产品）。它是衡量消费者生活方式的一个维度，以便营销人员更好地了解消费者的需求。

4.4.2 Situational Influences 情境因素

Other than internal factors that influence consumer behavior, the situational factors shape their purchase choice as well. Important cues in situational influences include the physical surroundings and time pressure.

除了影响消费者行为的内部因素外，情境因素也影响消费者的购买选择。情境因素包括物理环境和时间压力。

1. Physical Environment 物理环境

Light, smell, color, music, and temperature are elements in physical environment that significantly influence consumers' feelings and thus their purchase decisions. Think about having take-away food in your working place comparing with enjoying it in the well-decorated restaurant. The same dishes can give totally different impressions. Dreamworld, the gold coast's biggest theme park in Australia, people in there enjoy the benefits from the environmental control.

光线、气味、颜色、音乐和温度是物理环境中对消费者的感受甚至购买决定有重要影响的因素。想象一下，如果你在工作的地方吃外卖，而不是在装修精美的餐馆里享用，同样的菜会给人完全不同的印象。梦幻世界是澳大利亚黄金海岸最大的主题公园，人们在宜人的环境中保持着乐观的情绪，享受着环境带来的福利。

As to the sound, high-energy music, will attract a younger demographic, while effectively keeping boomers out of the store. Soft, medium-tempo music, on the other hand, has been found to encourage guests to not only stay in a restaurant longer, but also to consume more while there. Studies have shown that noisy environments, like those often found in quick-service restaurants, can encourage customers to overeat.

说到声音、激情满满的音乐，会吸引更年轻的人，同时也将老人有效地拒之门外。另一方面，人们发现，柔和的中速音乐不仅能使客人在餐馆逗留更长时间，而且促使他们在餐馆消费更多。研究表明，嘈杂的环境，比如快餐店，会让顾客吃得过多。

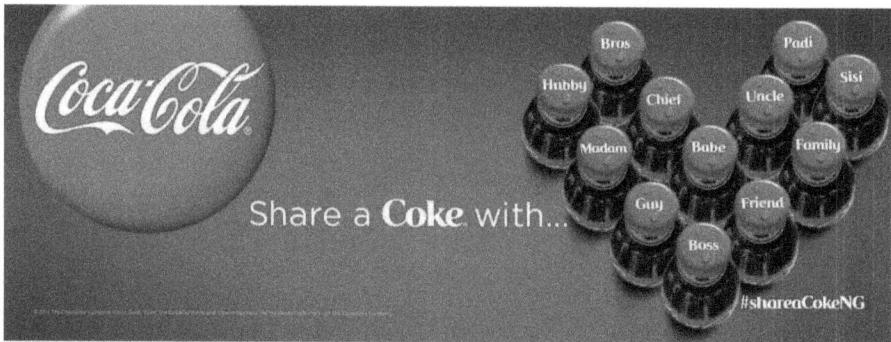

1885 年，美国政府发出了禁酒令，而为了让税务官一眼把可口可乐从含酒精的饮料中区分开，可口可乐的糖浆桶开始刷上了红色。这种红白相间的包装让可口可乐非常醒目，久而久之，这一配色也成为品牌激情、欢乐的象征

2. Time 时间

Time is something consumers give up for shopping. For buying a satisfying product or service, time seems to be a valuable thing. Time can affect consumption in three forms.

消费者购物就需要消耗时间。对于购买一个令人满意的产品或服务来说，时间似乎是一个宝贵的东西。时间可以以三种形式影响消费。

The first is time pressure. People reports more time pressure ever than before. When consumers do not have enough time, they tend to process less information. For example, if a businessman searching for a present for wife is right in a hurry to catch a plane, he may rely on clues like the best-known brand, or the product with the most exquisite package design, because he does not have time to consider the alternatives.

首先是时间压力。人们比以前有更多的时间压力。当消费者没有足够的时间时，他们倾向于处理较少的信息。例如，如果一个商务人士在赶飞机时急着给妻子买礼品，他可能会依靠一些线索，比如最知名的品牌或者包装设计最精美的产品，因为他没有时间考虑其他的选择。

The second is the time of the year. Consumption changes with the seasons, as we buy down jacket in winter and sunglasses in summer. Furthermore, the amount of daylight also affects consumer behavior. In winter time when the day is shorter, people tend to go shopping earlier. In summer, people are observed to spend more money.

第二个是一年中的时间。消费随着季节的变化而变化，我们在冬天买羽绒服，夏天买太阳镜。此外，日晒量也会影响消费者的行为。在冬季，白天较短，人们往往较早去购物。在夏天，据观察人们会花更多的钱。

The third is the time of the day. Most people rest during midnight to 6 a.m., and at noon time. Those who go shopping during this time appear to be less active, and may not make informed purchases. So, marketers provide shoppers with refreshments such as coffee or tea to cheer them up.

第三个是一天中的时间。大多数人在午夜到早上 6 点休息，中午午休。人们在这些时间似乎就不那么活跃，可能不会在清醒的情况下购物。因此，营销人员在这些时间段为顾客提供咖啡或茶等茶点，让他们打起精神来。

有许多发明旨在节省消费者的时间。宝丽来（Polaroid）拍立得是一款内部处理的即时相机，能在曝光后迅速生成成品照片，让朋友们在拍照后不久就能欣赏到自己的照片。速溶咖啡、方便面是现代快节奏生活的首选

4.4.3 Social Influences 社会因素

Besides internal and situational influences on consumer behavior, everyone lives in a society is inevitably affected by the comments made by families, friends, and other acquaintances we are connecting with.

消费者行为除了受内部和情境影响外，每个生活在社会中的人都不可避免地受到家人、朋友和其他熟人的影响。

1. Culture 文化

Culture is the most basic for human wants and behavior. It is the overall beliefs, values, and customs produced and practiced by a human society. A belief is a proposition that reflects a person's acknowledge and assessment. Values are general statements that guide behavior and influence beliefs. Customs are modes of behavior that constitutes culturally approved ways of behaving in specific situations.

文化是人类最基本的欲望和行为。它是人类社会生产和实践的共同信仰、价值观和习俗。信念是反映一个人的认知和评价的观点。价值观是指导行为和影响信念的一般性陈述。习俗是一种行为模式，它构成了文化上认可的在特定情况下的行为方式。

Consumers attitudes are different across western and eastern cultures. For example, Häagen-Dazs, an ice-cream brand sold in American supermarkets, successfully reinvented itself as a luxury ice cream brand sold in boutique stores in China. Its absolute price in China is more than twice that in the USA. Americans treat Häagen-Dazs as ice cream, but Chinese see it as part of a high-end lifestyle.

东西方文化中，消费者的态度有所不同。例如，在美国超市销售的冰激凌品牌哈根达斯，在中国成功转型为精品商店销售的奢侈冰激凌。它在中国的绝对价格是在美国的 2 倍多。美国人视哈根达斯为冰激凌，而中国人视其为高端生活方式的一部分。

Mattel 玩具公司成功地在许多国家销售了未作改动的芭比娃娃，但在日本的销售情况并不怎么好。他们的日本经销商对八年级的女孩进行调查后发现，她们认为芭比娃娃的胸部太大而腿又太长。经改造后的芭比娃娃大受欢迎，2 年卖出了 200 多万个

2. Subcultures 亚文化

Cultures can be divided into subcultures, which are smaller groups of people in a society whose members share a distinctive set of beliefs, traditions or common experiences. Each of us belongs to many subcultures. They can be religious groups, language groups, age groups, as well as iFans group formed by huge Apple fans, popular TV shows such as *Game of Thrones*, or computer game players leagues.

文化可以细分为亚文化，它是一个社会中较小的群体，其组织成员共享一套信仰、传统或经历。我们每个人都属于某些亚文化，可以是宗教团体、语言团体、年龄团体，也可以是由喜爱苹果公司产品的庞大群体所组成的"果粉"，或是喜爱热门电视剧《权力的游戏》的观众，或是热爱电玩的人组成的玩家联盟。

3. Social class 社会阶层

Social class is a social stratification in which people are grouped into a set of hierarchical social categories, whose members have shared values, interests, and behaviors.

社会阶层是一种社会分层，人们按照一个个等级森严的社会属性进行分组，每个组内的成员都拥有共同的价值观、兴趣，表现出类似的行为。

In western countries, social class can be grouped into three main categories: upper class, middle class, and lower class. Marketers are interested in this kind of classification for in many occasions, people are identified to share the same distinctive consumption patterns within a social class.

在西方国家，社会阶级可分为主要的三类：上层阶级、中产阶级和下层阶级。营销者对这种分类很感兴趣，因为在很多情况下，人们被认为在一个社会阶层中拥有着相同的独特的消费模式。

Upper class lives the social elite who accumulates a great amount of wealth and resources, such as senior cadres, wealthy traders, the big bankers. Wealthy traders are socially active, usually possess more than one property, buy high-performing cars, send children to greatest schools, and give donation to charity from time to time. They are more independent in making buying decisions, and they buy products that represent their status, usually those customized and in limited edition. Even though they may never use the product for what it is designed, either want to feel like they could or want others to think that they do. For example, an upper class member may buy a ¥4000 climbing jacket when he or she has no intention of ever summiting Everest.

在上层社会中，生活着积累了大量财富和资源的社会精英，包括高层干部、大富商、大银行家。富商大贾们积极参加社交活动，通常拥有不止一处房产，购买高性能的汽车，送孩子去最优质的学校，时不时地向慈善机构捐款。他们在购买决定上表现得更加独立，购买那些能够显示他们身份的产品，通常是定制版和限量版。尽管他们可能永远不会按照产品的设计来使用产品，但他们要么想让别人觉得他们可以，要么想让别人认为他们可以。例如，一个上层社会人士可能会买一件价值 4000 元的登山夹克，但根本就没有登上珠峰的打算。

There is a large population in middle class. Professionals, corporate managers, and the sizable working class fall into this group. They believe in education, will spend money on searching for better things in life such as good neighborhood and good social groups. When shopping, middle class consumers seek quality and value, but appreciate distinction. Practicality is paramount for the middle-class state of mind. These consumers will go a long way to justify their purchases—even pricey designer products such as Louis Vuitton handbags—as practical and durable. They buy popular products to keep up with the trends.

中产阶级人口众多。专业人士、公司经理和庞大的工人阶级都属于这个群体。他们相信教育，会花钱去寻找生活中更好的东西，比如好的邻居和好的社会群体。在购物时，中产阶级消费者追求质量和价值，但也尊重差异。对于中产阶级来说，实用性是最重要的。这些消费者将在很长一段时间内证明他们的购买——即使是昂贵的设计师产品，如路易威登手袋——是实用和耐用的。他们购买流行的产品，以跟上潮流。

Lower class is composed of people with less money available and low educational level. They live on daily wages, and spend most of their money on basic necessities such as food and shelter. They are less likely to purchase products for spiritual enjoyment, such as stylish furniture, beautiful paintings, fashionable dresses. Although many consumers in this class struggle to move upward into a higher class, they lack good education and are poorly paid for unskilled work. They have limited channel of receiving messages, so marketing communication to this class focuses on mass media such as radio and television.

下层阶级是指那些钱少、受教育程度低的人。他们靠日薪生活，把大部分的钱花在基本的必需品上，如食物和住所。他们不太可能购买精神产品，如时尚的家具、美丽的画作或时装。尽管这个阶层的许多消费者努力向上进入一个更高的阶层，但他们缺乏良好的教育，而且从非技术性工作中获得的报酬很低。他们接收信息的渠道有限，所以对这个阶层的营销传播主要集中在大众媒体，如广播和电视。

4. Reference groups 参照群体

A reference group is the set of people consumers like to get associated with, compare themselves with, want to please or imitate, and think themselves as a member of that group.

参照群体是消费者喜欢与之建立联系、与之进行比较、想要取悦或模仿并认为自己是该群体中的一员的群体。

Marketers find business opportunities created by reference groups. People shows conformity. Reference group influences people in two ways. First, they set levels of aspiration, and they are the models of what lifestyle should be achieved and as well as purchasing behavior. Second, they help define the physical items or services considered representative for those aspirations—the kind of housing, clothing, or car. Products with endorsement within a group, either through using or commenting, give a reason for those who look to the group to purchase that product.

营销人员通过参照群体发现商机。参照群体中的人们表现出从众性。参照群体通过两种方式影响人们。首先，他们设定了欲望的层次，他们是生活方式和购买行为的典范。其次，他们定义了那些被认为能代表这些欲望的产品或服务的种类，如住房、服装或汽车等。在一个参照群体中被购买的产品，无论通过使用还是评论的方式拥有了背书，都为群体中的人们提供了一个购买理由。

Moreover, an individual can also be a reference group, which is usually known as an opinion leader. An opinion leader is who people seek out for guidance in making purchase decisions, usually someone deemed to have a deeper expertise in a specific area than the average consumers.

此外，一个人也可以是一个参照群体，通常被称为意见领袖。意见领袖是指人们在做出购买决定时寻求指导的人，通常是那些被认为在某个特定领域比一般消费者有更多专业知识的人。

In many cases, consumers are unconsciously attracted by the products endorsed by their favorite celebrities. However, using celebrity as opinion leaders bears some risks. The reputation of the celebrity is strongly connected with the brand image. For example, the famous golf player Tiger Woods' image was ruined after he was caught cheating on his wife with multiple mistresses. He lost several endorsements and his career as a golfer has been downhill ever since. In order to stay out of his bad image, company such as Nike then slashed their contract with Tiger Woods by 50%, cutting his endorsement earnings to less than one-third of what had been previously reported.

在很多情况下，消费者会无意识地被他们喜爱的名人代言的产品所吸引。然而，利用名人作为意见领袖存在一些风险。名人的声誉与品牌形象密切相关。例如，当人们发现著名的高尔夫球运动员泰格·伍兹背着他的妻子与多个情妇偷情时，他的形象因此被毁。他失去了一些代言，从那以后，他的高尔夫职业生涯一直走下坡路。为了摆脱他的坏形象，耐克等公司随后将与老虎伍兹的合同削减了50%，将他的代言收入削减到此前的不到三分之一。

5. Gender Roles 性别角色

A Gender role is the set of societal norms dictating the types of behaviors which are generally considered acceptable, appropriate, or desirable for people based on their actual or perceived sex or sexuality.

性别角色是一套社会规范，规定了人们基于实际或感知的性别或性别行为，这些行为通常被认为是可接受的、适当的或可取的。

Gender roles deeply affect marketing communications. For example, Barbie and Hello Kitty targeting girl consumers subconsciously wear the color pink in order to look feminine. Credit card targeting female college students design colorful flowers and female symbols, those for male consumers often carry pictures with dark color and figures from computer games such as *League of Legends*.

性别角色深刻影响着营销传播。例如，针对女孩消费者的芭比娃娃和凯蒂猫下意识地穿粉红色，是为了看起来更女性化。针对女大学生的信用卡设计了五颜六色的花朵和女性符号，针对男性消费者的信用卡通常带有深色的图片和《英雄联盟》等电脑游戏中的人物形象。

◎ **阅读推荐**

德尔·霍金斯，戴维·马斯瑟伯.消费者行为学 [M]. 符国群，等译.北京：机械工业出版社，2014.

卢泰宏，等.消费者行为学：中国消费者透视 [M]. 北京：中国人民大学出版社，2015.

郑清元，等.从 1.0 到 3.0——移动社群如何重构社交关系与商业模式 [M]. 北京：人民邮电出版社，2016.

查克·马丁.决胜移动终端：移动互联时代影响消费者决策的 6 大关键 [M]. 向坤，译.杭州：浙江人民出版社，2014.

5

Business Markets

企业市场

知识解锁 Knowledge Unlocked

以下问题的答案，可在本章寻找：

1. 企业市场和消费者市场有什么不同？

2. 企业有什么样的需求？

3. 企业购买者是谁？企业在什么情况下购买？

4. 企业如何做出购买决策？

5.1 Characteristics of Business Markets 企业市场的特征

We are all familiar with a lot companies dealing with individual customers directly. Besides, there are more large companies, such as IBM, Alibaba, GE, and Philips that sell to other organizations, which is called business-to-business marketing (B to B). For example, a university would purchase thousands of and computers from Apple, garment manufacturers purchase components from Alibaba, and convenient stores purchase snacks from various brands. These are examples of B-to-B transactions. Business-to-business marketing involves any products or services a company purchases to resell, to use as components in their own products or services, or to support their daily operations.

我们都熟悉许多直接与个人客户打交道的公司。此外，还有更多的大公司，如 IBM、阿里巴巴、通用电气和飞利浦，它们向其他组织销售产品，这被称为企业对企业营销。例如，一所大学从苹果公司购买数千台电脑，服装制造商从阿里巴巴购买零部件，便利店向各种品牌购买零食，都是企业对企业交易的例子。企业对企业营销涉及企业购买的任意产品或服务，这些产品或服务可以转售、作为自身产品或服务的组成部分使用，或支持企业的日常运营。

Business buyer behavior refers to the buying behavior of the organizations that buy goods and services for use in the production of other products and services or to resell or rent them to others at a profit. Although business buyers also make decisions, they behave with a major difference. Let us look at some of the features of the business market.

企业购买行为是指购买商品和服务用于生产其他产品和服务，或将其转售或出租给他人以获取利润的组织的购买行为。虽然企业买家也会做决定，但他们的行为方式有很大的不同。让我们来看看企业市场的一些特点。

5.1.1 Multiple Buyers 多重买方

Products bought in business markets are often more than satisfying an individual's needs. There are diversified needs in an organization. For example, if you decide to buy a stereo system, furniture such as sofa for your apartment, you search information and choose from alternative brands, so you are the only person to serve. However, if the stereo system and furniture are for the government department use, it may take into consideration the requirements of the top managers, official workers, and others who may use them. Also, some products have to meet certain government-mandated criteria or local content guidelines. In companies, purchases of technical equipment are based on specific technical specifications made by expertise. So, it is more complicated and takes longer to make a business buying decision.

在企业市场上购买的产品往往不仅仅是为了满足个人的需要。组织中有各种各样的需求。例如，如果你决定为你的公寓购买音响系统、沙发等家具，你会搜索信息并从其他品牌中进行选择，所以你是唯一需要服务的人。但是，如果音响系统和家具是为政府部门使用而设计的，可能会考虑高层管理人员、正式工作人员、其他可能使用它们的人的需求。此外，一些产品必须符合某些政府规定的标准或地方内容指南。在企业中，技术设备的采购是根据专业知识制定的具体技术规范进行的。因此，做出商业购买的决定更加复杂，需要的时间也更长。

5.1.2 Number of Customers 客户数量

The amount of business customers is far less than individual buyers. According to national statistics, there are around 7 million companies and 325 million households in China. For example, LG who provides touch screens to Apple has a limited number of customers. This implies that the strategies use by the company vary greatly from that by consumer markets. In consumer markets, LG may use TV advertising and celebrity endorsement, but in its business markets personal selling is proved to be a better promotion strategy.

企业客户的数量远远少于个人买家。根据国家统计数据，中国约有 700 万家企业和 3.25 亿户家庭。举个例子，向苹果提供触摸屏的 LG 公司拥有有限的客户数量。这意味着企业所使用的营销策略与消费者市场的策略有很大不同。在消费者市场，LG 可能使用电视广告和名人代言，但在其商业市场，个人销售则是更好的促销策略。

5.1.3 Size of Purchases 购买规模

Business orderings often have a large scale with enormous quantity and preferential price. For example, a share-riding company purchase tens of thousands of bicycles from bicycle manufactures; a bakery company purchases tons of powder, sugar, butter, chocolate, and other ingredients every year. In contrast, even a baking fan who does the baking everyday at home cannot consume a box of each one of those ingredients within a day. Organizations can buy many types of products, such as professional human resource management system, working suits for employees, or production machinery, which are often expensive. Due to the big size of business purchase, marketing promotion turns to a strong sale force rather than mass media.

企业订单数量大、价格优惠。例如，一家股份公司每年从自行车制造商那里购买数万辆自行车，一家烘焙公司每年购买成吨的粉末、糖、黄油、巧克力和其他原料。相比之下，即使是一个每天在家烘焙的烘焙爱好者也不可能在一天之内吃完所有这些配料。组织可以购买许多类型的产品，如专业的人力资源管理系统、员工的工作套装或生产机器，这些往往是昂贵的。由于企业采购规模大，营销推广更多的是依靠强大的人员销售，而不是大众媒体。

5.1.4 Geographic Concentration 地理集中度

Business markets usually exhibit geographic concentration, for the improvement of industrial competitiveness, cooperation between businesses, and the development of the whole industry. For example, in China the major leather industry is located in Wenzhou, and the e-commerce industrial parks in Hangzhou make it the international e-business center. By concentrating, marketers are easy to concentrate their sales efforts for providing professional products and services, as well as benefit the growth of a company.

企业市场通常表现出地理上的集中，以提高行业竞争力、企业之间的合作和整个行业的发展。例如，在中国主要的皮革产业位于温州，以及杭州的电子商务产业园使其成为国际电子商务中心。通过地理上的集中，营销人员很容易集中他们在销售上所做的努力，为客户提供专业的产品和服务，有助于公司的成长。

Besides, an additional number of points can be concluded to distinguish business market and consumer market. Business markets have a more complex decision-making unit which may involve different specialists making contributions time and time again. Personal selling promotion strategy in business markets is superior to other marketing techniques, for the key in the exchanges is based on personal long-term relationship. Business products are judged by rational buyers on a set of technical specifications rather than the packaging and appearances as the consumer products.

此外，有另一些方面的差别区分商业市场和消费者市场。企业市场拥有一个更复杂的决策单元，可能需要不同的专家一次又一次地做出贡献。个人促销策略在企业市场上优于其他的营销手段，因为达成交易的关键在于销售员是否能维系和企业的长期关系。另外，理性的买家判断企业产品的标准是一套技术规格，而不是消费品的包装和外观。

5.2 Business-to-Business Demand 企业对企业的需求

Exchanges in business markets are initiated by the demand of business buyers. The few but large demand in business markets is derived, inelastic, fluctuating, and joint, making another difference between business and consumer markets. Let us take a look at these concepts one by one.

企业市场的交易始于企业买家的需求。企业消费者数量少但需求量很大，企业的需求是派生的、缺乏弹性的、波动的、连带的，这是企业市场和消费者市场之间的另一个区别。让我们一一解释一下这些概念。

5.2 1 Derived Demand 派生需求

Derived demand is probably the most fundamental concept to business marketing success. Business-to-business demand is derived demand that finally comes directly or indirectly from the demand of the end consumers. The demand for G-series high-speed trains is derived from the increasing consumer demand for quick and easy travel between cities in China, and the demand for building Free Trade Zone in Shanghai is derived from consumers' demand for imported lower-priced goods.

派生需求可能是企业营销成功最基本的概念。企业对企业的需求属于派生需求，它最终直接或间接地来自终端消费者的需求。对高铁的需求来源于中国城市间快速便捷出行的消费需求的增长，而上海自贸区的建设需求来源于消费者对进口低价商品的需求。

Value is added to each link of the derived demand value chain. Take a simple T-shirt production for example. There are companies who grow and pick up cotton, spinners who create textiles, weavers who make them into cloth, garment makers who tailor the cloth into shirts, then the shirts go to distributors and finally sell to the general public. We can see that, in this chain, none of the businesses buy the products for pure indulgence. They buy them with the ultimate aim of adding value in order that they can move the products down the chain until they finally reach us. Therefore, B2B marketing is about meeting the needs of other businesses, and the ultimate demand for the products made by these businesses is driven by consumers. So if business does not produce based on consumers' demands, the whole chain in the industry will be in big trouble.

价值被添加到派生需求价值链的每个环节。以简单的 T 恤生产为例。有种植和采摘棉花的公司，纺织工人制造纺织品，织布工把它们织成布，服装制造商把布缝制成衬衫，然后把衬衫卖给分销商，最后卖给公众。我们可以看到，在这个链条中，没有一个商家纯粹是为了享受而购买产品。他们购买这些产品的最终目的是增加产品的价值，这样他们就可以将产品从供应链上向下移动，直到最终到达我们这里。因此，B2B 营销就是满足其他企业的需求，而这些企业对产品的最终需求是由消费者来驱动的，如果企业不根据消费者的需求来生产，那么整个行业的链条都会陷入困境。

5.2.2　Inelastic Demand 非弹性需求

In economics, inelastic demand means demand for goods or services hardly increases or decreases in response to changes in price. In business market, demands are inelastic especially in the short term, because what is being sold is usually just one of many components that creates the finished product. For example, suppose Nike shoes are made of fiber, leather, rubber, plastic, etc., with each material sourced from individual suppliers. Other factors remaining the same, if the price of leather is reduced by 10%, the business will still buy the same amount of materials, and the demand for Nike shoes can hardly see an increase, for the price change of the raw material has little impact on the price of the finished shoes.

在经济学中，非弹性需求意味着对商品或服务的需求几乎不会随着价格的变化而增加或减少。在企业市场上，需求是无弹性的，尤其是在短期内，因为销售的产品通常只是制造最终产品的众多组成之一。例如，假设耐克鞋是由纤维、皮革、橡胶、塑料等制成的，每一种材料都来自独立供应商。其他因素保持不变，如果皮革的价格降低 10%，生产商仍将购买相同数量的材料，耐克鞋几乎看不到的需求增加，原材料的价格变化对成品鞋的价格影响不大。

However, this is not always the case. In business market, when the finished product is made of only one or a few materials, the price changes of the main material will affect the price of the finished products, the business would probably pass through the cost to the end-consumers which cause change in demand. The demand for shoes will increase until the price of the finished shoes is reduced.

然而，情况并非总是如此。在商业市场中，当成品仅由一种或几种材料制成时，主要材料的价格变化会影响成品的价格，企业可能会将成本转嫁给终端消费者，从而引起需求的变化。对鞋子的需求可能会增加，直到成品鞋的价格下降。

5.2.3　Fluctuating Demand 波动性需求

Another characteristic of business market is that business markets have more fluctuating demand, which means a small change in demand by consumers can have a big effect throughout the chain of businesses that supply all the goods and services that produce it. There are mainly two reasons for this. One is that there may be several companies satisfying one type of customer need. For example, the demand for borrowing money has promoted the development of the peer-to-peer lending platforms. Even a small increase in demand of lending and borrowing money can cause a dramatic increase in demand for platforms. That explains why peer-to-peer lending platforms are so popular over a period.

商业市场的另一个特点是，商业市场的波动性需求更大，这意味着消费者需求的一个小变化就可能会对供应所有产品和服务的整个商业链产生重大影响。这主要有两个原因。一个是可能有几家公司满足一种类型的客户需求。例如，借贷需求推动了 P2P 借贷平台的发展。即使是借贷需求的小幅增长也会导致平台需求的急剧增长。这就解释了为什么一段时间内 P2P 借贷平台如此受欢迎。

Another reason is that the life expectancy of some products from business market seems longer than consumer goods, such as the machinery used to produce packages can last 10 to 20 years. In this case, companies that sell the machinery can have high demands one year, but low for the rest several years. Unless the company owns large number of potential customers, or loyal customers that have long-term cooperation, the demand will always be fluctuating.

另一个原因是，商业市场上的一些产品的寿命似乎比消费品长，比如用于生产包装的机器可以使用 10 到 20 年。在这种情况下，销售机器的公司可能有一年的高需求，但接下来几年都是低需求。除非公司拥有大量的潜在客户，或者有长期合作的忠诚客户，否则需求会一直波动。

5.2.4 Joint Demand 联合需求

Joint demand is the demand when two or more goods are used together to create a product. For example, steel and glass are made together into a window. If the supply of either one of them decreases, it will not be able to produce as many windows. So the demand for one material affects the other, their demands are joint together.

联合需求是指两个或多个商品一起使用，来生产一个产品。例如，用钢铁和玻璃一起制成窗户。如果其中任何一种材料的供应减少，都不能生产同样多的窗户。所以对一种材料的需求会影响到另一种，它们的需求是联合在一起的。

5.3 Types of Business Buyers 企业购买者的类型

Business-to-Business marketing is often directed to individuals within an organization who act on behalf of a company. Many companies purchase to produce other goods and resell to support their operations, or integrate products from other companies for business expansion. There are mainly three types of business customers we will introduce as follows.

企业对企业的营销通常针对组织中代表公司的个人。许多公司购买其他产品进行生产并转售，以支持公司的运作，或者整合其他公司的产品来扩展业务。我们主要介绍以下三种类型的企业客户。

5.3.1 Producers 生产者

Producers are the individuals or organizations that purchase for use in the production of other goods and services, in return, they make a profit. Agricultural, fishing, animal husbandry, and logging industries are among producers. Service providers such as McDonald's buys beef and potatoes to provide a meal; hotel like Radisson purchases beddings, decorations, household appliances, furniture, and hundreds of recreational facilities that make guests feel not only comfortable but also distinguished; a dentist needs drugs such as Novocain, oral tools, and X-ray machines to practice dental treatment. Manufacturers such as BMW needs steel, glass, rubber, and many other materials to make a car; Dell needs electronic components, circuit board, metal to produce a laptop.

生产者是购买产品（原材料）用于生产其他产品和服务的个人或组织。作为回报，他们会获得利润。农业、渔业、畜牧业、伐木业都在生产者之列。像麦当劳这样的服务供应商购买牛肉和土豆来提供餐饮；像雷迪森这样的酒店会购买床上用品、装饰品、家用电器、家具和数百种娱乐设施，给客人提供舒适且尊贵的居住感受；牙医需要药物，如诺佛卡因、口腔工具和 X 光机来进行牙科治疗。像宝马这样的制造商需要钢铁、玻璃、橡胶和许多其他材料来制造汽车；戴尔需要电子元件、电路板、金属来制造笔记本电脑。

5.3.2 Resellers 经销商

While producers transform materials into other products, resellers are the companies that sell goods and services produced by other firms without materially changing them. Being distribution channel firms, resellers do not produce, they purchase with the intention of reselling rather than consuming or using them. Resellers consist of wholesalers, distributors, and retailers. They are the ones who help producers find customers and make sales to them.

当生产者将材料转化为其他产品时，经销商是那些销售其他公司生产的产品和服务而不进行实质性改变的公司。作为分销渠道，经销商不生产，它们购买的目的是转售，而不是消费或使用它们。经销商包括批发商、分销商和零售商。他们是帮助生产者找到客户并向他们销售产品的人。

Wholesaler is a trader that buys bulk quantity of goods from various producers or vendors, warehouses them, and resells. them in smaller ones. Although wholesalers do not involve in promotional activities, a good wholesaler can really cut down on your overhead costs and allow you to reach much greater profits.

批发商是一种贸易商，从各种各样的生产商或销售商那里购买大量的货物，把其储存起来，然后进行零售。虽然批发商不参与促销活动，一个好的批发商可以切实减少开支，让你获得更大的利润。

Distributor, usually with strong manpower and cash support to suppliers and manufacturers, is an agent that distributes products and services to various parties in different locations. It provides a range of services such as product information, technical support, after-sale service. For example, physical distribution firms help the company to stock and move goods from their points of origin to where they want. Marketing services agencies such as the marketing research firms, advertising agencies, media firms, and marketing consulting firms help the company target and promote its products to the right markets. Financial institutions include banks, credit companies, and insurance companies, facilitate finance transactions or insure against the risks associated with the buying and selling of goods. Having a good distributor can ensure your products in high demand.

分销商通常为供应商和制造商提供强大的人力和现金支持，它们是在不同地点向各方分销产品和服务的代理商。它提供一系列的服务，如产品信息、技术支持、售后服务。例如，物流公司帮助公司储存货物，并将货物从产地运到它们想去的地方。营销服务机构，如营销研究公司、广告公司、媒体公司和营销咨询公司，帮助公司确定目标，并将产品推向合适的市场。金融机构包括银行、信贷公司和保险公司，为金融交易提供便利，或为与买卖商品有关的风险提供保险。有一个好的经销商可以确保你的产品处于高需求中。

Retailer is a service provider fills the small orders of a large number of individuals, who are end-users, rather than large orders of a small number of wholesale. In the digital age, an increasing number of retailers are seeking to reach broader markets by selling through multiple channels, including online retailing.

Some brands have independent and small retailers, others turn to big retailers such as Wal-Mart, Carrefour, and Amazon, who have great number of potential customers and stores that operate in many countries around the world.

零售商是满足大量个人小订单的服务提供商，它们面对的是最终用户，而不是大批量的批发订单。在数字时代，越来越多的零售商正寻求通过多种渠道销售，包括网上零售，以拓展更广阔的市场。一些品牌有独立的小零售商，另一些则向沃尔玛、家乐福、亚马逊这样的大零售商寻求帮助，这些大零售商拥有大量的潜在客户，在世界各地的许多国家都有分店。

5.3.3 Organizations 组织机构

Government and non-profit institutions make up two types of organizations in the business market. Government markets refer to the various levels of government units that purchase or rent goods to carry out the main functions of government. It may surprise you that the biggest purchaser of goods and services in the world is the US government. It not only purchases small items such as ballpoint pens, notepads, tax machines as individual customers do, but also large items such as nuclear weapons, highway construction services, medical services, garbage collections, and transportations. Many government entities specify their requirements, and standard procedure in a guidance, so that ensure all suppliers are treated fairly and equally.

在商业市场中，政府和非营利机构构成了两种类型的组织。政府市场是指那些为执行政府的主要职能而采购或租用商品的各级政府单位。你可能会感到惊讶，世界上最大的商品和服务买家是美国政府。它不仅像个人客户那样购买圆珠笔、记事本、收税机等小件物品，而且还购买核武器、公路建设服务、医疗服务、垃圾收集和运输等大型物品。许多政府实体都在指南中规定了它们的要求和标准程序，以确保所有供应商得到公平和平等的待遇。

Non-profit institutional markets consist of organizations such as the Red Cross, churches, hospitals, charitable organizations. Holding low costs for these institutions is especially important. Unlike for-profit companies, most of the non-profit institutions use their small profits to fund all their activities. The lower the price a business can offer, the greater the opportunities that deal is made. Purchases in these markets are often made by non-professional employees who have duties other than making purchases. So these people rely more on advice and assistant given by marketers.

非营利机构市场由红十字会、教会、医院、慈善组织等组织组成。保持这些机构的低成本运行尤其重要。与营利性公司不同的是，大多数非营利机构利用其微薄的利润来资助所有的活动。企业提供的价格越低，成交的机会就越大。在这些市场购物的人通常是非专业的雇员，购物并不是他们的主要职责。所以这些人更依赖于营销人员提供的建议和帮助。

5.4　Major Types of Business Buying 企业购买的主要类型

5.4.1　The Buying Center 采购中心

The buying center is also called decision-making unit (DMU). It is noted that the buying center is not a place at all. It is a cross-functional team made up by people within an organization that work together to reach a business buying decision. The buying center is a fundamental concept in creating customer value and influence in organizational efficiency and effectiveness. Generally, participants in the buying center include supervisors, workers, expertise, engineers, secretaries, etc., all have varying influence on the B2B buying decision. The members can undertake one or more of the following roles.

采购中心也被称为决策单元。值得注意的是，采购中心根本不是一个地方。它是一个由组织内的人员组成的跨功能团队，他们一起工作以完成企业购买决策。采购中心是一个基本概念，可创造客户价值和影响组织的效率和效果。一般来说，购买中心的参与者包括主管、工人、专家、工程师、秘书等，他们对B2B采购决策都有不同程度的影响。成员可以承担以下一个或多个角色。

5.4.2　Initiator 发起者

Initiator is the person who recognizes the need for making a business buying decision. A factory worker may find the machine too old to work properly and need a replacement, then report to the supervisor. A salesperson may require the purchase of a more advanced computer system for large orders, in order to improve the company's efficiency. Sometimes, consultant will act as an initiator that suggests a purchase.

发起者是指认识到需要做出企业购买决策的人。工厂的工人可能会发现机器太旧，不能正常工作，需要更换，然后向主管报告。为了提高公司的效率，销售人员可能需要购买更先进的计算机系统来处理大订单。有时候，顾问会作为发起者提出购买建议。

5.4.3 User 用户

User is the one who needs the product. A user usually knows the performance condition of the product, and can offer advices and make suggestions on what to buy. Marketers need to inform the benefits of their product that help solve user's problem.

用户是指需要产品的人。用户通常了解产品的性能状况，并能提出购买建议。营销人员需要告知产品的好处，帮助解决用户的问题。

5.4.4 Gatekeeper 把关人

A gatekeeper controls the access of information to other members. It is the person responsible for keeping a decision-maker from being bothered by what he or she considers to be irrelevant and bothersome visitors and callers. Marketers learn to develop a relationship with the gatekeeper, because gatekeepers often hold a level of hostility toward salespeople.

把关人控制其他成员的信息获取。它是负责使决策者不被他或她认为不相关的和麻烦的访客和呼叫者打扰的人。营销人员要学会与"看门人"建立关系，因为"看门人"往往对销售人员怀有一定程度的敌意。

5.4.5 Influencer 影响者

An influencer affects the buying decision by offering expertise. Technical people develop specs and do the evaluation of alternative products. Marketers need to identify influencers in an organization and persuade them of their superiority to competitors.

影响者通过提供专业知识来影响购买决策。技术人员制定规格并对替代产品进行评估。营销人员需要识别组织中的影响者，并说服他们，使自己的产品看起来比竞争对手更有优势。

5.4.6　Decider 决定者

Decider makes the final purchase decision. Person taking this role usually has great power within an organization. Routine purchase will be made by some procurement agent, while complex purchase decision is usually made by a manager, a director, an executive officer who takes charge of a department or a company.

决定者做出最后的购买决定。担任这一职务的人通常在组织中有很大的权力。日常采购将由采购代理进行，复杂的采购决策通常由经理、董事，或管理某个部门或公司的领导做出。

5.4.7　Buyer 采购员

Buyer selects suppliers, negotiate the terms of purchase, and is responsible for the details of the purchase. Buyers negotiate price, confirm contract, arrange shipment, and make payment. Marketers should prepare negotiating details of the purchase to successfully sell the product and even establish a relationship with the buyers.

采购员选择供应商，协商采购条款，并负责采购的细节。采购员谈判价格，确认合同，安排装运和付款。营销人员应该准备交易的谈判细节，以成功地销售产品，甚至建立与买家的关系。

5.5　Three Buying Situations 三种采购情况

Business buyers have various levels of experience and information to use in purchasing products and services. Two organizations may develop different purchasing strategies in the same purchase if the buying situation is different. Buying situation concerns how much efforts, time, and money to put into the buying process. There are mainly three types of buying situations in the business market.

商业买家有不同层次的经验和信息，可用于购买产品和服务。如果采购情况不同，两个组织可能会在同样的采购中制定不同的采购策略。采购情况涉及在采购过程中投入多少精力、时间和金钱。商业市场上主要有三种采购情况。

5.5.1 Straight Rebuy 直接复购

It is a business buying situation in which the buyer routinely orders products. The buyer just needs additional units of the products that have been bought in the past. For straight rebuy, the buyer must be satisfied with the products bought. The buyer then simply orders products with the same quality and the same quantity from the same list of suppliers. For example, State Grid Corporation of China orders uniforms for its staff, government departments purchase stationery, all on a regular basis. This process usually takes little time, because there is no need for another evaluation and negotiation.

这是买方经常订购某产品的情况。购买者只需要增加过去购买的该产品的数量。对于直接再购，购买者一定是对所购买的产品感到满意的。然后，买方只需向相同的供应商订购相同质量和数量的产品。例如，中国国家电网公司为其员工订购制服，政府部门购买文具等，所有这些都是定期的再购买。这个过程通常花费很少的时间，因为不需要再进行评估和协商。

Straight rebuy often occurs to maintain a regular operation of the business, and most business purchases are done in this category. Companies that often engage in a straight rebuy of a product are an attractive target to marketers. For getting stable income from these regular purchases, marketers should make efforts in maintaining a sustainable relationship with the buyers.

直接回购通常是为了维持企业的正常运营而发生的，企业的大部分购买都属于这一范畴。对营销人员来说，经常进行直接回购的公司是一个具有吸引力的目标。为了从这些定期购买中获得稳定的收入，营销人员应该努力与买家保持可持续的关系。

5.5.2 Modified Rebuy 修订复购

As the production develops, straight rebuy would not last for too long. When the buyer finds there is a need for products with a lower price and better quality, other favorable terms of exchange, modified rebuy occurs. For example, if a company finds the cost has to be reduced in order to raise profit, it will look for a similar cheaper product. Modified rebuy also takes place when technological progress generates a need for more advanced products. A company may find the old computer cannot adapt to new requirements, and decide to turn to another supplier.

随着生产的发展，直接回购不会持续太久。当买方发现需要更低的价格和更高的质量的产品，或者其他有利的交易条款，就会发生修订重购。例如，如果一家公司发现必须降低成本才能提高利润，它就会寻找类似的更便宜的产品。当技术进步带来了对更先进产品的需求时，修订重购也会发生。一个公司可能会发现旧电脑不能适应新的技术要求，并决定转向另一个供应商。

Modified rebuy needs more decision making participants, and takes more energy and time than straight rebuy. Marketers who are not in the list of straight rebuy sees the modified rebuy as a golden opportunity to gain new businesses.

调整后的再购买需要更多的决策参与者，比直接再购更耗费精力和时间。不在"直接再购"名单上的市场营销人员认为，修订重购是获取新业务的好机会。

5.5.3 New-task Buy 新任务购买

A company faces new-task buy when it purchases a product or service for the first time. The company lacks experiences and product information to reach a deal with alternative suppliers. It takes the highest risks, the most time and energy in new-task buy. The higher the risks it takes, the more participants are involved, the greater efforts it takes. They spend time searching information from all kinds of sources, such as professionals and other buyers, before making a decision. For example, if a traditional financial institution wants to establish their online business, it has to start from gathering information about online financial business.

当一个公司第一次购买产品或服务时，它面临着新任务购买。该公司缺乏与多家供应商达成交易的经验和产品信息。公司在新任务的购买中承担着最大的风险，花费最多的时间和精力。风险越大，参与的人越多，付出的努力就越多。在做决定之前，他们会花时间从各种来源搜索信息，比如从专业人士和其他买家那里。例如，一个传统的金融机构要想建立在线业务，必须从收集有关在线金融业务的信息开始。

New-task buy is a challenge for a company are either unfamiliar with the suppliers, or lack experience with the product. However, it is a big opportunity for marketers. Due to the amount of efforts put in new-task rebuy, the company must have taken a careful consideration in choosing the right supplier. Once the company has a cooperation with this supplier, it may continue to use their product or services. To marketers, developing these new business customers could mean a potential flow of future revenue.

新任务购买对于不熟悉供应商或缺乏产品经验的公司来说是一个挑战。然而，这对市场营销人员来说是一个巨大的机会。由于在新任务回购上投入了大量的努力，公司在选择合适的供应商时必须仔细考虑。一旦该公司与该供应商合作，它可以继续使用他们的产品或服务。对营销人员来说，开发这些新的业务客户可能意味着未来潜在的收入流。

5.6 Business Buying Process 企业购买过程

Playing different roles in business buying, members in the buying center take another challenge as they go through several stages in business buying process. The process lists five distinct steps that are similar to that of individual customers. Different members are involved in each stage, depending on the cost and strategic importance of the purchase.

购买中心的成员在企业购买过程中扮演不同的角色，他们在经历业务购买过程的几个阶段时面临另一个挑战。该流程列出了与个体消费者类似的 5 个步骤。每个阶段都涉及不同的成员，这取决于购买的成本和购买战略的重要性。

5.6.1 Problem Recognition 问题识别

Firstly, the business process buying begins with the company identifying a problem that can be solved by initiating a purchase. If the company runs out of daily supply such as paper, bags, or it wants to renew an old item, straight rebuy occurs. The company places an order and replenish its stocks. Problem recognition in modified rebuy starts when the company finds there is a new product or service with a more favorable offer, or when there is new technology creates the needs for a more advanced product. Users are usually the persons who find the need, and write a report to the supervisor. In this stage, the buying center may be informed to make a written request or requisition if necessary.

首先，企业购买从公司决定通过启动一次采购来解决问题开始。如果公司的日常用品如纸、袋子用完了，或者想要更换旧的物品，就会直接进行再购，公司会直接下单以补充库存。当公司发现有新产品或服务提供了更优惠的报价，或者有新技术产生了对更先进产品的需求时，就会开始在修订重购中识别问题。用户通常是发现需求并向主管写报告的人。在这个阶段，如有必要，采购中心可以提出书面请求。

The need for new-task buy is created by the company's intention to enhance its operation and improve its efficiency. Smart salespersons can also stimulate the need that the company may not be aware of by advising them of issues and challenges that other companies in their industry face. Smart marketers can quickly identify customers with different needs, and lead the stage by inviting the members from the buying center, including especially the decision maker, to a discussion or workshop on the topic.

新任务购买的需求是由于公司有提升运营和提高效率的意图而产生的。聪明的销售人员还可以通过向他们提供行业内其他公司面临的问题和挑战的建议，来激发公司潜在的需求。聪明的营销人员能够迅速识别出有不同需求的客户，并通过邀请来自采购中心的成员（特别是决策人员）参加有关该主题的讨论或研讨会来主导这一阶段的工作。

5.6.2 Information Search 信息搜索

Information about the product and the supplier has to be collected. The members of the buying center refer to reports in trade magazines and journals, advices from consultants and experts, marketing intelligence from competitors, and advertisement from suppliers. Marketers try to place information when and where the business customers want. Mailing brochures and other printed materials, and telemarketing are the most commonly used tactics.

企业必须收集关于产品和供应商的信息。采购中心的成员参考行业杂志和期刊上的产品报告，咨询顾问和专家的建议，收集竞争对手的情报，以及供应商的广告。营销人员试图在客户需要的时间和地点投放产品信息。邮寄小册子和其他印刷材料、电话营销等是最常用的战术。

The information is collected to develop product specifications, a written statement of the characteristics of a product such as quality, size, weight, and other parameters, to facilitate its procurement. It contains a critical information about a product, how much of it is needed, where it is needed, and a list of rules, bans, and standards that apply to the item. By documenting the product and its features, the specification can be a useful screening tool to identify when a pre-production product differs from one on the store shelf, signaling the possibility of a material or design change, and potentially a non-compliant product. It can notify the manufacturer that whether an off-the-shelf product do, or must it be customized. Users and influencers come into play here.

收集这些信息是为了制定产品规格，书面陈述产品的特征，如质量、尺寸、重量和其他参数，以方便其采购。它包含关于产品的重要信息、需要多少产品、哪里需要，以及适用于该产品的规则、禁令和标准的列表。通过记录产品及其特性，该规范可以成为一个有利的筛选工具。它可以帮助识别预生产产品与商店货架上产品的不同，这表明材料或设计需要进一步更改，或者存在潜在的不兼容产品。它可以通知制造商一个现成的产品是否合格，或者它是否必须是定制的。用户和有影响力的人在这里发挥作用。

With the product specifications in hand, potential suppliers are identified. Most business buyers search online to find vendors and products, attend trade shows and conventions, seek information on trade magazines, or send e-mails and make calls to the suppliers they have relationships. Sometimes they even pay visit to the facilities. The most competitive candidates should be reliable, financially stable, and located properly.

有了产品规格，就可以确定潜在的供应商。大多数商业买家在网上寻找供应商和产品，参加贸易展览和会议，在贸易杂志上寻找信息，或发送电子邮件和打电话给他们有关系的供应商。有时他们甚至参观厂家设施。最有竞争力的候选人应该是可靠的、财务稳定的并有合理的定位。

A request for proposal (RFP) is sent to each member that makes the cut. A RFP is an invitation to submit a bid, which outlines the products' quality, price, delivery, after-sales service, whether it can be customized or returned, and even the product's disposal, in some cases. Marketing professionals focus not only on the proposal itself but also solutions to the problem the company is facing.

提案请求被发送给每个被选中的成员。RFP 是一种投标邀请，它概述了产品的质量、价格、交货、售后服务、是否可以定制或退货，甚至在某些情况下产品的处理。营销专家不仅关注提案本身，还关注公司所面临的问题的解决方案。

5.6.3 Evaluation of Alternatives 评估备选方案

During this stage, the proposals from different vendors are reviewed and one or more vendors are selected, all executed by the buying center. Companies set their own criteria in the evaluation. Different companies weight different dimensions of the proposal, but all estimate the benefits and total costs paid to each vendor. For most of them, price is the primary consideration, because the business purchase entails enormous expenses that can have a great impact on the company's profitability. Pricing evaluation includes discount policies, refund policies, the cost of repair and maintenance, the cost of inventory and delivery, the cost of financing large purchases, and terms of payment, etc.

在此阶段，来自不同供应商的建议将被审查，并选择一个或多个供应商，所有这些都由采购中心执行。公司在评估中有自己的标准。不同的公司对提案的不同维度进行权衡，但都对每个供应商的收益和总成本进行了评估。对于他们中的大多数人来说，价格是首要考虑的因素，因为业务采购需要大量的开支，这对公司的盈利能力有很大的影响。价格评估包括折扣政策、返点政策、维修保养成本、库存和配送成本、大宗采购融资成本、付款方式等。

As customer buying, some business buying decisions are based on other factors. With adequate capital, a company may pursuit the quality of the product and the services the vendor can offer. Some high-end devices may be produced by the only manufacturer who owns the technology, and thus will be sold at a premium. Companies also assess the life expectancy of some large facilities and the future resale value. Other companies pay attention to the reputation and reliability most, for the reason that any man-made delay in the supply chain may result in irretrievable injury to the profits. In the long run, organizations want to be sure that the suppliers have a strong production capacity, develops sustainably and will always be around in the future.

作为客户购买，一些企业购买决策是基于其他因素的。有了足够的资金，公司可以追求供应商的产品质量和所提供的服务。一些高端设备可能由唯一拥有该技术的制造商生产，因此将溢价出售。公司还评估了一些大型设施的预期寿命和未来的转售价值。其他公司最注重的是信誉和可靠性，因为供应链中任何人为的延误都可能导致不可挽回的利润损失。从长远来看，组织希望能确保供应商有强大的生产能力，能可持续发展，并在未来一直存在。

Usually, in purchasing less complex products, the vendors are asked to present samples for examination and the future inspection and test. In case of large and complex products, the vendors invite their potential customers to try out the product, have a discussion with them on how to make it more adapted.

通常情况下，在购买不太复杂的产品时，供应商被要求提供样品以供检验和未来的检测。对于大型和复杂的产品，供应商邀请他们的潜在客户试用该产品，并与他们讨论如何使其更适合。

5.6.4 Product and Supplier Selection 选择产品和供应商

Being a link in the supply chain, a business sees the on-time deliveries with the required quality and quantity as the critical factor in selecting suppliers. The just in time (JIT), created by Toyota in the 1970s, is a scientific inventory management method adopted to increase the efficiency and reduce the cost of warehousing by forecasting demand precisely. It ensures the business customer to receive goods only when they are needed in the production process. Through JIT systems, a company spends less on raw materials as they only buy just enough to produce and no more. Disadvantages occur when the supplier cannot make the delivery on time, causing disruptions in the supply chain.

作为供应链中的一个环节，企业将按时交货与所需的质量和数量视为选择供应商的关键因素。准时制是 20 世纪 70 年代由丰田公司发明的一种科学的库存管理方法，通过精确预测需求来提高效率和降低仓储成本。它确保客户只在生产过程中的需要之时接收货物。通过 JIT 制度，一个公司在原材料上的费用减少了，因为他们仅购入正好够生产产品的原材料，不多不少。该制度的不足在于，当供应商不能按时交货时，会造成供应链的中断。

Some traditional purchasing companies who fear of the disruption caused by delivery may choose multi-sourcing—buying a particular product from many suppliers, so as to protect themselves from supply failures. In multi-sourcing, there are more than one supplier, so the price is relatively competitive. At the same time, the purchasing company has others to rely on if one of the suppliers cuts off their supplies. However, there is less trust between customers and suppliers. The business volume per transaction is low for the suppliers unless several firms order the same, but the supplier may wait for bunching of orders from several customers thus delaying the delivery in some cases. Suppliers have low incentive to improve their performance and hesitate to invest their efforts in solving a business customer's problem.

一些传统的采购公司担心发货会造成中断，可能会选择多源采购——从许多供应商那里购买特定的产品，以保护自己不受供应不足的影响。在多源采购中有多个供应商，因此价格相对有竞争力。与此同时，如果某个供应商切断了供应，采购公司还有其他的供应商可以依靠。然而，客户和供应商之间的信任较少。除非有几家公司下同样的订单，否则供应商每笔交易的业务量都很低，但供应商可能会等待多家客户的订单统一生产，从而在某些情况下延迟交货。供应商没什么动力去提高它们的业绩，也不愿意投入精力去解决客户的问题。

Other companies choose single-sourcing, whereby a purchase part is supplied by only one supplier. The only supplier can provide focus attention to the customer, and the two parties establish close and stable relationship during the process. This method fosters products with higher quality and reliability, shorter lead times. More importantly, it is easier to control as there is only one supplier involved. The suppliers are more willing to improve performance and create specialized product to meet the customer's special needs. The disadvantages may lie that it has lower variability of products.

其他公司选择单一来源，即一个采购部分只由一个供应商提供。唯一的供应商可以将注意力集中在客户身上，双方在此过程中建立了密切稳定的关系。这种方法可以提高产品的质量和可靠性，缩短交货期。更重要的是，它更容易控制，因为只涉及一个供应商。供应商也更愿意提高性能，生产专门的产品来满足客户的特殊需求。其缺点可能是产品的可变空间较小。

Another type of partnership between buyers and sellers is outsourcing, when a company contracts out a part of their existing internal activities to another company who specializes in those activities. Outsourcing can reduce business managerial expenses, lower energy costs and labor costs, and improve efficient allocation of resources within a company. Outsourcing allows a company to focus its own competencies and hire outside resources to handle other tasks. However, outsourcing requires a high degree of standardization and management control in order to be effective. Some common outsourcing activities include: facilities management, human resource management, accounting, customer support and service, computer aided design, research, design, engineering, and legal documentation.

买方和卖方之间的另一种伙伴关系是外包，即一家公司将其内部的一部分业务外包给另一家专门从事这些业务的公司。外包可以减少企业的管理费用，降低能源成本和劳动力成本，提高企业内部资源的有效配置。外包使公司能够专注于自己的能力，并雇佣外部资源来处理其他任务。然而，外包需要高度的标准化和管理控制才能有效。一些常见的外包活动包括：设施管理、人力资源管理、会计、客户支持和服务、计算机辅助设计、研究、设计、工程和法律文件。

5.6.5 Post-purchase Evaluation 购后评价

This process is mainly used with new-task buy. The buyer assesses suppliers' proposals against criteria such as product performance to see whether the suppliers are living up to expectations. Some companies routinely survey the users of the products to see how satisfied they were with it, in aspects such as the installation, delivery, and services. Others provide vendors with information on their performance by writing customer satisfaction report or sharing data with them on a regular basis. It is viewed as an exchange for the suppliers' commitment to a long-term collaboration with the value chain. The evaluation results become feedback for future business buying decisions.

此过程主要用于新采购任务。买方根据产品性能等标准对供应商的建议进行评估，以确定供应商是否符合预期。一些公司经常对产品的用户进行调查，以了解他们在安装、交付和服务等方面对产品的满意度。其他公司通过编写客户满意度报告或定期与供应商共享数据，向供应商提供有关其业绩的信息。它被视为供应商承诺与价值链长期合作的交换物。评估结果将成为未来业务购买决策的依据。

A supplier with poor performance record may not be entirely to blame. For example, if the tea merchants contract with a tea farmer to purchase a batch of first-class tea next year, but a large number of the tea is not in high quality and has been delayed in delivery. It may not be the tea farmer's fault. Perhaps there are some factors that beyond human control such as a drought in the tea region in that particular year which caused the low quality of the tea, shipping volumes were unusually high, or the delivery experienced a natural disaster. The buyers and sellers need to work together to improve the overall performance so as to satisfy the end-customers' needs.

交易是否满意不能完全归咎于供应商。例如，如果茶商与茶农签订了明年购买一批上等茶叶的合同，但是大量的茶叶质量不高，而且已经延误了交货时间，这可能不是茶农的错。也许有一些因素是人类无法控制的，比如那年产茶区发生了干旱，导致茶叶质量下降，或者运输量异常高，运输过程中又发生了自然灾害。买方和卖方需要共同配合来提高产品的整体性能，以满足最终客户的需求。

In order to successfully navigate the buying decisions, marketers need to precisely identify the buying stages, as well as contact the right decision-makers, and offer the right type of information and guidance to them.

为了成功地促成采购决策，营销人员需要准确地识别采购阶段，并联系正确的决策者，为他们提供正确的信息和指导。

◎ **阅读推荐**

弗拉姆·毫茨，兰德尔. 企业成长之痛 [M]. 黄震亚，董航，译. 北京：清华大学出版社，2011.

史蒂芬森. 中小企业营销完美指导手册 [M]. 屈云波，毛圆媛，王林建，译. 北京：企业管理出版社，2007.

金焕民，刘春雄. 销量为王 [M]. 北京：企业管理出版社，2008.

6

Target Marketing

目标市场战略

Today, the STP strategy, also known as target marketing strategy, is one of the most commonly applied strategic approaches in modern marketing. The letters STP stand for segmentation, targeting, and positioning. It demonstrates the links between an overall market and how a company chooses to compete in that market.

今天，STP 策略，也被称为目标营销策略，是现代营销中最常用的策略方法之一。STP 是市场细分、目标市场和市场定位的缩写，它展示了一个整体市场和公司如何选择在这个市场上竞争之间的联系。

STP strategy does not come into being out of nowhere. The marketing strategy has experienced three stages in history: mass marketing, product-variety marketing, and target marketing.

STP 策略不是凭空产生的。营销策略在历史上经历了大众营销、产品多样化营销和目标营销三个阶段。

Mass marketing occurs when the seller mass produces, mass distributes, and mass promotes one product to all buyers. In the very beginning, McDonald's offered just one type of hamburger to everyone, and Coca-cola only produced coke in one flavor. Mass marketing focuses on lowest costs and prices, and aims to create the largest potential market. But due to today's increased competition and the complexity of consumers' needs, mass marketing is less likely to be successful, as consumers have a range of personalized requirements that they can satisfy themselves in a range of alternative competing products.

大众营销中，卖方大规模生产、大规模分销和大规模向所有买家推销一种产品。起初，麦当劳只提供一种类型的汉堡包给每个人，可口可乐只生产一种口味的可乐。大众营销专注于以最低的成本和价格，创造最大的潜在市场。但是，由于当今竞争的加剧和消费者需求的复杂性，大规模营销不太可能成功，因为消费者有一系列个性化的需求，他们可以在一系列可替代的竞争产品中满足这些需求。

In product-variety marketing, the seller produces two or more products that have different features, styles, qualities, sizes, etc. For example, later, McDonald's produced Big Mac to offer variety to buyers rather than appealing to different market segments. Product-variety marketing supports consumers who seek variety and change over time.

在产品多样化营销中，卖方生产两种或两种以上具有不同特征、风格、品质、尺寸等的产品。例如，后来，麦当劳生产巨无霸是为了向消费者提供多样化选择，而不是吸引不同的细分市场。产品多样化营销被那些寻求多样化和喜欢不断变化的消费者所喜欢。

Then it comes to target marketing. It becomes popular when seller identifies market segments, selects one or more of them, and develops products and marketing mixes for each. As you can see today, McDonald's offers different menus for different markets. Today, companies are using this strategy for it helps to precisely locate potential consumers.

然后是目标营销。当卖家确定细分市场，选择其中一个或多个，并为每个细分市场开发产品和营销组合时，它就会变得流行起来。正如你今天看到的，麦当劳为不同市场的消费者提供不同的菜单。如今，企业正在使用这种策略，因为它有助于准确定位潜在消费者。

The STP process goes with three steps: First, the overall market being split into submarkets; then the selection of one or more markets as a target; and finally the implementation of brand or product positioning strategy in relation to the market segment(s). Going through this process it allows a business management and marketing consultants or employees to formulate an appropriate marketing mix that ties company, brand, and product benefits to specific customer market segments.

STP过程分为三个步骤：首先，将整个市场划分为几个子市场；其次，选择一个或多个子市场作为目标；最后，针对细分市场实施品牌或产品定位策略。通过这个过程，企业管理和营销顾问或员工可以制定一个合理的营销组合，将公司、品牌和产品利益与特定的客户细分市场联系起来。

The segmentation of the overall market, the derived target markets, together with the positioning are the basis for determining any particular marketing mix. With the STP, marketers can prioritize propositions and deliver personalized messages to engage with commercially appealing audiences. Now let's look at the three steps one by one.

整体市场的细分、由此选定的目标市场，以及该市场的定位，是确定一切特定营销组合的基础。有了 STP，营销人员可以给各种提议确定优先顺序，并提供定制的信息，以吸引有利可图的受众群体。现在让我们一一来看这三个步骤。

6.1 Segmentation 市场细分

6.1.1 Definition 定义

Is a bottle of wine a perfect birthday gift for everyone? How about a basketball or a pair of sneakers? The answer is no. Buyers are not homogenous and products have to be tailored to specific customer needs. Market segmentation is the process of dividing a market into similar and identifiable segments based on some dimensions. In each segment, the members have common needs, characteristics, buying behavior, and may be attracted by similar type of marketing communication program. A market segment is a subgroup of people or organizations that have one or more types of shared characteristics such as interests, lifestyle, and demographic profiles that cause them to have the same product needs. Those dimensions that used to divide the total market into subgroups are called segmentation variables. Each of the consumers falls into different categories of segmentation variables, enabling marketers to set a target and meet their needs and wants.

一瓶葡萄酒对每个人来说都是完美的生日礼物吗？一个篮球或一双运动鞋呢？答案是否定的。并非所有买家都是同质的，产品必须根据特定的客户需求来定制。市场细分是根据某些标准将市场划分为相似的、可识别的细分市场的过程。在每个细分市场，成员有共同的需求、特点、购买行为，并可能被同一类的营销传播方案所吸引。一个细分市场是由一群人或组织组成的子市场，他们具有一种或多种类型的共同特征，如兴趣、生活方式和人口统计特性等，这些特征使他们具有相同的产品需求。那些将整个市场划分为子市场的维度被称为细分变量。每个消费者都属于不同的细分变量类别，这使营销人员能够设定目标，满足他们的需求和愿望。

The ultimate goal of segmentation is to identify the most high-yield potential market segments for company growth. Here, it brings about a question: Who actually segment the market? Does the marketers segment the market, or do the consumers naturally fall into segments by themselves? Let's take an example. Everyone must have an age that is unchangeable, and a living address which classifies you into a certain geographic area. Marketers segmenting consumers based on these dimensions do not give you an age or an area. Likewise, some consumers are pioneers in pursuing products with advanced technology, and others are playing followers. Marketers do not make them to be a pioneer or a follower, marketers only identify them and separate them into two different segments. As a matter of fact, segmentation happens naturally. There are a number of various predefined criteria used to subdivide a market. A touch challenge of segmentation that marketers face is to isolate the traits, identify the most meaningful criteria by which to analyze the market so that segments are determined.

市场细分的最终目标是为公司增长找到最具高收益潜力的细分市场。这就带来了一个问题：到底是谁在细分市场？是营销人员细分市场，还是消费者自然地归于与某些细分市场？我们来举个例子。每个人都有确定的、无法更改的年龄，以及一个可以将你划分到某个地理区域的居住地址。营销人员只是根据这些现有的维度对消费者进行细分，而不是给消费者分配一个年龄或地区。同样，一些消费者是追求先进技术产品的先锋，其他人则是跟随者。不是营销人员使他们成为先锋或跟随者，营销人员只是识别出他们的角色，并将他们分成两个不同的部分。因此，事实上，细分是自然发生的。许多现成的标准可以用来做市场细分。营销人员所面临的挑战是分辨这些特征，选择最有意义的标准来分析市场，从而确定如何细分。

It is not an easy task. Sometimes a marketer has to try different segmentation variables in order to find a useful one. Accordingly, marketing strategy is adjusted based on identified consumer segments. However, not all segmentation ways are meaningful. Cold medicine producers carry out segmentations based upon gender or age is obviously meaningless. Fashion brands divide market on the basis of gender may fail in building brand.

这不是一项简单的工作。有时候，为了找到一个有用的细分变量，营销人员不得不进行各种尝试。相应地，市场营销策略是根据已确定的消费群体进行调整的。然而，并不是所有的细分方法都有意义。比如，感冒药生产企业对市场进行性别或年龄的划分显然是没有意义的。时尚品牌在建立品牌时如果根据性别来划分市场，可能会失败。

6.1.2　Ways to Segment Consumer Markets 消费市场细分方法

To focus their energy on what they can do, the following questions are the most important to marketers: Who are the potential customers? How old are they? What is their income level? What are their occupations and education backgrounds? Do they have their own houses or do they rent houses? How do they look at the market? What do they usually buy? So on and so forth. There is no single way of segmenting the market. It is developing into a more subtle tactic as new consumer needs continue to arise in this ever-changing market. Lipsticks makers consider the use in different scenarios, keyboard makers consider game players and non-gamers, and camera producers take people who like selfies into consideration. Here, we simply look at four commonly used variables of segmentation: geographic, demographic, psychographic, and behavioral variables.

为了把精力集中在他们能做的事情上，以下问题对营销人员来说是最重要的：谁是潜在客户？他们多大了？他们的收入水平如何？他们的职业和教育背景是什么？他们拥有自己的房子还是租房子住？他们如何看待市场？他们通常买什么东西？等等。细分市场不是唯一的。在这个瞬息万变的市场中，随着新的消费者需求不断涌现，它正在发展成为一种更加微妙的策略。口红制造商考虑让消费者在不同场景下都能使用他们的产品，键盘制造商同时面向游戏玩家和非游戏玩家，相机制造商把目标对准了那些喜欢自拍的人。在这里，我们介绍四个常用的细分变量：地理、人口、心理和行为变量。

1. Geographic Segmentation 地理细分

Geographic segmentation involves dividing a market using geographic variables such as region, country, climate, or neighborhood. Where potential consumers live, work, and entertain largely influence how they buy products. For example, according to a Chinese national survey, Android mobile phone is the best-seller in Beijing; people in Shanghai love fashion product most; people in Gansu consumers like to buy jeans; Anhui has the largest consumer group who loves pets; people in Taiwan compose the biggest group of shutterbug. In some industry, companies specially target consumers who live in a certain region. The Swedish-founded multinational group IKEA uses the national colors of Sweden in their furniture designs. Researchers find that people near the neighborhood of a crowdfunding company are most likely to make the investment.

地理细分包括使用地理变量（如地区、国家、气候或邻近地区）划分市场。潜在消费者的生活、工作和娱乐场所在很大程度上影响着他们购买产品的方式。例如，根据中国的一项全国性调查，安卓系统的手机是北京最畅销的手机；上海人最喜欢时尚产品；甘肃消费者喜欢购买牛仔裤；安徽拥有最大的宠物消费群体；台湾的摄影爱好者人数最多。在某些行业，公司会特别以某一地区的消费者为目标。瑞典成立的跨国集团宜家在其家具设计中使用了瑞典的民族色彩。研究人员发现，众筹公司附近的人最有可能进行投资。

But there is no other effective way of geographic segmenting the market. There are basically two categories: market scope and geographic nature. Market scope constrains market to a state, a region, a province, or places with the same postcode. Geographic nature considers urban and rural areas, density of population, seasons etc. For example, seasonal products, such as coats, winter gear, swimwear and beach attire, often are marketed to geographic segments. Winter gear is promoted for several months leading up to late winter in northern China where harsh weather is common. Beach attire and swimwear is often targeted year-round in southern coastal provinces such as Hainan.

然而市场上有效的地理细分方法较少，常用的基本上有两类：市场范围和地理性质。市场范围将市场限制在一个州、一个地区、一个省或具有相同邮政编码的地方。地理特征考虑城乡、人口密度、季节等因素。例如，季节性产品，如大衣、冬装、泳装和沙滩装，往往是针对地理区域销售的。在中国北方，恶劣的天气是很常见的，冬季装备促销会持续几个月，直到暮冬。在海南等南部沿海省份，沙滩装和泳装通常是全年销售的。

Analyzing geographic elements is the simplest way of breaking down the market, as it is usually easy to collect geographic data through government census report. So most marketers take geographic segmentation as the first choice.

无论如何，分析地理因素是细分市场最简单的方法，因为通常很容易通过政府人口普查报告收集地理数据。因此，大多数营销人员将地理细分作为第一选择。

2. Demographic Segmentation 人口细分

A market split into sub-segments on the basis of variables such as age, gender, sex, family, income, education, religion, culture, occupation, profession, ethnicity is known as demographic segmentation. Demographic segmentation is a popular approach for dividing the consumer market. One reason is that consumer needs, wants, and usage rates often vary closely with the demographic variables. Moreover, demographic factors are easier to measure than most other type of variables.

根据年龄、性别、性别、家庭、收入、教育、宗教、文化、职业、职业、种族等变量将市场细分为若干子市场，称为人口细分。人口细分是划分消费市场的一种流行的方法。原因之一是，消费者的需求和使用率往往与人口统计变量密切相关。此外，人口因素比大多数其他类型的变量更容易测量。

3. Age 年龄

Age is probably the most identifiable variable in demographic segmentation. Modern companies use this as a very useful marketing tactic to create and retain their customers right from birth to death. At the age of 1 to 2, companies shall try to offer stuff like nappies for new born, baby cream, anti colic, baby clothes. With the passage of time, these may change to toys (a lot of sub-division) then bikes, balls, sport, jeans, school, then university, car, insurance, employment, then retirement, healthcare products, pension, and even death (funeral services).

年龄可能是人口细分中最容易识别的变量。现代企业把这作为一种非常有用的营销策略，从人的出生到死亡，公司都在努力创造和留住客户。1~2 岁时，公司应尽量提供新生儿尿布、婴儿乳霜、抗绞痛药、婴儿服装等。随着时间的推移，这些可能会变成玩具（很多细分领域），接着是自行车、球、运动、牛仔裤、学校，然后是大学、汽车、保险、就业，再然后是退休、医疗产品、养老金，甚至死亡（葬礼服务）。

4. Gender 性别

Gender segmentation is another powerful and successful segmentation and can be seen in areas like clothing, cosmetics, beauty products, hair styles, careers, cars, insurance, and now even education. There are several separate male and female schools. Again in Europe, schools for girls only have successfully targeted the part of the ethnic population who are averse to co-education. Car designers know that subtleties make difference, so Nissan's Micra and Mini Cooper have special attractions for ladies. In some cases, manufacturers develop parallel products to appeal to each sex, as more genders are recognized in some developed countries.

性别细分是另一个强大而成功的细分方法，它可以适用于服装、化妆品、美容产品、发型、职业、汽车、保险甚至现在的教育等领域。甚至有一些学校分为男校和女校。同样在欧洲，女子学校仅仅成功地招收了反对男女同校的少数民族学生。汽车设计师知道细微之处会带来差异，所以尼桑的 Micra 和 Mini Cooper 两款车对女性有特殊的吸引力。在某些情况下，由于一些发达国家意识到了更多性别的存在，制造商开发同类产品以吸引每一种性别。

银行按性别细分设计的信用卡

5. Income 收入

Income segmentation is the way to having a homogeneous group of people with similar annual or monthly incomes. The distribution of wealth is important, for it determines the purchasing power of the consumers. An indicator used is disposable income, or the money available to be spent or saved as one wishes. The more disposable income you have, the more attractive you are to some brands. Luxury products are offered to people who have an income above a certain level. For example, a premium car with exclusive features like powerful engine, luxurious interiors, personalized styling, prioritized after sales service, would target to people with high disposable income. Other companies target low-income groups for large volume of sales and quick turnover will still increase their revenue despite small profits from each product. Examples are Walmart supermarket and InTime discount shopping mall.

收入细分是将年收入或月收入相似的人群归类的方法。财富的分配很重要，因为它决定了消费者的购买力。常见的指标是可支配收入，即可用来消费或按个人意愿储蓄的钱。你的可支配收入越多，你对某些品牌的吸引力就越大。奢侈品是提供给那些收入超过一定水平的人的。例如，一辆拥有强大引擎、豪华内饰、个性化造型、优先享受售后服务等专属特色的高档车，其目标客户是高可支配收入人群。其他公司的定位于低收入群体的大量销售量和快速周转，尽管单品利润很少，但依然可以增加收入，如沃尔玛超市和银泰折扣购物中心。

Income is not a precise predictor of consumer purchase behavior. People can buy any products what they wish. Consumers with high income do not necessarily like luxury goods, and vice versa.

收入并不能准确地预测消费者的购买行为。人们可以买任何他们想要的产品。高收入的消费者不一定喜欢奢侈品，反之亦然。

6. Education and Occupation 教育和职业

In the time of education being a life-time process, people receive more education at all levels than ever before, and enjoy longer time of attending school. Schools and businesses offer courses not only to improve job skills but also for self-improvement.

The increased interest in education may lead many people to higher paying job positions. This means they will have more discretionary income to spend on goods and services. People in certain occupation form ideal segments for related goods and services. The marketers of career related goods and services target potential customers according to their occupations.

在倡导终身教育的时代，人们接受的各个层次的教育比以往任何时候都多，上学的时间也更长。学校和企业提供的课程不仅是为了提高工作技能，也是为了自我提升。对教育的兴趣的增加可能会使许多人找到薪水更高的工作。这意味着他们将有更多的可支配收入用于购买商品和服务。于是，特定职业的人产生了对某些商品和服务的需求，从而形成了理想的细分市场。与职业相关的商品和服务的营销者根据职业这一维度去定位潜在的客户。

7. Race and Ethnic Background 种族和民族背景

People from the same race or ethnic group have shared physical traits, ancestry, genetics, language and social or cultural traits. Everyone is a member of at least one ethnic group. and For example, Blacks are the most fashion-conscious of all racial and ethnic groups, and they are the most likely to be willing to travel an hour or more to shop at their favorite store and almost twice as likely as the average consumer to go out of their way to find new stores, especially if a bargain is to be had. Hispanics tend to make shopping a family affair. Their kids have a significant impact on the brands they buy. Whites are the most likely to plan far ahead to buy expensive items, and go shopping only when they absolutely need something. Asians are the most brand-conscious, for they always look for a brand name when they shop. Asians also 125 percent more likely than the average consumer to rely heavily on the Internet to help them plan their shopping trips.

来自同一种族或民族的人有共同的身体特征、血统、遗传、语言和社会或文化特征。每个人至少是一个民族的成员。例如，黑人是最追求时尚的族群，他们是最有可能愿意花一个多小时在他们最喜欢的商店购物，几乎是花两倍于普通消费的精力去寻找新的商店，尤其是能讨价还价的时候。西班牙人则倾向于把购物当成一件家庭事务。他们的孩子对他们购买的品牌有重大影响。白人最有可能提前计划购买昂贵的物品，且只有在十分需要的时候才去购物。亚洲人是最有品牌意识的，因为他们总是在购物时寻找特定的品牌。此外，亚洲人严重依赖互联网购物，比普通消费者高出 125%。

In marketing communications, marketers adapt themselves by using spokespersons of similar ethnic background in advertisements, hiring ethnic salespeople, or using ethnic language, music, art, national flags, or other cultural symbols as part of the brand or promotion.

在营销传播中，营销者通过使用具有相似民族背景的代言人进行广告宣传，雇用民族销售人员，或使用民族语言、音乐、艺术、国旗或其他文化符号作为品牌或促销的一部分来进行自我调整。

8. Psychographic Segmentation 心理细分

Psychographic segmentation is dividing your market based upon consumer personality, values, attitudes, interests, and lifestyles. Psychographic segmentation include information that are deeper and richer than geographic and demographic segmentation. The consumer in psychographic segmentation may have the same income level and gender but they may have different inclinations and a unique style of living. They may have different personalities determining their likes and dislikes for a particular class of products. Suppose you produce and sell organic foods which are healthier and price-higher than normal foods. You may easily identify the high-income group by demographic segmentation, or locate customers with high acceptance of organic food in first-tier coastal cities by geographic segmentation, but you won't be able to tell whether these consumers buy organic food because it is healthier, tastes better, or good for environmental protection.

心理细分是根据消费者的个性、价值观、态度、兴趣和生活方式来划分市场。心理细分包括比地理和人口细分更深入、更丰富的信息。同一个心理细分子市场中的消费者可能具有相同的收入水平和性别，但可能有不同的偏好和独特的生活方式。他们性格的不同决定了他们对某一类产品的好恶。假设你生产和销售的有机食品比普通食品更健康，价格也更高，你可以很容易通过人口细分来确定高收入人群，或者通过地理细分来确定沿海一线城市对有机食品接受度高的消费者，但你无法分辨这些消费者购买有机食品是因为它更健康、味道更好，还是更有利于环保。

Psychographics are qualitative attributes of a market and can be difficult for marketers to segment their markets into these types of categories on their own. Marketers may need the help of third-party organizations in information search. Nielsen is one organization that offers services that can access to consumer lists based on their specific classifications. They have divided U.S. households into 66 distinct types or segments to help marketers focus on market segments based on psychographic characteristics.

心理统计特征是一个市场的定性属性，对于营销人员来说，很难靠自己将他们的市场做这样的划分。市场营销人员可能需要利用第三方机构来进行信息搜索。尼尔森是一个提供服务的组织，可以根据客户的具体分类提供客户列表。他们把美国家庭分为 66 种不同的细分子市场，来帮助营销者聚焦基于心理特征的细分市场。

The most well-known research methodology used for psychographic market segmentation is VALS, which stands for "Value and Lifestyle". The system was developed by SRI Consulting Business Intelligence in 1978. It divides the U.S. adults into nine segments. Marketers in the U.S. can go to its website and easily find out their VALS type by completing a VALS survey questionnaire. Later, SRI has improved the system by creating a revised version, which places less emphasis on activities and interests and more on a psychological base to tap relatively enduring attitudes and values. Companies can use this service to guide their strategic decisions.

最著名的用于心理细分的研究方法是"价值和生活方式"（VALS）。该方法由 SRI 咨询公司于 1978 年提出。它将美国成年人分为 9 个部分。美国的市场营销人员可以访问其网站，通过填写 VALS 调查问卷，轻松找到他们对应的 VASL 类型。后来，社会责任研究所改进了这一方法，制定了一个修订版，降低了对活动和兴趣的研究，更多地强调消费者心理，以挖掘相对持久的态度和价值观。

公司可以使用这项服务来指导自己的战略决策。

9. Behavioral Segmentation 行为细分

Even consumers living in the same neighborhood and brought up by the same culture can exhibit different buying habits. Behavioral segmentation aims to understand customers' purchasing habits, usage habits, and spending habits by studying how they act in the process of making buying decisions. There are phrases "make hay while the sun shines" and "strike when the iron's hot", meaning to take advantage of a window of opportunity when it opens.

即使是生活在同一个社区、在同一个文化背景下长大的消费者，也会表现出不同的购买习惯。行为细分的目的是通过研究消费者在购买决策过程中的行为来了解消费者的购买习惯、使用习惯和消费习惯。有"机不可失"和"趁热打铁"这两个成语，意思是当机会之门打开之时，要利用它。

10. Users Status 用户状态

One commonly used way of behavioral segmentation is categorizing consumers by users status. Non-users might need to be made aware that they have a problem or pain point in the first place; Prospects will need to learn why choosing your product or service is the better option; First-time buyers might need further instruction on how to use the product to get the most out of it; Regular users would benefit from being introduced to supplemental products or services that could help them attain their goals; Defectors, or ex-customers who have chosen a competitor's brand, might come back to a brand if the brand has recently fixed the issue that caused them to defect in the first place.

一种常用的行为细分方法是根据用户状态对消费者进行分类。对于非用户，营销人员首先需要知道他们的痛点所在；潜在客户则需要了解为什么你的产品或服务是更好的选择；首次购买的人可能需要进一步的指导，比如，如何使用产品以获得最大的好处；经常使用的用户将受益于能够帮助他们实现目标的额外的产品或服务；流失的客户或选择了竞争对手品牌的前客户，如果该品牌最近解决了最初导致他们流失的问题，他们可能重新购买该品牌。

11. Usage Rate 使用率

Another way to segment a market based on behavioral segmentation is to look at usage rate. Heavy users are the most reliable customers who provide a company with a bulk consumer generated revenue. As much as a company rely on them for revenue, they also heavily rely on the company for the services you provide. Think of the benefits airlines provide frequent fliers: as thanks for their continued patronage, these individuals are usually given free upgrades and other discounts fairly often.

另一种基于行为细分来细分市场的方法是看使用频率。重度用户是最可靠的客户，他们为公司提供大量的收入。就像公司在收入上依赖他们一样，他们也在很大程度上依赖于你所提供的服务。想想航空公司为飞行常客提供的好处：由于他们的持续光顾，这些人经常会得到免费升舱和其他折扣。

Mid-level users are customers who can be counted on to make purchases at regular—but not frequent intervals. Mid-level users might make purchases during times that are significant to them, such as birthdays or anniversaries. Companies that offer birthday freebies understand the importance of contacting mid-level users during such occasions to keep them interested and engaged with their brand.

中度用户是指定期购物的顾客——但不是频繁地购买。中度用户可能会在对他们来说很重要的时间购物，比如生日或纪念日。提供生日礼品的公司明白在这样的场合联系中度用户的重要性，以保持他们对自己品牌的兴趣和参与度。

Light users are similar to rare-personal occasion customers: They will likely be one-off customers, unless the company makes an offer they cannot refuse. This is why many companies offer discounts and other freebies for first-time customers: They know they need to provide immediate value in order to keep individuals coming back for more. The goal of any company is to get light users to become mid-level users and get mid-level users to become heavy users.

轻度用户类似于非常私人场合的客户：他们很可能是一次性的客户，除非公司提出一个令他们无法拒绝的报价。这就是为什么许多公司会为初次顾客提供折扣和其他免费赠品：他们知道，他们需要提供即时价值，以吸引顾客再次光顾。任何公司的目标都是让轻度用户变成中度用户，让中度用户变成重度用户。

12. Loyalty Status 忠诚状态

Generating the bulk of the revenue, loyal customers continually purchase products or services from their favorite brands rather than a competitor's, and they cost little to keep around. The best example of behavioral segmentation by loyalty is observed in the hospitality sector where airlines, hotels, restaurants and others give their best service to provide the most excellent experience possible such that they can retain their customers. By getting to know the loyal customers on a deeper level, a company will discover the best way in which to thank them for their patronage, in turn incentivizing to engage even further with the brand.

忠实的客户创造了大部分的收入。他们不断地从自己喜欢的品牌而不是竞争对手那里购买产品或服务，而且维护忠实客户的成本很低。根据忠诚度进行行为细分的最好例子是在服务业，航空公司、酒店、餐厅等都试图提供最佳的服务，以带来最优质的体验，这样他们才能留住客户。通过更深层次地了解忠诚的客户，公司会挖掘出感谢他们惠顾的最佳方式，从而激励他们进一步与品牌建立联系。

13. Benefits 利益

Many products are targeted towards the benefits sought by the customer. Benefit segmentation offers more utility than the traditional methods. There has been a market war between Colgate and Sensodyne to target the people who have sensitive teeth, and there are still other toothpastes are targeted towards whitening of teeth. Marketers need to identify the benefit customers are seeking. For example, a lady who cycles and walks rather than drives to keep fit will buy organic foods for her perceived health benefits. Suppose she is not an environmentalist, the reason she gives up driving is not for reducing CO_2 emission, but for the fit and health of herself, then an ample parking lot and free home delivery would not be of benefit to her.

许多产品都以客户所追求的利益为目标。利益细分比传统方法提供了更多的效用。高露洁和舒适达之间曾针对牙齿敏感人群进行了市场大战，还有一些牙膏是针对牙齿美白的。市场营销人员需要识别客户所寻求的价值。例如，一个骑自行车和步行而不是开车来健身的女士会购买有机食品，因为她认为有机食品对健康有益。假设她不是一个环保主义者，她放弃开车的原因不是为了减少二氧化碳的排放，而是为了自己的身体健康，那么一个车位充足的停车场和免费送货上门对她来说是没有价值的。

6.2 Targeting 设定目标

Targeting is the second step of STP strategy. After segmenting the entire market into small groups that share certain characteristics, the next step marketers need to do is to find out which group or groups to select, or rather, to target. The group or groups that a company selects to turn into customers as a result of segmentation and targeting is called target market.

设定目标是 STP 战略的第二步。在将整个市场分割成具有某些共同特征的小群体之后，市场营销者下一步需要做的是找出应该选择哪些群体，或者更确切地说，应该瞄准哪些目标群体。由于细分和目标定位，公司选择成为客户的一个或多个群体被称为目标市场。

6.2.1 Evaluating Market Segments 评估细分市场

In the former section, we have learned that a company is not able to serve everyone while making a profit. With limited resources, companies have to carefully select a segment or series of segments and target it/them. All the marketing efforts are to put into these segments as to generate the greatest revenue. There are two key aspects (the attractiveness of the segmentation and the competitiveness of the company) that marketers need to consider in evaluating market segments and to find out the most suitable one or ones.

在前一部分中，我们了解到一个公司不可能在盈利的同时服务好每一个人。在资源有限的情况下，企业必须谨慎地选择一个或几个细分市场，并将其作为目标。所有的营销努力都是为了在这些细分市场上获得最大的收益。市场营销人员在评估细分市场和找出最合适的细分市场时，需要考虑细分市场的吸引力、公司竞争优势两个关键方面。

6.2.2 Selecting and Entering Market Segments 选择和进入

There are mainly four targeting strategies as follows.

主要有以下 4 种目标策略。

1. Undifferentiated Marketing 无差异市场营销

Undifferentiated targeting strategy is also called mass marketing. It aims to appeal to a broad spectrum of people. The company decides to develop a single marketing mix for all customers. Typical examples are that local government promotes the city as a historic destination by placing ads in widely read newspapers, and companies selling basic commodities such as sugar, salts or most staples. In business scenarios, if the strategy is successful, it will be benefit from reaching the economies of scale by producing one single product or one promotional campaign, thus significantly lowering the cost. Google, Facebook, Microsoft, and Apple are excellent companies adopting undifferentiated marketing strategy.

无差异定位策略也被称为大众营销。它的目标是吸引广泛的人群。公司决定为所有客户开发同一个营销组合。典型的例子是，当地政府通过在读者广泛阅读的报纸上刊登广告，将该市作为历史旅游胜地来宣传，以及把广告发布在销售糖、盐或大多数主食等基本商品的公司。在商业情景中，如果战略成功，通过生产一种产品或一种促销活动来达到规模经济，这将会使公司受益，从而大大降低成本。谷歌，脸书、微软、苹果公司等都是采用无差异营销策略的优秀公司。

2. Differentiated Marketing 差异化营销

On the contrary, differentiated targeting strategy exploits the differences of each target segments. It is a strategy used when a company develops several distinct offerings to each segment it targets. The products in each segment must be kept separate by implementing particular marketing mix that communicates unique benefits.

　　与此相反，差异化目标策略利用了各个目标细分市场的差异。当一个公司为它的每个目标市场开发几个不同的产品时，就会采用这种策略。每个部门的产品必须通过实施特定的营销组合来保持独立，以传达独特的价值。

Newly-rising companies often use this strategy to lure customers away from existencing players for winning market share. Although it is a smart approach for new companies to choose differentiated marketing strategy when entering into a market, it carries higher cost. A company has to create its own marketing plan, do significant amount of researches on competitors, design and develop a single product, and invest heavily in product promotion. Cost adds up quickly especially there are more than one target markets. What is more, it faces high risks if competitors create similar product at a higher speed or there sees inconsistent theme for a brand. However, once it is successful, not only does it initiate lucrative business, but also it creates an overwhelmingly strong and a firm market presence with absolute domination that is hard for competitors to replace.

　　新兴公司经常使用这种策略来吸引顾客离开现有的商家以赢得市场份额。虽然对于新公司来说，在进入一个市场时选择差异化的营销策略是一种聪明的做法，但是这样做的成本较高。一个公司必须制订自己的营销计划，对竞争对手进行大量的研究，设计和开发单一的产品，在产品推广上投入大量资金。成本增加很快，尤其是有一个以上的目标市场时。更重要的是，如果竞争对手以更快的速度创造出相似的产品，或者本公司的品牌系列产品风格不统一，那么它将面临很大的风险。然而，一旦它成功了，不仅能开启利润丰厚的业务，而且还能创造一个具有绝对优势的强大而稳固的市场地位，这是竞争对手难以取代的。

奥利奥 (Oreo) 饼干针对中国市场的特点，开发了多种口味的饼干。消费者可以享受绿茶冰激凌、覆盆子蓝莓、芒果橙和葡萄桃、樱花抹茶等口味的奥利奥

3. Concentrated Marketing 集中性营销策略

Concentrated targeting strategy, or niche marketing, is a type of marketing strategy where a firm chooses to offer one or more products to one particular market segment. The primary goal of this strategy is to achieve high penetration among the narrowly defined target segments. Concentrated targeting is suitable for small businesses with limited budget or no desire to serve more than one segments. Making every penny counts, concentrated targeting focuses all efforts on meeting the needs of a single, well-defined and well-understood segment, which effectively distinguish a business from its competitors.

集中性营销策略，或利基营销，是一种企业选择向一个特定的细分市场提供一种或多种产品的营销策略。该战略的主要目标是在狭义的目标市场中实现高渗透。集中目标适合于预算有限或不希望服务于多个细分市场的小型企业。为了让每一分钱都发挥价值，集中目标将所有的努力都集中在满足单一的、定义明确的、容易理解的细分市场的需求上，这些细分市场有效地将企业与其竞争对手区分开来。

The main disadvantage of concentrated marketing strategy lies the vulnerability of responding to the changing market. Unlike large companies, either economy recession or change of customer taste can be fatal to businesses targeting only one segment. For example, luxury brands such as Chanel, Prada, Burberry are good examples of this strategy. With more diversified consumers needs, these brands are losing their glory-days status.

集中式营销策略的主要缺点是易受市场变化的影响。与大公司不同的是，无论是经济衰退还是顾客口味的改变，对于只瞄准一个细分市场的企业来说都是致命的。例如，香奈儿、普拉达、博柏利等奢侈品牌就是这种策略的好例子。随着消费者需求的多样化，这些品牌正在失去往日的辉煌。

4. Customized Marketing 定制营销

Customing marketing strategy is an approach that tailors specific product or service to suit the taste of individuals. It is believed to be the ultimate form of target marketing. Ideally, products or services are designed to meet the unique needs of every customer. This strategy is commonly used in business marketing where large orders are placed on specialized products that only certain clients will use.

定制营销策略是以定制的产品或服务，来适应个人的口味。它被认为是目标营销的最终形式。理想情况下，产品或服务的设计是为了满足每个客户的独特需求。这种策略通常用于商业营销，在这种营销中，只有特定客户才会使用特定产品的大订单。

Another bright side of customized marketing is that it ties the relationship between companies and customers. Customer-oriented companies are seeking ways to win over more of loyalty customers by tailoring products or services to their set of needs.

定制营销的另一个好处是它将公司和客户联系起来。以客户为导向的公司正在寻找方法，通过根据客户的需求定制产品或服务来赢得更多的忠诚客户。

宝马 MINI Cooper 和丰田等品牌都在最大程度上鼓励消费者选择自己汽车的颜色和配件。在赛百味（Subway），人们可以根据自己喜欢的食材、口味和大小制作自己喜欢的三明治。可口可乐 (Coca-cola) 推出 "昵称瓶"，每个可乐瓶都印有千禧一代最受欢迎的名字之一，这让新一代更容易记住这个品牌

Yet, the practice of this strategy is easier said than done. Sometimes customized marketing can cause public-relation disasters. Hotels predicting the needs of coming guests by using big data may make it appear they are spying on them.

然而，这种策略的实施说起来容易做起来难。有时候，定制营销可能会导致公关灾难。酒店通过大数据来预测客人的需求，可能会让人觉得他们在监视客人。

6.3　Positioning 定位

The final part of the STP strategy is positioning. Marketers proceed to identify concepts for each target segment, select the best, and communicate it.

STP 策略的最后一部分是定位。营销人员开始为每个目标细分市场确定产品概念，选择最好的进行营销传播。

The concept of positioning traces back before 1950s. Yet, it is Al Ries and Trout that advanced several definitions of positioning in their articles and books, making the concept highly influential. Positioning is a marketing strategy making a brand or a product occupy a distinct position in the mind of the consumers.

定位的概念可以追溯到 20 世纪 50 年代以前。然而，艾尔里斯和特劳特在他们的文章和书籍中提出了定位的几个定义，使这一概念极具影响力。定位是一种营销策略，使一个品牌或一个产品在消费者心中占据一个独特的位置。

Sometimes we hear people say "product positioning" or "brand positioning". They are just part of positioning with limited description focusing on either product or brand, while positioning is a marketing technique mainly deals with consumers' minds.

有时我们会听到人们说"产品定位"或"品牌定位"。它们只是定位的一部分，只是对产品或品牌的描述。而定位是一种营销技巧，主要针对的是消费者的心理。

Positioning process can be broken down into steps to effectively help companies to target consumers. By following the steps, it will not necessarily make the execution any easier, for the success of a positioning strategy requires a great deal of clarity and strong belief to follow through. The steps are listed below.

定位过程可以分解为几个步骤来有效地帮助公司定位消费者。遵循这些步骤，并不一定会使执行变得更容易，因为一个定位策略的成功需要大量的清晰的思路和坚定的信念来贯彻到底。具体步骤如下。

6.3.1 Competitor Analysis 竞争对手分析

Before deciding what kind of message to convey to potential consumers, marketers have to understand the current position of competitors. Who are the competitors out there, what strategies do they use, how are they perceived by the target consumers, and how will your actions cause their response accordingly? A thorough competitor analysis aids the development of your own marketing strategies.

在决定向潜在消费者传递什么样的信息之前，营销人员必须了解竞争对手的当前地位。你的竞争对手是谁，他们采用什么策略，他们如何被目标消费者感知，你的行为将如何引起他们相应的反应？彻底的竞争对手分析有助于你制定自己的营销策略。

Competitor positioning analysis should be conducted in this stage as well. Michael Porter forwards a Five Forces Framework saying that there are five forces of competitive position analysis that determine the competitive intensity and attractiveness of a market. They are: (1) Supplier power. The number of suppliers, the uniqueness of their products or services, their relative size and strength in the market, how easy it is for suppliers to raise prices, and the cost of switching between suppliers. (2) Buyer power. The number of buyers in the market, the importance of their patronage to the supplier, how easy it is for buyers to bargain over the price, and the buyer's cost of switching between suppliers. (3) Competitive rivalry. It includes factors such as sustainable competitive advantage through innovation, level of advertising expense, competition between online and offline companies, firm concentration ratio. The more competitors there are offering similar products or services, the less attractive the market is. (4) Threat of substitution. Number of similar products available in the market, their prices, perceived level of differentiation, ease of substitution, etc. Where an abundance of similar products exists, the likelihood of price-driven brand switches runs high. Suppliers have less power in saturated markets, so those markets are less attractive. (5) Threat of new entrance. High industry profitability will be a major attraction, unless there are barriers such as high customer loyalty to established brands, government policy, capital requirement, patents, economies of scale.

竞争对手的定位分析也应该在这个阶段进行。迈克尔·波特提出了一个五力模型，他说有五种竞争地位分析的力量决定了一个市场的竞争规模和程度。它们是：（1）供应商权力。供应商的数量、他们的产品或服务的独特性、他们在市场上的相对规模和实力、供应商提高价格的容易程度，以及在供应商之间转换的成本。（2）买方势力。市场上买家的数量、其对供应商的支持的重要性、买家讨价还价的容易程度，以及买家在供应商之间切换的成本。（3）竞争对手。它包括通过创新获得持续竞争优势、广告费用水平、线上和线下公司之间的竞争、企业集中度等因素。提供类似产品或服务的竞争者越多，市场吸引力就越低。（4）替代威胁。市场上同类产品的数量、价格、感知的差异化程度、替代的难易程度等。在存在大量类似产品的地方，价格驱动型品牌转换的可能性很大。供应商在饱和市场的影响力较小，因此这些市场的吸引力较小。（5）新入口威胁。高行业盈利能力将是一个主要的吸引力，除非存在一些障碍，如对知名品牌的高客户忠诚度、政府政策、资本要求、专利、规模经济等。

6.3.2 Identifing Your Current Position and Competitiveness 确定你目前的职位和竞争力

There are several questions should be answered: Who are you as a brand and what do you stand for? Who are your target audience and what do they need? How will you reliably meet those needs?

有几个问题需要回答：作为一个品牌，你是谁？你代表什么？你的目标受众是谁？他们需要什么？你如何持续稳定地满足这些需求？

Knowing your unique attributes will set you apart from the competition, and give the potential customers a better perception of value for your brands. Companies choose various forms of competitive advantage. Some companies position themselves as affordable options for selling low-price goods by offers more favorable price than parallel-quality products. For example, Meituan.com offers a selection of local restaurants, bars, cinemas, KTV, SPA, salon, and other specialty businesses with discounts, making the on-demand service platform a strong competitor with Chinese leading e-commerce firms in offline retail. Some companies use high-price strategy to make consumers believe there is an additional value in the product. This strategy aims at people who associate higher-priced products with better quality. A yoga instructor teaching private classes may charge more to present himself/herself as a highly professional coach. Another positioning technique is developed on specific demography which makes product a specialty for a certain group, or physical distribution strategy which makes your product special by placing it in perceivably deserved stores. Others differentiate themselves based on advanced technology, large customer base, user-friendly interface, etc.

了解你的独特属性会让你在竞争中脱颖而出，让潜在客户更好地了解你的品牌价值。公司选择各种形式的竞争优势。一些公司把自己定位为一般人负担得起的廉价商品，因为他们能提供比同类产品更优惠的价格。例如，美团网提供本地精选的餐厅、酒吧、电影院、KTV、SPA、沙龙等特色折扣业务，使其成为中国线下零售电商的有力竞争对手。一些公司使用高价策略让消费者相信产品具有额外的价值。这种策略针对的是那些将价格更高的产品与质量更好的产品联系在一起的人。一个教授私人课程的瑜伽教练可能会收取更多的费用来表明自己是一个高度专业的教练。另一种定位技术是基于人口统计学发展起来的，它使产品成为某一群体的特色产品，或者是基于一种实体分销策略：将产品放置在某一群体公认的商店中而使你的产品与众不同。另一些公司则凭借先进的技术、庞大的客户群、友好的用户界面等优势脱颖而出。

6.3.3　Developing a Positioning Idea 设计定位理念

Once the ideal market position is identified, it is time to establish a unique impression in the minds of potential customers for your company or products. For one thing, with all the information in hand, you should clearly state who you are as a company, how you differ from the competitors, what problems exist in the market, and how you are going to solve them, how to present yourself as an image that is most recognizable. All these facts can be condensed into a positioning statement. A positioning statement is an internal statement of distinction expressing how a product or service meets consumer needs in a way that competitors do not. Target says "style on a budget". Whatever products Target supplies, social offers they make, they have to ask themselves, "Does this help us provide style on a budget?" Volvo automobile positions themselves as "best in safety", so they conduct consumer reports saying that consumers think of Volvo when they think of car safety, as supporting components.

一旦确定了理想的市场定位，就是时候在潜在客户的心目中为你的公司或产品打造一个独特的印象了。首先，有了所有的信息，你应该清楚地说明：作为一家公司你是谁，你与竞争对手有什么不同，市场上存在什么问题，你将如何解决这些问题，如何把自己塑造成一个最容易识别的形象。所有这些事实都可以浓缩成一个定位声明。定位声明是一种内部声明，以区分与竞争者的不同。它表达了产品或服务如何满足消费者的需求，而竞争对手则没有。塔吉特百货公司说"风格要精打细算"。无论产品的目标供应是什么，提供什么样的社交服务，他们都必须问问自己："这能帮助我们在预算之内展现时尚的理念吗？"沃尔沃汽车将自己定位为"最安全的汽车"，因此他们在发布消费者报告时表示，消费者在想到汽车安全时会想到沃尔沃，那么这个定位已经成为消费者决策的依据。

6.3.4 Testing the Market Responses 测试市场反应

In the final step, marketers evaluate the effectiveness of its positioning concept. Testing models have to be built in respect of the company and target audience. Qualitative and quantitative researches are carried out mainly on planned purchase of the brand or product (given its implicit positioning), the image projected by the brand, the planned frequency of usage, pricing expectations, distribution expectations, potential problems, and so forth. The data gathered will tell if the company can move on with the current positioning concept or it needs to modify the key benefits and features in the present positioning to make it more meaningful to the target audience. The major change in positioning for the product or brand is called repositioning. Burberry was suffering from a bad reputation, being associated as gang wear until its new director Christopher Bailey introduced swimwear and trench coats that are unrelated to the former goods, and made it into a high-end luxury fashion.

在最后一步，营销者评估其定位概念的有效性。必须根据公司和目标受众构建测试模型。定性和定量研究主要针对品牌或产品的购买计划（鉴于其隐含的定位）、品牌所投射的形象、计划使用频率、定价预期、分销预期、潜在问题等。收集的数据将告诉公司是否可以继续当前的定位概念，或者它需要修改当前定位的关键利益和特点，使其对目标受众更有意义。产品或品牌定位的主要变化称为重新定位。博柏利曾经一度名声不佳，被认为是黑帮服装，直到新任总监克里斯托弗·贝利推出了与前两款产品无关的泳衣和风衣，并将其打造成一种高端奢侈时尚，博柏利才得以以新形象示人。

◎ **阅读推荐**

阿尔·里斯，杰克·特劳特.定位——有史以来对美国营销影响最大的观念 [M]. 谢伟山，等译.北京：机械工业出版社，2016.

艾·里斯，杰克·特劳特.营销战 [M]. 李正栓，等译.北京：中国财政经济出版社，

2002.

阿尔·里斯，杰克·特劳特 . 营销革命 [M]. 左占平，等译 . 北京：中国财政经济出版社，2002.

杰克·特劳特，史蒂夫·里夫金 . 重新定位——定位支付杰克特劳特封笔之作 [M]. 谢伟山，等译 . 北京：机械工业出版社，2016.

W. 钱·金，勒妮·莫伯涅 . 蓝海战略 [M]. 吉宓，译 . 北京：商务印书馆，2016.

克里斯·安德森 . 长尾理论 [M]. 乔江涛，译 . 北京：中信出版社，2006.

托德·A. 穆拉安迪，库尔特·马茨勒，劳伦斯·J. 林 . 战略营销 [M]. 郑晓亚，等译 . 上海：格致出版社，2014.

格雷厄姆·胡利，奈杰尔·皮尔西，布里吉特·尼库洛 . 营销战略与竞争定位 [M]. 楼尊，译 . 北京：中国人民大学出版社，2014.

7

Product Strategy

产品策略

知识解锁 Knowledge Unlocked

以下问题的答案，可在本章寻找：

1. 产品是怎么分类的？

2. 产品计划有哪几个阶段？

3. 如何根据产品生命周期进行营销？

4. 品牌、包装及商标在产品形象的建立中扮演什么样的角色？

5. 特殊产品——服务有什么特征？

6. 服务营销通常采用哪些战略？

7. 如何衡量服务的质量？

7.1 What Is a Product? 什么是产品？

A product is anything tangible or intangible (everything) that satisfies customers' needs, creating a benefit that a customer receives in an exchange. For example, a product can be a good, idea, method, information, object or service created as a result of a process and serves a need or satisfies a want. A good is a tangible product that we can see, touch, smell, hear or taste.

产品是满足客户需求的任何有形或无形的东西（一切），在交易中为客户创造价值。例如，产品可以是商品、主意、方法、信息、物体或服务，它是作为一个过程的结果（一组将输入转化为输出的相互关联或相互作用的活动）而创建的，可以服务于需要或满足欲望。商品是一种有形的产品，可以被看到、触摸到、闻到、听到或品尝到。

We buy and use products almost every day, but we do not have the chance to know what they actually are. In order to actively explore the nature of a product further, let's consider a product in three different layers: the core product, the actual product, and the augmented product.

我们几乎每天都在购买和使用产品，却没有机会知道它们到底是什么。为了进一步积极地探索产品的本质，让我们从三个不同的层次来考虑一个产品：核心产品、实际产品和延伸产品。

7.1.1 The Core Product 核心产品

The core product is not the tangible physical product that you can touch. It consists of all the main benefits that consumers seek. The best question asked by marketers to understand core product is "What is the buyer really buying?" Successful marketers will tell you that a marketer may produce and sell heating pads, but a customer buys warmth. That means people buy core product, and if there is a new portable heating device with a lower price or higher quality that provides the same benefit, the manufacturer of heating pads faces a slowdown in sales or their products become even unmarketable.

核心产品不是你可以触摸到的有形的实物产品。它包括消费者寻求的所有主要利益。营销人员要想了解核心产品，最好的问题是"购买者真正购买的是什么？"成功的市场营销人员会告诉你，一个市场营销人员可能生产和销售电热毯，但客户购买的是温暖。这意味着人们购买的是核心产品。如果有一种新的便携式加热设备，价格更低或质量更高，却能提供同样的好处，那么电热毯的制造商就会面临销售放缓或产品滞销的局面。

Most products provide a series of benefits. Women purchase luxury bags not only to carry stuff, but also enjoy the feeling of being admired by their friends. So luxury goods provide customers with good quality, functions as well as social status. Likewise, if you buy an iPad, you buy more than a mobile computer or a personal organizer. The core customer value you buy may be freedom, on-the-go connectivity and being viewed as a swinger.

大多数产品都为消费者提供了一系列的价值。女性购买奢侈品包不仅是为了装东西，也是为了享受被朋友羡慕的感觉。因此，奢侈品为消费者提供了良好的品质、功能及社会地位。同样地，如果你买了 iPad，你买的不仅仅是移动电脑或个人记事本。你购买的核心顾客价值可能是自由、即时连接网络和被视为一个时髦的人。

7.1.2　The Actual Product 实际产品

The second layer is the actual product. Marketers should turn the core benefits into a physical identifiable actual product. This involves developing product features, materials, a shape, a quality level, a packaging, and even a brand name. The smart phone you finally buy as well as the car are actual products. You buy the phone, the brand, the packaging, the design, the functionality, and so on. All actual product designs mean to relate to the core customer value. The appearance, design, styling, packaging of a smart phone are carefully combined together to deliver the core product of staying connected.

第二层是实际产品。营销人员应该把核心利益转化为有形的、可识别的实际产品。这包括开发产品的特性、材料、形状、质量水平、包装甚至品牌。你最终购买的智能手机和汽车都是实实在在的产品。你买手机买的是品牌、包装、设计、功能等。所有实际的产品设计都意味着与核心客户价值相关。智能手机的外观、设计、造型、包装都被精心组合在一起，传递出保持连接的核心产品。

7.1.3　The Augmented Product 延伸产品

Finally, the levels of product are completed with the augmented product. It is built around and are by-product of the core product and the actual product. By adding extra benefits such as warranty, after-sale support, delivery or installation to a product, companies can make themselves stand out from the competition.

最后，产品的层次是通过延伸产品来完成的。它是核心产品和实际产品的副产品。通过提供额外的利益，如保修、售后、按时交付或辅助安装的产品，公司可以使自己从竞争中脱颖而出。

7.2　Classifying Products 产品分类

Products are classified into categories because it affects how consumers purchase and use them. Classifying products into meaningful categories helps marketers decide which strategies and methods will help promote a business's product or service. There are many types of classification existing. The key is to categorize the products in ways that make sense for your own business. This allows you to design separate marketing campaigns for each category of product you offer. Using a one-size-fits-all marketing plan is often less effective than implementing several highly targeted plans. No simple recipe exists for categorizing products and services, but there are some common product classifications in marketing.

产品被分类是因为它影响了消费者购买和使用它们的方式。将产品分为有意义的类别有助于市场营销人员决定哪些战略和方法能提升企业的产品或服务。分类的方法有许多，关键是要使其对您自己的业务有意义。你可以为每一类产品设计单独的营销活动。使用一个放之四海而皆准的营销计划往往不如实施几个目标明确的计划有效。分类没有简单规律可循，但是市场营销中有一些常见的产品分类方法。

7.2.1　Defined by the Life of the Product 由产品的生命周期来定义

Some products will last for many years, and others are consumed on the spot when we purchase them. These are known as durable and non-durable goods.

有些产品可以使用多年，有些则是在购买时当场消费。这就是所谓的耐用品和非耐用品。

Durable goods have an extended product life from months to decades, and are not typically worn out or consumed quickly when you use them. Houses, cars, furniture, household appliances, jewelry, and electronic products fall into this category. It is not a rigid concept, for some people see a table cloth as fast moving consumer goods, but others use it for many years. Durable goods are purchased infrequently under conditions of high involvement situations. It involves longer decision-making time and more energy put in searching the product information. Marketers have to know what benefits consumers are exactly looking for and provide the information where consumers are most likely to search. Communicating the augmented products may help promoting the products.

耐用品的使用寿命可以从几个月延长到几十年，一般不会很快就用坏或消耗完。房屋、汽车、家具、家用电器、珠宝、电子产品都属于这一类。但这并不是一个严格的概念。有些人认为桌布是快消品，有些人却能使用很多年。耐用品很少在高参与度情况下购买。它需要更长的决策时间和更多的精力来搜索产品信息。营销人员必须知道消费者究竟在寻找什么帮助，并向消费者提供最有可能搜索的信息。传播延伸的产品可能有助于产品的推广。

Non-durable goods are products that are consumed or are only useable for a short period of time. Boxes of cereals, canned foods, clothing, disposable cups, socks, and paper plates are in this category. Consumers spend less energy in buying non-durable goods as they have low perceived risks. These low involvement decisions are made on the basis of learning, meaning good past experiences lead to repurchase and bad ones lead to abandonment. Business running convenient stores has a deep insight into consumer behavior of purchasing non-durable goods, as study shows that consumers spend 3 to 5 minutes on average in completing a purchase. Attractive packages and innovative ads can be their buying reasons.

非耐用品是指只能在短时间内消耗或使用的产品。谷类、罐头、衣服、一次性杯子、袜子、纸盘都属于这一类。消费者在购买非耐用品上花费的精力较少，因为他们的感知风险较低。这些低参与决策是在"学习"的基础上做出的，这意味着满意的经历会促使复购，而不满意的经历会导致放弃复购。便利店经营对消费者购买非耐用品的行为有着深刻的洞察。研究表明，在便利店里，消费者平均花费 3~5 分钟完成一次购买。有吸引力的包装和创意广告可能是他们购买的原因。

7.2.2　Defined by How Consumers Buy the Product 由消费者购买产品的方式决定

Another classification approach is based on how and where consumers buy the product. Consumer products can be thought of as convenience goods, shopping goods, specialty products or unsought goods. Focusing on how customers buy these goods is equally important as classifying products and developing the marketing campaigns.

另一种分类方法是基于消费者购买产品的方式和地点。消费品可以被认为是便利商品、购物商品、特色商品或冷门商品。顾客如何购买这些商品，与对产品进行分类和制订营销计划同样重要。

Those products your customers buy often and with little thought or planning are classified as convenience products. Convenience products are low-priced, widely scattered. Shampoo, staples, and bandages are common examples of convenience goods. Consumers typically make a choice once on their brand preference for these products and repeat that choice over many purchases. Making your convenience goods available for impulse purchase or emergency purchases can be particularly effective. Impulse products require that marketers create easily identifiable packaging to ensure highly visible of their products. Emergency product such as first aid kit requires suitable size for purchasing.

顾客经常购买却很少仔细考虑或计划的产品被归类为便利产品。便利产品价格低廉，分布广泛。洗发水、订书钉、绷带都是常见的便利商品。一般来说，消费者对这些产品的品牌偏好只会做出一次选择，并在许多次购买中重复这一选择。便利产品用于冲动购买或紧急购买的场景是特别有效的。冲动消费产品要求营销人员设计易于识别的包装，以确保产品高度可见。紧急用品，如急救包，需要考虑尺寸是否合适。

On the contrary, shopping products are those consumers will invest considerable time and effort in gathering information and comparing alternatives. Purchase decisions entails medium to high involvement. For example, a customer might compare ingredients, prices and safety information for a variety of laundry detergents before making a final purchase. For attribute-based shopping products, people look for the best combination of those attributes (features, warranty, performance, options, and other factors); for price-based shopping products with little differences in distinguished features, people look for the least expensive one. Often, the most effective marketing approach is to use heavy promotions and knowledgeable salespeople to develop brand preference and loyalty among customers.

相反，对于选购性产品，消费者会投入相当多的时间和精力来收集信息和比较替代品。购买决策需要中等到高参与度。例如，顾客可能会在最后购买之前比较各种洗衣剂的成分、价格和安全信息。对于基于属性的购物产品，人们寻找这些属性（功能、保证、性能、选项和其他因素）的最佳组合；基于价格的购物产品在特色上差别不大，人们寻找最便宜的。通常，最有效的营销方法是使用大量的促销活动和知识渊博的销售人员来开发品牌偏好和客户的忠诚度。

Specialty products are those with unique characteristics and to which consumers are brand loyal. They are fully aware of these products and their attributes prior to making a purchase decision. For getting the product, consumers are willing to wait or travel a long distance, so they are less price sensitive. Examples include exotic perfumes, famous paintings, hi-fi components, photographic equipment, molecular gastronomy, and the most high-end brands of cars. Consumers are willing to make a significant purchase effort to acquire the brand desired and will pay a higher price than competitive products, if necessary. For specialty goods, consumers will not make purchases if their brand is not available. Substitutes are not acceptable. In general, it is desirable for marketers to lift their product from the shopping to the specialty class and keep it there.

特色产品是指具有独特的特性，消费者对其品牌忠诚的产品。在做出购买决定之前，他们充分了解这些产品及其属性。为了得到产品，消费者愿意等待或远距离出行，所以他们对价格不太敏感。例如，异国香水、名画、高保真音响、摄影器材、分子美食，以及最高端的汽车品牌。消费者愿意做出重大的购买努力，以获得所需的品牌，并将支付比竞争产品更高的价格，如果必要的话。对于特殊商品，如果没有他们喜欢的品牌，消费者将不会购买，不接受代替品。一般来说，对营销人员来说，将他们的产品从购物商品提升到特色产品并保持下去是可取的策略。

Unsought products are goods or services that consumers have little awareness or do not often think about until there is a need. New products that have no brand recognition, certain types of life insurance, fire extinguisher, and prepaid funeral plans fall under this classification. Sauerkraut, a traditional fermented moist cabbage side dishes, was common as food given to American soldiers during World War I. However, due to concerns the American public would reject a product with a German name, American sauerkraut makers relabeled their product as "Liberty cabbage" for the duration of the war, successfully put across the food.

冷门产品，消费者很少意识到或不经常考虑，直到有需要的时候。没有品牌知名度的新产品、某些类型的人寿保险、灭火器和预付费的葬礼计划都属于这一类。酸菜是一种传统的发酵卷心菜配菜，在第一次世界大战期间被普遍用作美国士兵的食物。然而，由于担心美国公众会拒绝使用德文名字的产品，美国泡菜制造商在战争期间将他们的产品贴上"自由泡菜"的标签，并成功地将其用于食品之中。

7.3 Product Line Strategies 产品线策略

7.3.1 Product Mix Strategies 产品组合策略

Small companies may achieve temporary success by focusing on one product, but in any organization with a larger scale, there are numerous products present. If a company has only a single product, it is understood as the result of an extremely high demand of the product or the company lacks the resources to expand the number of products. Examples are Coca cola, Apple, Microsoft, Nestle, Unilever, Pharmaceutical companies, so on and so forth. Companies with multiple products need to think in terms of a wide product portfolio as the product strategies affect the whole range of products simultaneously.

小公司可能通过专注于一种产品而获得暂时的成功，但是在任何规模较大的组织中，都存在大量各色产品。如果一个公司只有一种产品，会被认为是由于市场对该产品有极高需求或者公司缺乏扩充产品品种的资源，如可口可乐、苹果、微软、雀巢、联合利华、制药公司等。拥有多种产品的公司需要考虑一个广泛的产品组合，因为产品战略会同时影响整个产品系列。

The complete range of products present within a company is known as the product mix. An organization with several product lines has a product mix. In developing a company's product mix strategy, companies usually think of product mix width, which refers to the number of different product lines the company carries. Some companies manage very complex product portfolios. For example, Sony corporation's diverse portfolio consists of four primary product businesses worldwide: Sony Electronics, Sony Electric Vehicles and Batteries, Sony Entertainment (pictures, music), and Sony Financial Services (life insurance, banking, and other offerings). Normally, companies developing a mix of product lines share common physical distribution channels or manufacturing facilities.

公司提供给市场的全部产品线和产品项目被称为产品组合。拥有多个产品线的组织就拥有了一个产品组合。在制定公司的产品组合战略时，公司通常会考虑产品组合宽度，即公司拥有的不同产品线的数量。有些公司拥有非常复杂的产品组合。例如，索尼公司的多元化投资组合包括全球范围内的4项主要产品业务：索尼电子、索尼电动汽车和电池、索尼娱乐（图片、音乐）和索尼金融服务（人寿保险、银行和其他产品）。通常情况下，开发多种产品线的公司之间共享分销渠道或生产设施设备。

7.3.2 Product Line Strategies 产品线策略

Product line generally refers to a series of related products defined by their functions and customer market, forming a "line" or a category. Large companies with many types of products have similar number of product lines. For example, in Nestle, there are milk based products like Milkmaid, food products like Maggi, chocolate products like Kitkat and other such product lines. Therefore, Nestle's product mix will be a combination of the all product lines within the company. To do a better job of meeting varying consumer needs, each brand goes with more than one flavor. For example, Kitkat in Japan has over 80 flavors covering strawberry, green tea, golden peach, sweet potato, etc., with soy sauce being the top selling.

产品线一般是指由其功能和客户市场定义的一系列相关产品，形成同一销售渠道。拥有多种产品的大公司有一些类似的产品线，如雀巢有以奶，制品为基础的一系列产品，如牛奶饮品 Milkmaid，食品如美极，巧克力如奇巧，以及其他类似的产品线。因此，雀巢的产品组合将是公司内部所有产品线的组合。为了更好地满足不同消费者的需求，每个品牌的食品都有不止一种口味。例如，奇巧在日本有超过 80 种口味，包括草莓、绿茶、金桃子、甘薯口味等。其中，酱油味是最畅销的。

A product line can contain one product or hundreds. The number of products in a product line refer to its product line depth, while the number of separate product lines owned by a company is the product line width (or breadth). A large number of variations in a product line is described as a full line, while a product line with fewer product variations is called a limited line.

一条产品线可以包含一个产品，也可以包含数百个产品。产品线的数量代表着产品线深度，而一个公司拥有的独立产品线的数量是产品线宽度。产品种类和变化多的产品线被称为一个完整的产品线，而产品种类和变化较少的产品线被称为有限的产品线。

高露洁旗下的各系列个人护理用品，销往全球 200 多个国家和地区

1.Stretching 产品线延伸

As a company grows, it may wish to extend its product line. Product line extensions occur when a company introduces additional items in the same product category under the same brand name, such as new flavors, forms, colors, added ingredients, or package sizes, that is, lengthens its product line beyond its current range. The strategies applied are upward line stretch, downward line stretch, or two-way stretch.

随着公司的发展，可能会希望扩展产品线。产品线延伸是指公司在同一品牌下，在相同的产品类别中引入新的产品，如新口味、形状、颜色、添加的成分或包装尺寸等，也就是说，将产品线扩展到当前的范围之外。其中所采用的策略有向上延伸、向下延伸或双向延伸。

When a business adds a line extension to the product line and if it is of a higher quality than the current products, it is considered as an upward stretch or trading up. It occurs when a company wishes to enter the high end of the market for more growth, higher margins or simply to position themselves as full-line manufacturers. Many companies have climbed up to reach higher-end segments. Starbucks in coffee, Haagen-Dazs in ice cream, and Evian in bottled water. Leading Japanese auto companiesall all have introduced upscale automobiles: Toyota's Lexus, Nissan's Infiniti, and Honda's Acura. Difficulties in an upward stretch may lie in that it may encounter obstacles as competitors in that market are defending themselves, volume of sales may not be sufficient as the turnover is generally less, and new distribution channels are to be developed.

当企业在产品线上增加了一个产品，如果它的质量比当前的产品更高，它就被认为是向上延伸或向上经营。当一家公司希望进入高端市场以获得更大的增长、更高的利润率或仅仅将自己定位为全线制造商时，就会出现这种情况。许多公司都已经向上攀升，进入了高端市场，如星巴克的咖啡、哈根达斯的冰激凌、依云的瓶装水。日本名列前茅的汽车公司都推出了高档汽车：丰田的雷克萨斯、日产的英菲尼迪和本田的讴歌。向上延伸的困难可能在于，当竞争对手在市场上进行自我保护时，可能会遇到障碍，销售量不足，营业额普遍较低，需要开发新的分销渠道。

向上延伸：雷克萨斯是日本丰田集团旗下全球著名豪华汽车品牌

Conversely, if the new added item is of lower quality compared to other existing products, it is known as a downward stretch or trading down. A company staying in the middle market may introduce a downward stretch line for the following three reasons: The company has noticed strong potential growth opportunities in the down markets; the company may wish to tie up lower-end competitors who might otherwise be a strong rival in higher-end segments; the company finds that the current market is turning down or even stagnating. It should be carefully taken in case the current prestige brand image is mixed up with the new lower one. For example, Samsung has done a lot of downward product line stretching. It has premium smart phones like the Edge series, it also has the series of cheaper smart phones so that it does not lose the massive consumption brought by cheap smart phones. Another example is Parker pens which have taken over the likes of Cross and Mont Blanc in terms of turnover and overall profitability. While competing with Cross and Mont Blanc who have their own premium brand equity, Parker on the other hand has covered the middle market by introducing Sonnet fountain pen.

相反，如果新增加的产品与其他现有产品相比品质较低，则称为向下延伸或向下经营。处于中间市场的公司可能会引入一条向下延伸的线，原因有以下3个：公司在下沉市场中发现了巨大的潜在增长机会；公司可能希望与较低端的竞争对手合作，而这些竞争对手原本可能是高端市场的强劲对手；公司发现目前的市场势头正在下降，甚至停滞不前。公司应该小心地采取向下延伸的策略，以防目前的颇有威望品牌形象与新的低端形象混为一谈。例如，三星做了很多向下延伸的产品线。它有高端智能手机，比如 Edge 系列，它也有一系列更便宜的智能手机，这样它就不会失去廉价智能手机的大量消费市场。另一个例子是派克笔，它已经在营业额和整体盈利能力方面取代了高仕和万宝龙。在与拥有自己的高端品牌资产的高仕和万宝龙竞争时，派克钢笔通过引入"卓尔"系列自来水笔来覆盖中间市场。

向下延伸：中国联合航空有限公司是中国东方航空集团有限公司（China Eastern Airlines）旗下子公司，定位于"创新经济型航空公司"

In some cases, companies introduce a new product into an already existing product line, and into both the lower and higher ends of that overall product line within the same period of time, which is called two-way stretch. This is generally rare and more likely happen in new markets or when companies are in rapidly expansion of their product line and trying to offer a full range of product offerings in order to reduce the incentive for new competitors. By doing so, the company is likely to dominate the product category. Texas Instruments launched calculators in both upper and lower range; Accor Hotels fills its product line by bringing in Ibis Hotels at the lower end and Sofitel Hotels at the upper end.

在某些情况下，公司将一种新产品引入已有的产品线中，并同时将其引入整个产品线的较低和较高的两端，这被称为双向延伸。这种情况比较罕见，更有可能发生在新兴市场或当公司在迅速扩大其产品线时，并试图提供全方位的产品，以减少对新的竞争对手的刺激。这样做该公司可能会主导产品类别。德州仪器推出了高、低端的计算器；雅高酒店则面向低端市场推出宜必思酒店，在高端市场推出索菲特酒店，从而充实了其产品线。

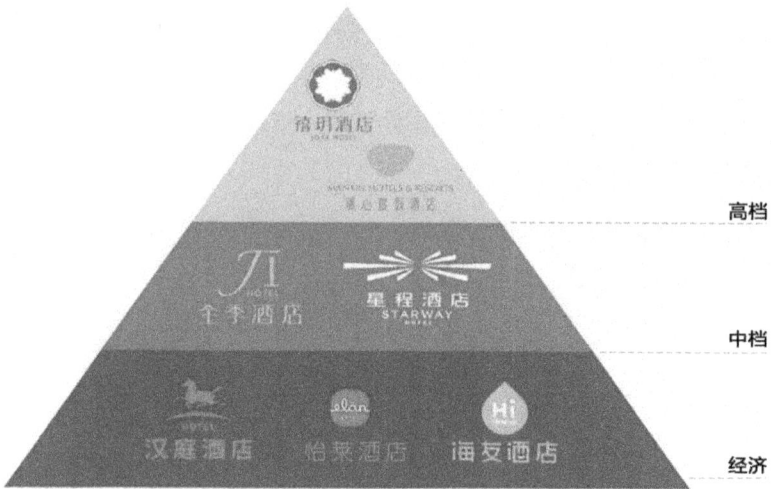

华住会旗下品牌分类

2.Line-filling 产品线填充

Sometimes, companies use a line-filling strategy by adding sizes or styles that weren't previously available in a product category. It occurs when a void in the existing product line has not been filled or a new void has developed due to the activities of competitors or the request of consumers. The most commonly used way of filling out the product line is product proliferation, the introduction of new varieties of the initial product or products that are similar. For example, a ketchup manufacturer introduces a hickory-flavored sauce, a pizza-flavored barbecue sauce, and a special hot dog sauce.

有时，公司会通过添加以前在产品类别中没有的尺寸或样式来实施产品线填充策略。当现有产品线中的一个空缺没有被填补，或者由于竞争对手的活动或消费者的要求而产生了一个新的产品空缺时，就会发生这种情况。最常用的丰富产品线的方式是产品增值，即引进新品种的产品或相似的产品。例如，番茄酱制造商引入了一种山核桃味的酱、一种比萨味的烧烤酱和一种特殊的热狗酱。

The risk of overfilling the product line is product cannibalization, a reduction in sales volume, sales revenue, or market share of one product as a result of the introduction of a new product by the same producer. Another risk is the pressures on the manufacturing, logistics system, and sales, and service staff, given too many products to manufacture and sell.

产品过剩的风险是侵蚀效应（也称品牌替换），即由于同一家生产商推出新产品，导致原有产品的销售量、销售收入或市场份额下降。另一个风险是制造、物流系统、销售和服务人员的压力，因为有太多的产品需要制造和销售。

3. Line-Pruning 产品线削减

Sometimes, companies try to get rid of products that no longer contribute to company profits by using line-pruning strategy. A simple fact of marketing is that sooner or later a product will decline in demand and require pruning. Timex has stopped selling home computers. Hallmark has stopped selling talking cards. A great many of the components used in the latest automobile have replaced far more expensive parts, due to the increased costs in other areas of the process, such as labor.

有时，公司试图通过产品线削减的策略来摆脱那些对公司利润不再有贡献的产品。市场营销的一个简单事实是，产品的需求迟早会下降，需要精简。天美时已经停止销售家用电脑。贺曼公司已经停止销售会说话的贺卡。最新汽车上使用的许多零部件已经取代了昂贵得多的零部件，这是由于生产过程中其他方面的成本有所增加，比如劳动力成本。

Using modern robotics technology has halved the manufacturing costs of several products. Through such implementation, Keebler Cookies moved from packaging their cookies totally by hand to 70% automation. Other possible ways a company might become more efficient are by replacing antiquated machinery, moving production closer to the point of sale, subcontracting out part of the manufacturing process, or hiring more productive employees.

现代机器人技术使一些产品的制造成本降低了一半。通过这些技术，奇宝饼干从全手工打包转变为 70% 的自动化打包。公司提高效率的其他方法可能是替换陈旧的机器，将生产地点转移到销售点附近，将部分制造流程外包出去，或者雇用更有生产力的员工。

7.4　Product Life Cycle 产品生命周期

The product life cycle (PLC) describes the life of a product in the market with respect to business costs and sales measures. Just like any living thing does, a product goes through stages from birth to death: Introduction, growth, maturity, and decline. Some products live longer, others shorter. However, each product has a limited life, and thus, every product has a life cycle. Although life expectancies of products can be extended in some way, each product has a natural phases through which it is expected to pass. Product features, growth of sales, financing, manufacturing, purchasing, and human resource requirements change over stages of product life cycle, so as product marketing strategies.

产品生命周期描述了产品在市场上的生命周期，包括商业成本和销售指标。就像任何生物一样，一个产品从诞生到死亡经历了几个阶段：引入期、成长期、成熟期和衰退期。有些产品寿命长，有些则短。然而，每个产品都有一个有限的生命周期，因此，每个产品都有一个生命周期。虽然产品的预期寿命可以以某种方式延长，但每个产品天然地都有阶段性，人们预期它会经历这个阶段。产品特性、销售增长、融资、制造、采购和人力资源需求随着产品生命周期的不同阶段而变化，产品营销策略也是如此。

7.4.1　Introduction 引入期

The product life cycle begins with the introduction stage. This stage comes after the completion of product development, which means the product has been designed and tested, and it is time to introduce the new product to the market.

产品生命周期从引入阶段开始。这个阶段是在产品开发完成后，也就是产品已经完成设计和测试，把新产品投入市场，就进入了引入期。

At this stage, the company usually do not make a profit, for the high research and development cost is not able to be recovered within a short period, and besides, the company is investing a good amount of money in initial marketing, advertising, and distribution to create consumers' awareness. The goal of this stage is to let people know about the product, inform them about its benefits, get them to try and finally to pay for the product. In order to achieve this goal, promotion and awareness campaigns are launched. The price of new products may be set high to recover the initial investment based on considerable demand, or low to realize a fast market penetration. If the new product has a clear advantage over its competitors, consumers are less concerned about the price.

在这个阶段，公司通常不盈利，因为高昂的研发成本无法在短时间内收回，而且公司在初期的营销、广告和分销上投入了大量资金，以提高消费者对品牌的认知度。这一阶段的目标是让人们了解产品，告诉他们产品的好处，让他们尝试并最终为产品付费。为了实现这一目标，营销方面将开展促销和宣传活动。新产品的价格可以在需求较大的情况下调高，以收回初始投资，也可以调低，以实现快速的市场渗透。如果新产品相对于竞争对手有明显的优势，消费者就不那么在意价格了。

Demands are created for the first time, but the market size is small thus making sales volumes small and increasing slowly. This period can last long and not all products can make it through. Wrong market forecast or consumers' dissatisfaction with the product performance will quickly lead to failure. For a well-established market, unless the company creates a brand new demand, it may be trapped in homogeneity, or highly competitive environment that makes itself hard to move on. Since most products assume great risks in this stage, the company has to carefully choose the best time for entry and market as precise as possible to the most potential segments.

在这个阶段，需求被第一次创造出来，但由于市场规模小、销量小，增长较为缓慢。引入期可能会持续很长时间，而且并不是所有产品都能度过这个阶段。错误的市场预测或消费者对产品性能的不满会很快导致失败。对于一个成熟的市场，除非该公司创造出一个全新的需求，否则它可能会陷入同质化，或高度竞争的环境使其难以前进。由于大多数产品在这一阶段都承担着很大的风险，公司必须谨慎选择最佳的进入时间，并尽可能精确地定位最有潜力的细分市场。

7.4.2 Growth 成长期

The growth stage is the period during which the product eventually and increasingly gains acceptance among consumers, the industry, and the wider general public. During this stage, the product or the innovation becomes widely accepted in the market. As a result, there is a strong growth in sales and profits, and because the company can start to benefit from economies of scale in production which lowers the cost of production, the profit margins, as well as the overall amount of profit, will increase.

成长期是指产品最终逐渐被消费者、行业和广大公众所接受的阶段。在这个阶段，产品或创新被市场广泛接受。因此，在销售和利润方面有一个强劲的增长，因为公司可以开始受益于生产成本降低带来的规模经济，利润率及总利润将会增加。

High profits attract more players to join in, forming a more competitive marketplace. In order to counter the competition, companies either try to look for new segments or lower their prices. The average price of products in the same category falls accordingly, driving the speed of growth down. Profit reaches its peak in the end of this stage.

高额的利润吸引了更多玩家的加入，形成了一个更有竞争力的市场。为了应对竞争，公司要么寻找新的细分市场，要么降低价格。同类产品平均价格随之下降，增速下降。利润在这个阶段结束时达到顶峰。

To maintain the growth stage, the company can look at ways to introduce new features, alterations, or other types of innovation to the product according to feedback from consumers and from the market in general. Other businesses choose to invest more money in the promotion activities to maximize the potential of this growth stage. In fact, the growth stage is seen as the best time to set up a brand image instead of to communicate product benefits. Customer loyalty is desirable.

为了维持成长期的涨势，公司可以根据消费者和市场的反馈，寻找方法来引入新功能或进行其他类型的创新。有一些企业选择在促销活动中投入更多的资金，以最大限度地发挥这一成长阶段的潜力。事实上，成长期被认为是树立品牌形象的最佳时期，但不是传达产品价值的最佳时期。这个阶段容易建立客户忠诚度。

7.4.3 Maturity 成熟期

The maturity stage of the product life cycle can take the longest time. It refers to the stage in the product life cycle where sales growth ultimately peaks, then slows as the product reaches widespread acceptance within the target markets, and competition is fierce. Similar products in different brands and styles keep turning up, squeezing profit margins. Prices tend to drop due to the proliferation of competing products. Demand for the product ultimately decreases due to competition and market saturation, as well as new technologies and changes in consumer tastes.

成熟期可能经历最长的时间。在这个阶段，销售增长最终达到顶峰，然后随着产品在目标市场的广泛接受和竞争的激烈而放缓。不同品牌和风格的类似产品不断出现，挤压了利润率。由于竞争产品的增加，价格有下降的趋势。由于竞争和市场饱，以及新技术和消费者口味的变化，对产品的需求最终会下降。

To maintain or increase market share, companies can resort to feature diversification. For example, being in the maturity stage, the car industry may include alloy wheels, new colors, sport or hybrid versions, or other changes in order to keep sales going. Other actions taken include lowering prices in order to fight off competition, intensifying distribution and promotional efforts, brand or product differentiation efforts, hopefully the new customers will start to buy the product.

为了保持或增加市场份额，企业可以采取特征多样化策略。例如，处于成熟阶段的汽车行业可能采用合金车轮、新颜色、运动或混合动力版本及变化以保持销售。其他措施包括降低价格以对抗竞争，加强分销和促销，加强品牌差异化或产品差异化，希望新客户会开始购买产品。

7.4.4 Decline 衰退期

Eventually, the market for a product will start to shrink, which is known as "decline". It is the stage of the product life style where low or negative sales growth, lower profits, and maximum competition occur, forcing the product into decline and "death". Changes in consumer tastes and emergence of new technologies can be the reasons eroding sales, which may make the popularity of the product falls. For example, CDs and DVDs are become ultimately obsolete. Video cassette has exited the market.

最终，一种产品的市场将走向萎缩，这被称为"衰退"。这是产品生命周期的一个阶段，在这个阶段，销售增长缓慢或负增长，利润下降，竞争加剧，迫使产品走向衰落和"死亡"。消费者口味的变化和新技术的出现可能是销售下降的原因，这可能会使产品的受欢迎程度下降。例如，CD 和 DVD 最终被淘汰，录像带已退出市场。

It is important to note that product termination is not usually the end of the business cycle; rather, it is only the termination of a single product that can no longer compete as it has reached the end of its life. While this decline may be inevitable, it may still be possible for companies to manage it in some ways. The company can keep the product on the market and reducing production if there is some residual demand. For a product sees quick turndown, the company completely gives up by cutting production and operation, to let the existing stocks run out. All in all, the idea is to do the final clear out without any support from marketing efforts.

需要注意的是，产品终止通常不是商业周期的结束；相反，它只是一种产品的终止，因为它已经到了生命的尽头，不再具有竞争力。虽然销量下降有时是不可避免的，但企业仍有可能在某些方面加以控制。如果有一些剩余的需求，公司可以将产品留在市场上，减少生产。对于销量下降很快的产品，公司就会完全放弃生产和经营，把现有的库存消耗完。总而言之，在没有任何营销支持的情况下完成最后的清场工作。

7.5 Branding 品牌化

7.5.1 What Is a Brand? 什么是品牌？

While marketers keep an eye on the life cycle of their products, they also plan to give an identity to the products. This is where the products need branding. Everybody can easily recognize some brands, more or less. But what is a brand? It seems like a simple question, but the answer is anything but simple. If you are confused by your brand, your customers will be confused, too.

当营销人员关注他们产品的生命周期时，他们也计划给产品一个身份。这就是产品需要建立品牌的原因。每个人，或多或少都能很容易地认出一些品牌，但什么是品牌呢？这似乎是一个简单的问题，但答案绝不简单。如果你对自己的品牌感到困惑，你的客户也会感到困惑。

Brand is a set of perceptions and images that identifies a company, its products or services and differentiates it from the competition. We recognize a brand by a brand name (McDonald's), a trade character (the M&M chocolate men), a brand mark (Twitter logo), or packaging. A brand consists of several elements: (1) Brand promise.

At its core, a brand is a promise to consumers. A brand makes a commitment to what consumers will get when they purchase a product or service under your brand. It also incorporates the feelings that consumers get when they use your products and services. Nike promises that the brand might represent athleticism, performance, strength, good health, and fun. (2) Brand perceptions. Brands are the way that consumers perceive and define your company and products. Marketers work to develop consumer perceptions that accurately reflect the brand. (3) Brand expectations. When consumers pull their hard-earned money out of their pockets and purchase your products or services, they assume their expectations for your brand will be met. If the brand does not meet their expectations in every interaction, consumers will become confused and turn away to another brand that does meet their expectations. If Rolls Royce launches a car at 60,000 RMB, consumers will be confused because it does not meet their expectations for a luxury brand. (4) Brand personality. It is a set of human characteristics attributed to a brand name to which the consumer can relate. From appearance to personality and everything in between, brand personality is one that consumers will evaluate and judge before making an exchange. For example, Tencent and Alibaba.com have very different brand personalities, as brand personality determines who you would rather spend time with.

　　品牌是一套识别公司、产品或服务的，能将产品与竞争对手区分开来的认知和形象设计。我们通过品牌名称（麦当劳）、商业角色（M&M巧克力人）、品牌标志（Twitter标志）或包装来识别一个品牌。品牌包含几个要素：（1）品牌承诺。品牌的核心是对消费者的承诺。品牌承诺消费者在购买你品牌下的产品或服务时会得到什么。它还包含了消费者在使用你的产品和服务时的感受。耐克承诺，他们的品牌代表着运动能力、性能、力量、健康和乐趣。（2）品牌认知。品牌是消费者感知和定义你的公司和产品的方式。市场营销人员努力培养能准确反映品牌的消费者认知。（3）品牌期望。当消费者从口袋里掏出辛苦赚来的钱来购买你的产品或服务时，他们假设自己对品牌的期望会得到满足。如果品牌在每一次互动中都没有达到他们的期望，消费者就会变得困惑，从而转向另一个能满足他们期望的品牌。如果劳斯莱斯以6万元的价格推出一辆车，消费者会感到困惑，因为这并不能满足他们对奢侈品牌的期望。（4）品牌个性。

它是品牌所具有的一系列人类的人格特质。从外观到个性，以及其中的一切，品牌个性是消费者在进行交易之前会进行评价和判断的。例如，腾讯和阿里巴巴的品牌个性非常不同，品牌个性决定了你愿意和谁在一起。

Therefore, a brand is represented by intangible elements (promise, perception, expectation) as well as tangible elements (name, term, logo, symbol, design, packaging). They work together as a psychological trigger that causes an association to all other thoughts we have about a brand. A brand is clear, reliable, and believable to both consumers and employees. However, brands are not built overnight. You must understand your competitors and audience, so you can develop a brand that promises the right things to the right people. Research should be first, definition, strategy, and execution should follow, and the brand will grow over time. The objectives that a good brand will achieve include being clear, confirming credibility, emotionally connecting target audience with your product and/or service, motivating the buyer to buy, and creating loyalty, etc.

因此，品牌是由无形元素（承诺、感知、期望）和有形元素（名称、术语、标识、符号、设计、包装）组成的。它们作为一种心理触发因素共同产生作用，使我们建立对一个品牌的所有想象。品牌对消费者和员工来说是清晰、可靠、可信的。然而，品牌不是一夜之间建立起来的。你必须了解你的竞争对手和受众，才能建立一个能够向正确的人承诺正确的事情的品牌形象。研究是首要的任务，其次是定义、战略和执行，品牌会随着时间的推移而成长。一个好的品牌所要达到的目标包括：清晰、确定的可信度、在情感上把目标受众与你的产品或服务联系起来、激励买家购买、建立忠诚度等。

7.5.2　Value of Branding 品牌的价值

Branding is the process of establishing a brand through researching, developing, and implementing brand names, brand marks, trade characters, and trademarks. Branding is so powerful that it is a key element of differentiating from the competition.

品牌化是通过研究、开发和实施品牌名称、品牌标识、商业角色和商标来建立一个品牌的过程。品牌的作用非常强大，它是区别于竞争对手的一个关键因素。

The value of a brand that is well-known and conjures positive mental and emotional associations is called brand equity. For any given product, service, or company, brand equity is considered as a key asset because it helps it remain relevant and competitive. Brand equity can manifest itself in consumer recognition of logos or other visual elements, brand language associations made by consumers' perception of quality, and value among other relevant brand attributes.

品牌中富有价值的产品或服务，能唤起积极的精神和情感联想，这就是品牌资产。对于任何给定的产品、服务或公司，品牌资产被认为是关键资产，因为它有助于保持相关性和竞争力。品牌资产可以表现为消费者对商标或其他视觉元素的认知，消费者对质量的感知所产生的品牌语言联想，以及其他相关品牌属性的价值。

Satisfied customers become brand loyals and are willing to pay a higher price or even a premium for their favorite brands as compared to mass-market brands. In consumer markets, branding can influence whether consumers will buy the product. Branding can also help in the development of a new product by facilitating the extension of a product line or mix, through building on the consumers' perception of the values and character represented by the brand name.

满意的顾客会成为品牌忠诚者，愿意为他们喜爱的品牌支付比大众市场品牌更高的价格甚至溢价。在消费市场，品牌影响着消费者是否购买产品。品牌化也有助于新产品的开发，通过建立在消费者对品牌名称所代表的价值和特征的感知上，促进产品线或产品组合的扩展。

2021	2020	Logo	Name	Country	2021	
1 ∧	3	Apple	Apple		$263,375M	
2 ∨	1	amazon	Amazon		$254,188M	
3 ∨	2	Google	Google		$191,215M	
4 =	4	Microsoft	Microsoft		$140,435M	
5 =	5	SAMSUNG	Samsung Group		$102,623M	
6 ∧	8	Walmart	Walmart		$93,185M	
7 =	7	facebook	Facebook		$81,476M	
8 ∨	6	ICBC	ICBC		$72,788M	
9 ∧	12	verizon	Verizon		$68,890M	
10 ∧	19		WeChat		$67,902M	
11 ∧	13		China Construction Bank		$59,649M	
12 ∧	15		Toyota		$59,479M	
13 ∨	11		Mercedes-Benz		$58,225M	
14 ∧	26		Tencent		$56,432M	
15 ∨	10		Huawei		$55,396M	

2021 年 1 月 26 日，全球领先的品牌估值与咨询机构 Brand Finance 发布了《2021 年全球品牌价值 500 强报告》。苹果、亚马逊、谷歌位列前三，华为第十五

1. Benefits of Branding for the Consumers 品牌给消费者带来的利益

Effective branding of a product enables consumers to easily identify the product. This means when a customer is shopping for a particular product or considering a company to perform a service, they recognize your company in the running. Consumers are far more likely to choose a brand that they recognize over something unfamiliar, even if they don't know a great deal about your company at the time. This will increase the probability that the product will be accessible and therefore purchased and consumed. For example, the cross-border e-commerce logistics corporation, SF Express, is a brand that has an established logo and imagery that is familiar to most Chinese consumers. The vivid colors and image of the "Three Squirrels" are easily recognized and distinguished from competitors.

有效的品牌化可以使消费者很容易地识别产品。这意味着，当客户在购买

特定产品或考虑一家公司提供的服务时，他们已经认可了你的公司。消费者更有可能选择他们熟悉的品牌，而不是他们不熟悉的东西，即使他们当时对你的公司不是很了解。这将增加接触产品的可能性，进而购买和消费。例如，跨境电子商务物流公司顺丰快递就是一个品牌，它的标识和形象已经为大多数中国消费者所熟知。"三只松鼠"鲜艳的色彩和生动的形象很容易被人识别和区别于竞争对手。

2. Benefits of Branding for the Manufacturers and Retailers 品牌给制造商和零售商带来的利益

Branding helps create loyalty, decreases the risk of losing market share to the competition by establishing a differential advantage, and allows premium pricing that is acceptable by the consumer because of the perceived value of the brand. Good branding also allows for effective targeting and positioning. For example, Starbucks is a brand known for its premium coffee. Starbucks has a solid fan base due to its established global branding that communicates value.

品牌有助于建立忠诚度，通过建立差异化优势，来降低市场份额流失给竞争对手的风险。同时，由于消费者感知到了品牌价值，他们能够接受品牌溢价。良好的品牌也能够有助于建立有效的目标和定位。例如，星巴克就是一个以优质咖啡闻名的品牌。星巴克拥有坚实的粉丝基础，因为它所建立的国际品牌有效地传播了价值。

Brand names and images arouse emotions and wishes that retailers can benefit from. For example, a customer who truly values organic brands might decide to visit a store to shop for organic household cleaners that are safe to use around babies. This customer might have learned that a company is called BabyGanics, which positions itself as making "safe, effective, natural household solutions", and its cleaners are only available at this particular retailer.

品牌名称和形象能够唤起零售商的情感和愿望，使他们从中受益。例如，一个真正重视有机品牌的顾客可能会决定去商店购买有机家用清洁剂，这种清洁剂在婴儿周围使用是安全的。这位顾客可能已经了解到，一家名为甘尼克的公司, 其产品定位是提供 "安全、有效、天然的家居解决方案", 他们的清洁剂只在特定的零售商那里售卖。

3. Benefits of Branding for the Company Itself 品牌对公司自身的好处

The brand is what differentiates a company in the marketplace. When customers recognize and favor a brand, it helps lend a competitive edge to the company. The more recognition a brand receives and the more effort in building a brand, the more competitive it becomes. Strong branding also facilitates introduction of new products or test them out before you further invest in them. If a brand has a loyal brand following, its customers will often be interested in the newly launched products and even anticipate them being released. Loyal customers share values with their families and friends, and the brand loyalty often lasts a lifetime and even transfers to future generations.

品牌是使一个公司在市场上与众不同的东西。当顾客认可并喜欢某个品牌时, 这有助于公司获得竞争优势。一个品牌获得的认知度越高, 在建立一个品牌上付出的努力越多, 它的竞争力就越强。强大的品牌还有助于新产品的推出或在进一步投资之前进行测试。如果品牌拥有忠实的品牌追随者, 它的客户通常会对新推出的产品感兴趣, 甚至会期待它们的发布。忠诚的顾客会与他们的家人和朋友分享品牌价值, 那么品牌忠诚往往会持续一生, 甚至会传递给下一代。

7.5.3 Branding Strategies 品牌策略

1. Individual Branding and Family Branding 单一品牌和家族品牌

Individual and family branding strategies are beneficial for organizations who want to extend their brand portfolio by launching new products on the market or adapting the old ones. Individual branding is a branding strategy in which products are given separate and unique brand names. Individual brand names are newly created and generally not connected to names of existing brands offered by the company. A company which approaches individual branding strategy can avoid the failure of the whole organization's brand image and reputation. For example, if customers develop a negative perception towards a brand product it will only affect the individual brand

and not all the organization's products as in the case of family brands. Furthermore, during times of crisis, an individual brand can be a lifesaver for any organization because it does not operate under the shadow of its corporate brand. Due to the individual branding strategy the consumers would not associate it with the corporate brand under crisis. Researchers found that negative evaluations of a brand product by its customers may lead to decrease in sales due to the unfavorable attitudes toward all products under the same brand name.

单一和家族的品牌战略对那些想要通过在市场上推出新产品或改造旧产品来扩展其品牌组合的组织是有益的。单一品牌是一种品牌战略，其中产品被赋予单独和独特的品牌名称。单一品牌名称是新创建的，通常与公司提供的现有品牌名称没有关联。企业采用个性化的品牌战略可以避免整个组织的品牌形象和声誉的失败。例如，如果顾客对一个品牌产品产生了负面的看法，那么它只会影响单一品牌，而不会像家族品牌那样影响整个组织的产品。此外，在危机时期，单一品牌可以成为组织的救星，因为它没有在公司品牌的阴影下运作。由于个人品牌使用特殊的策略，消费者不会将其与危机下的企业品牌联系起来。研究人员发现，顾客对某产品的负面评价可能会导致整个品牌的销售量下降，因为他们对同一品牌下的所有产品都持负面态度。

In contrast, family branding, also called umbrella branding, uses a single brand name for the sale of two or more related products. The family or umbrella branding strategy offers economic advantages to those companies that have established strong brand identity in the minds of the consumers. The family brand has a strong brand value and a reputation. It is more likely for an organization with strong brand equity to adopt the family branding strategy rather than an individual branding strategy. Using the brand family name enhances brand awareness, perception, and loyalty among customers. People are willing to try new products from the same brand especially when the ones that sit under the family branding built a positive impact on the audience. Creating a strong brand image and equity from the beginning makes the family branding strategy cost-effective for the company.

与此相反，家族品牌，也称为品牌伞，使用同一个品牌名称来销售两个或两个以上的相关产品。家族品牌或伞形品牌战略为那些在消费者心目中建立了强大品牌识别的公司提供了经济优势。家族品牌具有较强的品牌价值和声誉。拥有强大品牌资产的组织更有可能采取家族品牌战略，而不是单一品牌战略。使用家族姓氏建立品牌可以提高消费者对品牌的知名度、感知度和忠诚度。人们更愿意尝试同一品牌的新产品，特别是当家族品牌下的产品对受众产生了积极影响的时候。从一开始就建立强大的品牌形象和资产，使家族品牌战略产生成本效益。

2. National and Store Brands 全国及门店品牌

Retailers control what brands to store and promote. A national brand is the brand name of a product that is distributed nationally under a brand name owned by the producer or distributor, as opposed to local brands or private label brands. National brands are produced by, widely distributed by, and carry the name of the manufacturer. A national brand's greatest strength is its broader recognition relative to store brands. A national brand is distributed through various retail outlets nationwide. It is also commonly promoted on national television and through other media. Carrying a national brand that is highly recognized and sought-after may attract customers that otherwise would not visit your store. Retailers carry national brands to remain competitive and to provide what customers want, but they do not actually make a profit on them because there is no exclusive marketing rights.

零售商控制着备用和要推广的品牌。全国品牌是生产者或分销商拥有的在全国范围内销售的品牌，与当地品牌或私人标签品牌相反。全国品牌是由生产厂家生产，广泛销售，并冠以厂家的名称。全国品牌最大的优势是，它相对于门店品牌而言，具有更广泛的认知度。全国品牌通过全国各地的零售店销售，也经常在国家电视台和其他媒体上宣传。人们高度认可并且欢迎全国性的品牌，这可能会吸引那些本不会到店消费的客户们。零售商经营全国品牌是为了保持竞争力和提供顾客想要的东西，但他们实际上并不能从中获利，因为没有独家销售权。

Although national brands have long dominated the retail scene, retailers generally use their national brands to draw customers to their stores. Recently department stores, supermarkets, service stations, clothiers, and chemists have started to increase more store brands. Store brands are manufactured or acquired by a particular firm for exclusive sale to consumers. A core benefit of a store brand is that it is unique to your store that you can market as your own. Wal-mart has introduced more than 40 store brands such as "Great Value", "Mainstays", "Simply Basic" under its name. The convenient store franchise chain Seven-Eleven has a store brand called "iseLect", selling beers, frozen foods, snacks etc. Store brands also usually allow for higher profit margins. When you control the production and development, costs are typically lower. Not all store brands are made by the company that brands and sells them. Some "private label" products are made by a single manufacturer, but sold by various retailers, each putting its own store brand on the products. Store brands are often placed at lower prices than national brands, but yield higher profit.

虽然长期以来，全国品牌一直主导着零售市场，但零售商通常会利用全国品牌来吸引顾客。最近，百货商店、超市、服务站、服装店和药店开始增加更多的门店品牌。门店品牌是由特定的公司生产或收购，独家销售给消费者。门店品牌的一个核心优势是，它是你的商店所独有的，你可以像推销自己的品牌一样推销它。沃尔玛已经推出了40多个商店品牌，如"惠宜""明庭""简适"等。便利店连锁店7-11有一个门店品牌叫"iseLect"，销售啤酒、冷冻食品、零食等。门店品牌通常也有更高的利润率。当你控制了生产和开发时，成本通常较低。并不是所有的门店品牌都是由品牌公司生产和销售的。一些自有品牌的产品是由一个单独的制造商生产的，但由不同的零售商销售，每个零售商都在产品上印上自己的门店品牌。门店品牌的售价往往低于全国品牌，但利润却更高。

3. Generic Brands 通用品牌

As oppose to national or store branding, generic brand is a type of consumer product that lacks a widely recognized name or logo, and is sometimes called the "house brand". Generic brands have no branding and are less expensive due to lack of promotion. Known for their trimmed-down packaging, and plain labels, generic-branded products are designed to be substitutes for more expensive brand-name goods. Sellers place generic goods next to branded goods to attract customers who are in favor of cheaper ones. Examples include toilet papers, dairy products, vegetables, over-the-counter medications, and cereals selling by kilo. Generic brands are popular during times that consumers are price-conscious.

与全国品牌或门店品牌相反，通用品牌的名称和标志缺乏广泛认知度，有时也被称为"自有品牌"。通用品牌没有品牌，而且由于缺乏促销，价格更低。以简洁的包装和简单的标签而闻名的通用品牌产品，被视为昂贵的名牌产品的替代品。卖家把通用商品放在品牌商品旁边，以吸引那些喜欢便宜商品的顾客。例如卫生纸、乳制品、蔬菜、非处方药和按公斤出售的谷物。在消费者对价格敏感时，通用品牌很受欢迎。

4. Licensing 许可

Licensing means renting or leasing of an intangible asset. Brand licensing leases a brand name to a company other than the owner of that particular brand. Licensing is used by brand owners to extend a trademark or character onto products of a completely different nature. An arrangement to license a brand requires a licensing agreement, which authorizes a company which markets a product or service to lease a brand from a brand owner who operates a licensing program. Disney consumer products always deliver strong retail sales growth. Driven by Disney movies such as *Finding Nemo, Winnie the Pooh,* related products with brand licensing appear in stores. *Harry Potter* movies even create Harry Potter Lands around the world, allowing fans to walk in the footsteps of Harry Potter and explore the wonders of the wizard world. However, brand licensing is among the least explored methods to enter a new product category by most brands.

许可是指租赁或出租无形资产。品牌授权许可指将一个品牌名称租给该特定品牌所有者以外的公司。品牌所有者使用许可将商标或字体扩展到性质完全不同的产品上。许可品牌需要许可协议，该协议授权销售产品或服务的公司从运营许可程序的品牌所有者那里租赁品牌。迪士尼消费产品总是表现出强劲的零售增长。在《海底总动员》《小熊维尼》等迪士尼电影的带动下，获得品牌授权的相关产品出现在商店里。"哈利·波特"系列电影甚至在世界各地创造了"哈利·波特世界"，让粉丝们跟随哈利·波特的脚步，探索魔法世界的奇迹。然而，品牌授权是大多数品牌引进新产品时最不常用的方法之一。

5. Co-branding 联合品牌

Co-branding is an arrangement that associates a single product or service with more than one brand name in marketing a new product. Music-streaming app Spotify partnered with ride-hailing app Uber to create "a soundtrack for your ride". This is a great example of a co-branding partnership between two very different products with very similar goals—to earn more users. The co-branding partnership of Apple and Nike started as a way to bring music from Apple to Nike customers' workouts using the power of technology: Nike + iPod created fitness trackers and sneakers and clothing that tracked activity while connecting people to their tunes.

联合品牌是在营销新产品时，将某个产品或服务与另外几个品牌建立联系的一种商业策略。音乐流媒体应用 Spotify 与叫车软件优步合作，"为你的出行配乐"。这是两个有着相似目标的不同产品之间的品牌合作得很好的例子——赢得更多的用户。苹果和耐克的联合品牌合作最初是为了利用科技的力量，将苹果的音乐带到耐克客户的健身活动中：耐克 + iPod 发明了健身追踪器、运动鞋和服装，可以追踪人们的活动，同时将人们与他们的音乐联系起来。

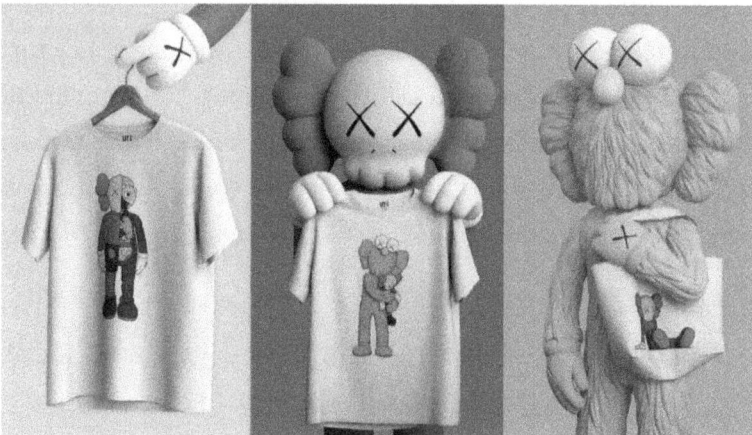

优衣库 UT 系列和潮牌 Kaws 发布品牌联名产品，引众人疯抢

7.6 Packaging and Labeling 包装与标识

Packaging and labeling are of the same importance as branding in the identification of the products in marketing. They play a vital role in developing your image and brand within your target market. Failing to pay attention to the design of your packaging and labeling can decrease the visibility and attractiveness of your products, which can be devastating for sales.

在市场营销中，包装和标签与品牌同样重要，在目标市场中形成公司形象和建立品牌起着至关重要的作用。不注意包装和标签的设计会降低产品的知名度和吸引力，这对销售来说是毁灭性的。

7.6.1 Functions of Packaging 包装的功能

Studies show that, in a typical supermarket, a shopper passes about 600 items per minute, or one item every tenth of a second. Therefore, the only way to get some consumers to notice the product is through displays, shelf hangers, tear-off coupon blocks, point-of-purchase devices, and, last but not least, effective packages. A package is more than the container or covering for a product. It facilitates brand recognition, communicates product benefits, augments the product with information on the recipes and warranties. Here, we list the main functions of packaging that cannot be missed out for successful marketing.

研究表明，在一个有代表性的超市里，一个购物者每分钟浏览大约 600 件商品，也就是 1/10 秒浏览一件商品。因此，让一些消费者注意到产品的唯一方法是通过显示器、货架挂钩、撕掉的优惠券、手绘海报，以及最后不得不提的，有效的包装。包装不仅仅是一个产品的容器或覆盖物，它能增加品牌识别度，传达产品价值，增加产品的配方和保证信息。这里，我们列出了包装的主要功能，它是成功的营销不可错过的重要组成。

Physical protection: Electronic objects enclosed in the package may require protection from damage of shipping, electrostatic discharge, vibration, compression etc. Foods remain clean and fresh if the package material provides protection from water vapor, dust, thus extending their shelf life.

物理保护：包装内的电子物品可能需要保护，防止运输、静电放电、振动、压缩等造成的损坏。如果包装材料能保护食品不受水汽、灰尘的侵害，那么食品就会保持干净和新鲜，从而延长食品的保质期。

Information transmission: Packages communicate how to use, transport, recycle, or dispose of the package or product. With pharmaceuticals, food, medical, and chemical products, some types of information are required by governments. Some packages and labels also are used for track and trace purposes.

信息传递：包装传达了如何使用、运输、回收或处理包装或产品的信息。对于药品、食品、医疗和化工产品，政府要求标注某些信息。一些包装和标签也具备追踪溯源的功能。

Marketing communication: The packaging and labels can be used by marketers to attract potential buyers to purchase the product. Marketing communications and package graphic design are applied to the surface of the package and the point of sale display.

营销传播：营销人员可以利用包装和标签来吸引潜在的购买者购买产品。营销传播和包装平面设计可应用于包装的表面和销售点的展示。

Convenience: Packages can have features that add convenience in distribution, handling, stacking, display, sale, opening, re-closing, use, dispensing, reuse, recycling, and ease of disposal.

便利性：包装可以在配送、处理、堆放、展示、销售、打开、重新关上、使用、配药、重复使用、回收和易于处理等方面增加便利性。

Security: Packaging can play a vital role in reducing the security risks of shipment. Packages can be made with improved tamper resistance to deter tampering and also can have tamper-evident features to help indicate tampering. Packages can be engineered to help reduce the risks of package pilferage.

安全性：包装在降低运输安全风险方面起着至关重要的作用。优良的包装可以防止被擅自拆封，也可以具有明显的拆封提示。包装可以被设计来帮助降低包装被盗的风险。

7.6.2　Packaging Considerations 包装注意事项

What are the product's critical attributes? Does the package meet the level of quality of the product? Does the presence straightforward enough to deliver the message? What is the material and package size? Does it environmentally friendly? Can it be scaled up or down? An effective packaging decision requires much thought.

产品的关键属性是什么？包装符合产品的质量标准吗？包装的外观是否足够直接地传递了信息？材料和包装尺寸是多少？它环保吗？它可以按比例放大或缩小吗？一个有效的包装决策需要深思熟虑。

The Environment. Package development takes environment protection and sustainability into consideration. It may involve a life cycle assessment which considers the material and energy inputs and outputs to the package, the packaged contents, the packaging process, the logistics system, and waste management. It is necessary to know the relevant regulatory requirements for point of manufacture, sale, and use. The traditional "three R's" of reduce, reuse, and recycle are part of a waste hierarchy which may be considered in product and package development. The typical snack chip bag is made from up to seven layers of foil and plastic. Companies like this because these bags are light, reduce shipping volume, do not take up much space on a shelf, and are graphics friendly. However, the downside is that there is currently no machinery to separate these layers, and they are not recyclable to be environmentally friendly. Other examples are toothpaste tube and the toothbrush and white plastic bottles. If environmental impact is a priority for you, the sustainability of your packaging is to be considered.

环境包装设计应考虑到环境保护和可持续性。它可能涉及包装材料的生命周期评估，考虑耗材的能量输入和输出、包装的内容、包装过程、物流系统和废物管理等。了解生产、销售和使用点的相关法规要求是必要的。传统的"三R"，即减少、重复使用和回收，是废品层次结构的一部分，可以在产品和包装开发中考虑。典型的零食袋是由多达7层的箔纸和塑料制成的。公司喜欢这种袋子，因为它们很轻，减少了运输量，不占用太多的货架空间，而且适合放各种图案。然而，这种包装的缺点是，目前没有机器来分离这么多层包装，它们是不可回收的，因此对环境不友好。其他的例子是牙膏管、牙刷盒和白色塑料瓶。如果公司重点考虑产品对环境的影响，那么包装的可持续性是必须考虑的。

The cost. Keeping the cost down is important especially to small businesses. Quality assured, one should choose the most basic packaging. Besides, the true cost of packaging comes from the whole supply chain rather than the unit price. To understand the true cost of your operation you need to review labor, storage, transportation, administration, postage, damages and returns. Waste prevention also reduces cost. Packaging should be used only where needed. Furthermore, the mass and volume of packaging per unit of contents can be measured and used as one of the criteria to minimize during the package design process. Usually, "reduced" packaging also helps minimize costs.

成本。保持低成本对小企业尤其重要。在保证质量的前提下，应选择最基本的包装。此外，包装的真正成本来自整个供应链，而不是单价。要了解真实的营业成本，你需要审查劳动力、储存、运输、管理、邮费、损坏和退货的成本。杜绝浪费也能降低成本。包装应该只在需要的地方使用。此外，每单位内容物的包装质量和体积应该可测量，并作为最小化包装的设计标准之一。通常，"简化的"包装也有助于降低成本。

The appearance. Many product providers may think that the product and its performance is more important than what the packaging looks like, but the product packaging can play a role in the success or failure of the sales of the product. Good packaging has aesthetic considerations. A product's packaging should appeal to its target markets and tell customers what your brand is. For luxury brand items that deliver high value, quality materials and metallic print over the top with smooth finishes can instantly add a touch of quality and style that elevates the brand's positioning. For eco-friendly brands, using bio plastics, recycled papers, and earth colors would be more suitable.

外观。许多产品供应商可能认为和包装比起来，性能更重要，但产品包装的确可以成为产品销售的成功或失败的关键。优质的包装要考虑美观。产品包装应该吸引它的目标市场群体，并告诉客户你的品牌是什么。对于提供高价值的奢侈品牌产品，优质的材料和表面光滑的金属印花可以立即增加质感，强化风格，提升品牌的定位。对于环保品牌来说，使用生物塑料、再生纸和土色会更合适。

What about color? Color is such a visual medium that it is one of the most tangible representations of a package. Packaging designers need to have the relevant knowledge of color psychology. White color stands for safe, basic, unadventurous, and conservative, and it is a good choice where you want to create the impression of cleanliness, purity, efficiency or simplicity. Black is the color of power, authority, and control. It tends to stand out when used as a packaging color as it makes products appear heavier and more expensive and transmits a higher perceived value. Black adds a degree of mystery and intimidation on one hand and elegance and class on the other. In 1997, when Steve Jobs returned to Apple, he axed the multicolored logo and gave it monochromatic look. The era when the colorful logo was in use, the company was facing financial losses and was seen as a failing company. Steve used the monochrome styled logo to transform the image into a company that manufactured cutting edge sleek products.

那么包装的颜色呢？色彩是一种视觉媒介，是包装最有形的表现形式之一。包装设计师需要具备色彩心理学的相关知识。白色代表着安全、基本、不冒险和保守。如果你想给人留下干净、纯洁、高效或简单的印象，白色是个不错的选择。黑色是代表权力、权威和控制的颜色。当作为包装颜色时，它往往会脱颖而出，因为它使产品看起来更重、更贵，并传递更高的感觉上的价值。黑色一方面增加了一定程度的神秘感和威慑力，另一方面又增加了优雅和阶级感。1997年，当史蒂夫·乔布斯重返苹果公司时，他砍掉了多色标识，并赋予其单色外观。在使用彩色标志的时代，苹果公司面临财务损失，被视为一家失败的公司。史蒂夫使用单色风格的标识，把苹果的形象转化成一个生产先锋时髦产品的公司。

Blue relates to trust, honesty and reliability, strength and unity. Red means energy, action, passion, excitement, and strength. Using red can stimulate the senses and excite the potential purchaser. Green, yellow, pink, brown, purple, magenta, gold, silver, gray, all have their psychological meanings in business. Imagine seeing a soft drink can in signature red with a white swirl, missing its brand mark "Coca Cola". Nearly everyone around the world would call the brand to mind. Many brands are instantly recognized because of their signature colors.

蓝色代表信任、诚实可靠、力量和团结。红色意味着能量、行动、激情、兴奋和力量。使用红色可以刺激感官，激发潜在的购买者。绿色、黄色、粉色、棕色、紫色、品红、金色、银色、灰色，在商业中都有它们的心理含义。想象一下，你看到一个带有白色漩涡的红色标志的饮料罐，即使上面没有"可口可乐"的商标，世界上几乎每个人都会想起这个品牌。许多品牌因为其标志性的颜色而被立即识别。

星巴克的标志以白色和深绿色为特色。两条鱼尾巴是白色的，而绿色是标志性的设计背景

The shape of packaging is considered for it affects the ease of carry, open, reclose, store, thus having an impact on consumer behavior. If you have a package that is difficult to open, find a packaging material and design that allows for an easy-open seal. A zip-lock package is more appealing to a consumer than a package that cannot be easily re-closed. Find little tips to delight a prospective consumer like this and you will open the opportunity for brand loyalty. The shape of your package can say a lot about your product if you use it to your advantage. Masculinity, for example, is most often implicitly associated with angular shapes and designs while femininity can be visualized in curved shapes. A smaller package may be perceived as higher quality, while larger or bulky packaging can also be perceived as higher value in the more-bang-for-your-buck sense.

另外要考虑包装的形状，因为它影响携带、打开、重新封口和存储的便利性，从而对消费者的行为产生影响。如果你的产品包装很难打开，那么就需要重新寻找容易打开和密封的材料和设计。对于消费者来说，自封式包装比重新封口的包装更有吸引力。找到一些小技巧来取悦潜在的消费者，你就会拥有打开品牌忠诚度的机会。如果你利用包装的优势，那么它就能帮助展示产品。例如，男性特征通常与棱角形状和设计联系在一起，而女性特征则可以用曲线来表现。小包装可能意味着更高的质量，大或笨重的包装可能意味着更高的性价比。

7.6.3　Product Labeling 产品标签

In some countries, many products, including food and pharmaceuticals, are required by law to contain certain labels such as manufacturer of the product, ingredients, nutritional information, date of manufacture, date of expiration, or usage warning information. In China, product packaging labeling has been legally required by the Product Quality Law and Food Safety Law.

在一些国家，许多产品，包括食品和药品，法律要求必须在包装上标明某些信息，如产品制造商、成分、营养信息、生产日期、过期日期或使用警告信息。在我国，《产品质量法》和《食品安全法》已经对产品包装标识做出了法律规定。

Through labeling, benefits and values of the products are shared with customers. For instance, images of happy families, healthy athletes, and green pastures each speak to different types of consumers. Labels also must fulfill your legal obligations. Food manufacturers, for example, must publish detailed nutritional information in a specific format and employ marketing terms, such as "low-fat" or "reduced cholesterol".

通过贴标签，公司与顾客分享产品的利益和价值。例如，幸福的家庭、健康的运动员和绿色牧场的形象能吸引不同类型的消费者。标签也必须履行公司的法律义务。例如，食品制造商必须以特定的格式公开详细的营养信息，并采用"低脂"或"低胆固醇"等规范的营销术语。

Besides, the product might need a Universal Product Code (UPC), especially if it will be sold in high-volume retail outlets. It consists of a strip of black bars and white spaces above a sequence of 12 numerical digits, uniquely assigned to each trade item. When the cashier in the supermarket scans the barcode at the checkout for you, the retailer is able to track sales and control their inventory.

此外，该产品可能需要一个通用产品代码（UPC），特别是在大型零售店销售的情况下。它由 12 个宽度不等的黑色条码组成，每个商品都有唯一的代码。当超市的收银员为你扫描商品的条形码时，零售商就能够跟踪销售并控制库存。

◎ **阅读推荐**

凯文·莱恩凯勒 . 战略品牌管理 [M]. 吴水龙，等译 . 北京：中国人民大学出版社，2014.

霍华德·舒尔兹 . 多莉·琼斯·扬 . 将心注入——一杯咖啡成就星巴克传奇 [M]. 文敏，译 . 北京：中信出版社，2015.

吴晓波 . 腾讯传（1998—2016）——中国互联网公司进化史 [M]. 杭州：浙江大学出版社，2017.

马克·彭德格拉斯 . 可口可乐转——一部浩荡的品牌发展史诗 [M]. 高增安，等译 . 北京：文汇出版社，2017.

约翰·斯达克 . 产品生命周期管理 [M]. 杨青海，等译 . 北京：机械工业出版社，2017.

保罗·特洛特 . 创新管理与新产品开发 [M]. 陈劲，译 . 北京：清华大学出版社，2015.

哈雷·曼宁，凯丽·博丁 . 体验为王：伟大产品与公司的创生逻辑 [M]. 高洁，译 . 北京：中信出版社，2014.

罗宾·卡罗尔，毕比·尼尔逊 . 新产品开发 [M]. 冯丽丽，等译 . 北京：人民邮电出版社，2015.

8

Pricing Strategy

定价策略

知识解锁 Knowledge Unlocked

以下问题的答案，可在本章寻找：

1. 什么是价格的非货币价值？

2. 定价目标如何为定价战略打基础？

3. 有哪些因素会影响定价？

4. 如何根据不同情况应用不同的定价策略？

8.1　Price Definition 定义价格

8.1.1　Defining Price 什么是价格

Price is something the customer is willing to give up to receive a good or service. To a business, it is the money it charges for a good or service. Price is not the cost, but a business needs to take account of cost when setting price to ensure that it is making a profit on the products it offers. When marketers talk about what they do as part of their responsibilities for marketing products, the tasks associated with setting price are often not at the top of the list. However, pricing decisions have great significance for the marketing organization, and the attention given by the marketer to pricing is just as important as the attention given to more recognizable marketing activities.

价格是顾客为了得到一种商品或服务而愿意放弃的一些东西。对一家企业来说，它是指为一种商品或服务付费。价格不是成本，但企业在定价时需要考虑成本，以确保其提供的产品是盈利的。当营销人员谈到他们所做的工作是营销产品职责的一部分时，与定价相关的工作往往不是最重要的。然而，定价决策对营销组织具有重要意义，营销人员对定价的关注与对其他更容易识别的营销活动的关注同样重要。

8.1.2 Monetary and Non-monetary Price 货币价格与非货币价格

To get a deeper insight into price, we examine monetary and non-monetary price. The amount of money that a product or service costs a consumer to purchase is known as monetary price. The most commonly used exchange of value is based on cash. But in some marketing practices, payment can be non-monetary.

为了更深入地了解价格，我们考察了货币价格和非货币价格。消费者为购买一个产品或服务所花费的钱被称为货币价格。最常用的价值交换是基于现金的。但在一些营销实践中，支付可以是非货币的。

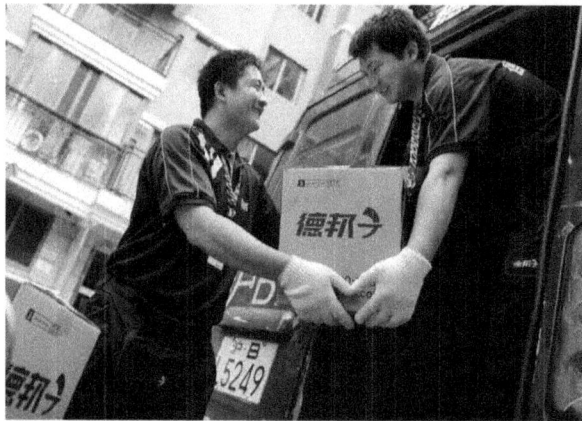

物流服务价格不等于服务质量，涉及更多主观体验因素，因此无法单纯用货币衡量

Non-monetary price refers to what it costs a customer, other than money, to buy a product. For example, one professional agrees to perform tax accounting for another professional in exchange for cleaning services. During the exchange, no money changes hands, but there is an exchange of value. Moreover, time spent on shopping, risk taken, search cost, convenient cost, and psychological cost are considered to be non-monetary cost.

非货币价格指的是除金钱以外，顾客购买产品所付出的成本。例如，一个专业人员同意替另一个专业人员做税务会计工作，以换取清洁服务。在交换过程中，没有货币易手，但有价值的交换。此外，花费在购物上的时间、承担的风险、搜索成本、便利性和心理成本都被认为是非货币成本。

Non-monetary price also takes the form of opportunity cost, which means a benefit, profit, or value of something that must be given up to acquire or achieve something else. For example, if you spend time and money going to a movie, you cannot spend that time at home reading a book, and you cannot spend the money on something else. A player attends baseball training to be a better player instead of taking a vacation. The non-monetary price he pays is the benefit from vacation. If you decide not to go to work, the non-monetary price or opportunity cost is the lost wages. In real world practice, authorities raise the opportunity cost to reduce certain kind of behavior. For example, hefty fines for manufacturers contaminating environment can effectively reduce such behavior.

非货币价格也以机会成本的形式出现，这意味着必须放弃某物的利益、利润或价值来获得或实现其他目的。例如，如果你花时间和金钱去看电影，你就不能把这些时间用于在家里读书，你也不能把这些钱花在其他事情上。球员参加棒球训练是为了成为更好的球员，而不是去度假。他付出的非金钱的代价就是度假的好处。如果你决定不去工作，非货币价格或机会成本就是你失去的工资。在现实世界中，政府提高机会成本来减少某种行为。例如，对污染环境的制造商处以巨额罚款可以有效地减少这种行为。

8.2　Steps in Price Planning 定价计划的步骤

8.2.1　Develoing Pricing Objectives 制定定价目标

1. Sales-related Objectives 以销售为导向的定价目标

Sales-oriented pricing objectives seek to boost sales volume or market share. It is assumed that sales growth has a direct positive impact on profits so pricing decisions are taken in way that sales volume can be raised. Setting a price, altering or modifying policies are targeted to improve sales. Demand management is applied in order to regulate exchanges or sales. In some cases, price and pricing are taken as the tools to increase market share. When you realize that your market share is lower than expected it can be raised by appropriate pricing; pricing is aimed at improving market share.

以销售为导向的定价目标目的是提高销售量或市场份额。假设销售增长对利润有直接的积极影响，那么定价决策的方式是提高销售量。制定价格、改变或修改政策的目标是提高销售。公司用需求管理来规范交易或销售。在某些情况下，价格和定价被视为增加市场份额的工具。当你意识到你的市场份额低于预期时，可以通过适当的定价来提高市场份额，这也是定价的目的所在。

2. Profit Objectives 利润目标

Profit objectives aim at setting a specific level of profit for the business. Anything less will ensure failure. It also aims to maximize price for long-term profitability. Price has both a direct and indirect effect on your profits. The direct effect relates to whether the price actually covers the cost of producing the product. Price affects profits indirectly by influencing how many units sell. The number of products sold also influences profits through economies of scale, that is, the relative ability of selling more units. Profit margin maximization seeks to maximize the per unit profit margin of a product. This is typically applied when the total number of units sold is expected to be low. Profit maximization, on the other hand, seeks to earn the greatest total amount in profits.

利润目标是为企业设定一个特定的利润水平。任何情况下的利润不足都会导致失败。它还旨在最大限度地提高价格，以实现长期盈利。价格对利润有直接和间接的影响。直接影响是指价格是否实际覆盖了生产产品的成本。价格通过影响销售量来间接影响利润。销售量也通过规模经济来影响利润，即销售更多产品的相应能力。一方面，利润率最大化追求产品的单位利润率最大化，这通常适用于预计销售的总单元数较低的情况；另一方面，利润最大化追求利润总额的最大化。

3. Competitiveness Objectives 竞争力的目标

To gain an advantage over its competitors, a company is likely to take a series of actions to broaden the market share. Decreasing price may increase demand and lead to higher market share. ofo, the Chinese ride-sharing bike leading company, uses the strategy of setting a low price of 50 cents for half-hour and the convenience of being able to "pick up and park bikes wherever you want", giving the company the edge on its American competitors, such as BCycle and Spin. However, low price could also provoke a competitive response, since competitors can set price even lower to gain a larger market share. Enhancement of competitiveness does not necessarily mean setting a low price. Products with higher prices in the high-end market are thought to be of superior quality.

为了获得相对于竞争对手的优势，公司可能会采取一系列行动来扩大市场份额。价格下降一般会导致需求量扩大，从而获得更高的市场份额。中国共享单车行业的领军企业 ofo 采用的策略是，设定每半小时 50 美分的低收费，并提供 "随时随地取车和停放自行车" 的便利，这让该公司在与 BCycle 和 Spin 等美国竞争对手的竞争中占据了优势。然而，低价也会引发竞争反应，因为竞争对手可以设置更低的价格来获得更大的市场份额。提高竞争力的途径不仅限于设定较低的价格。在高端市场，价格较高的产品被认为质量更上乘。

4. Customer Satisfaction Objectives 客户满意度目标

Customer satisfaction is the lifeline of a company, especially to a service firm. Being the most sensitive element in shopping, price gives a signal of product and service quality that arouse certain emotions. For example, the traditional pricing strategy for general merchandise is ending the price by the figure 9, making the product look cheaper. But the fast fashion designer brand MINISO, set its price at a subversive integer. MINISO is not only favored by young generations who dislike the 1 dime change, for the small changes drive them away from the "middle class", but also a new idea of building customer loyalty. Now it has opened over 1,000 stores in less than three years in the international market, earning love from the target customers aged from 18 to 35.

客户满意度是一个公司的生命线，尤其是对服务类企业来说。价格是购物中最敏感的元素，它是产品和服务质量的信号，能激起一定的情绪反应。例如，一般商品的传统定价策略是以数字 9 结尾，使产品看起来更便宜。但快时尚设计师品牌名创优品将其价格设定为一个颠覆性的整数。名创优品不仅受到不喜欢一毛钱变化的年轻一代的青睐——因为这些微小的变化使他们远离了"中产阶级"，同时也形成了一种建立客户忠诚度的新理念。在不到 3 年的时间里，名创优品在全球市场上开设了 1000 多家门店，深受 18~35 岁目标客户的喜爱。

5. Image Objectives 形象目标

Being a highly visible communicator, price reflects a firm's position of respect and esteem in its community. Although image is not directly established by pricing in the lower-end markets, it is believed that image enhancement function of pricing is particularly remarkable with prestige products. Luxury goods with high prices can appeal to customers who are conscious of social and brand status.

作为显性营销传播工具，价格反映了公司在该领域受尊重的程度和社会地位。在低端市场，定价并不能直接树立形象，但在高档产品中，定价的形象增强功能十分显著。高价的奢侈品可以吸引那些注重社会地位和品牌地位的顾客。

8.2.2 Estimating Demand 评估需求

1. Estimation of Demand 需求的评估

The purpose of demand estimation is to find a business's potential demand so managers can make accurate decisions about pricing, business growth, market potential, as well as inventory management. Managers base pricing on demand trends in the market.

需求评估的目的是发现企业的潜在需求，以便管理者能够对定价、业务增长、市场潜力及库存管理做出准确的决策。经理们根据市场的需求趋势来定价。

Managers and business owners use multiple techniques for demand estimation. Using historical data is one method to determine the potential demand for a product or service. Businesses with high-end merchandise might examine census information to determine the average income of an area.

经理和业务所有者使用多种技术进行需求评估。利用历史数据是确定产品或服务潜在需求的一种方法。拥有高端商品的企业可能会检查人口普查信息，以确定一个地区的平均收入。

When demand is specified to be linear in form, the coefficients on each of the explanatory variables measure the rate of change in quantity demanded as that explanatory variable changes, holding all other explanatory variables constant. Take a start-up dumpling restaurant who wants to estimate demand for example. The number of estimated buyers in the whole market is 32,000, and the average number of each buyer consuming is 15 bowl of dumplings per year. The annual demand for dumplings in the market equals 480,000. For the demand forecasting, the seller needs to know what its market share is. Assuming the predicted market share for this particular restaurant is 2.5%, its annual demand equals 12,000, then a provision of 1,000 bowls of dumplings per month would be reasonable. In practice, the restaurant should also take other factors into consideration in order to determine demand, such as the entering of new competitors, the change of customer taste, the delivery services upgrade, or the food safety issues.

当需求为线性形式时，每个解释变量的系数衡量的是当解释变量发生变化时需求量的变化率，此时保持所有其他解释变量不变。以一家新开张的饺子店为例，这家店想要估算饺子的需求。整个市场估计有 3.2 万个买家，平均每个买家每年消费 15 碗饺子，那么市场对饺子的年需求量为 48 万碗。对于需求预测，卖方需要知道它的市场份额是多少。假设这家餐厅的预测市场份额是2.5%，它的年需求量是 1.2 万碗，那么合理的量是每月提供 1000 碗饺子。在实践中，餐厅也应该考虑其他因素来确定需求，如新的竞争对手的进入、顾客口味的改变、送货服务的升级或食品安全问题。

2. The Price Elasticity of Demand 需求的价格弹性

We already know that the price change will cause the change in demand. But how much does quantity demanded change when price changes? By a lot or a little? Elasticity can help understand this issue.

我们已经知道价格的变化会引起需求的变化。但需求量随价格变化多少呢？是多还是少？弹性可以帮助理解这个问题。

Price elasticity of demand (PED) measures the change in the quantity demanded relative to a change in price for a good or service. It is calculated as the percentage change in quantity demanded divided by percentage change in price. The formula goes: Price Elasticity = Percentage Change in Quantity / Percentage Change in Price = $[(Q_1-Q_0) / Q_0] / [(P_1-P_0) / P_0]$. Where P stands for price, Q stands for quantity. P_0 and Q_0 represent the initial or starting price and quantity combination, and P_1 and Q_1 represent the ending price and quantity combination.

需求的价格弹性衡量需求量相对于一种商品或服务价格的变化。它的计算方法是需求量变化除以价格变化。公式为：价格弹性 = 数量变化 / 价格变化 = $[(Q_1-Q_0) / Q_0] / [(P-P_0) / P_0]$。其中 P 代表价格，Q 代表数量。P_0 和 Q_0 表示初始价格和数量组合，P_1 和 Q_1 表示最终价格和数量组合。

8.2.3 Determining Costs 确定成本

Cost is another concept that must be taken into consideration by marketers. There are mainly two types of analysis used in pricing: break-even analysis and marginal analysis. Before introducing the analytical methods, marketers need to have some basic knowledge about cost.

成本是营销人员必须考虑的另一个概念。定价中主要使用两种分析：盈亏平衡分析和边际分析。在介绍分析方法之前，营销人员需要对成本有一些基本的了解。

1. Types of Cost 成本的类型

Fixed cost and variable cost make up the two components of total cost. In marketing, it is necessary to know how costs divide between variable and fixed. This distinction is crucial in forecasting the earnings generated by various changes in unit sales and thus the financial impact of proposed marketing campaigns.

固定成本和变动成本构成总成本的两个组成部分。在市场营销中，有必要知道成本是如何在可变成本和固定成本之间进行分配的。它们在预测单位销售额的各种变化所产生的收益时至关重要，从而预测将要开展的营销活动对财务影响。

Variable cost. The variable cost is the per-unit cost of production that change in proportion to output. Generally, variable costs are directly tied to the activities of producing volume, which rises when these activities increase and falls when activities decrease. Variable costs may include the cost of raw materials and components, packaging and distribution cost, sales commission cost, the cost of electricity and gas, and the depreciation of capital inputs due to wear and tear, etc. For example, a business manufacturing widgets pays raw material for production. Assuming it takes $0.5 worth of raw materials to produce one pen, then it will take $1 worth of raw materials to produce two pens. When the activity increases, the usage of raw material also increases thereby increasing the expenditure. For the production of pens, variable costs would also include the cost of timber and paint, plus the cost of the wages of part-time staff or employees paid by the hour.

可变成本。可变成本是生产的单位成本，它与产量成比例变化。一般来说，可变成本与生产活动直接相关，生产活动增加时可变成本上升，生产活动减少时可变成本下降。可变成本主要包括原材料和部件的成本、包装和配送成本、销售佣金成本、电费和煤气费，以及由于损耗而产生的资本投入的折旧等。例如，一家生产小部件的企业为生产提供原材料。假设生产一支笔需要价值 0.5 美元的原材料，那么生产两支笔需要价值 1 美元的原材料。当生产增加时，原材料的使用也增加，从而增加了支出。对于笔的生产，可变费用还包括木材和油漆的费用，加上按小时支付的非全日工作人员或雇员工资的费用。

Calculating variable cost per unit and total variable cost for a company gives a standard of comparison in respect of running efficiency. Higher per-unit variable costs may suggest that a company is less efficient than others, whereas a lower per-unit variable cost might represent a competitive advantage. For example, assuming a simple manufacturing operation of pen has three variable costs over a one-year period: $30,000 for raw materials, $20,000 for packaging and shipping, and $85,000 for sales commission. Summing up all of the three gives total variable cost for one year which is $135,000. Dividing the total variable cost for a given time period by that period's production volume will yield the unit variable cost. So if the business above produces 27,000 units of pens that year, its unit variable cost is $135,000 / 27,000, that means the variable cost of pen is $5 per units. It is the extra cost incurred by producing each additional unit. For example, if the business above produced 100 more units, it would expect to incur additional production cost of $500.

单位可变成本和总可变成本的计算，为公司运行效率提供了比较标准。较高的单位可变成本可能意味着公司的效率低于其他公司，而较低的单位可变成本则意味着竞争优势。例如，假设一支笔的简单制造在一年内有 3 个可变成本：原材料费 3 万美元、包装和运输费 2 万美元，以及 8.5 万美元的销售佣金。把这 3 种成本加起来，一年的可变成本是 13.5 万美元。用给定时期的总可变成本除以该时期的产量，就得到单位可变成本。如果一年生产 27000 支笔，单位可变成本是 135000 / 27000 美元，这意味着每支笔的可变成本是 5 美元。它是生产每一额外产品所产生的额外成本。如果这家企业额外生产了 100 支笔，它将会产生 500 美元的额外生产成本。

It should be remembered that rising cost is not necessarily a troubling sign. Whenever sales rise, more units must first be produced, which in turn means that the variable production cost must also increase. Thus, for revenues to climb, expenses must also rise accordingly. More importantly, to make a profit, revenues must increase at a faster rate than expenses. For example, assuming the variable cost for a business were $40,000 last month with a revenue of $70,000. This month, the company reports the variable cost double, while sales volume only increases by 20%, then the business is losing money. So companies are looking for ways to reduce the input cost associated with producing each item it sells, for its profitability improvement.

要记住，成本上升不一定是一个令人不安的迹象。当销售上升时，首先必须生产更多的产品，这反过来意味着可变生产成本也必须增加。因此，为了增加收入，支出也必须相应增加。更重要的是，为了盈利，收入的增长速度必须快于支出。例如，假设上个月企业的可变成本为 4 万美元，收入为 7 万美元。这个月，公司报告可变成本翻了一番，而销售量只增加了 20%，那么就是亏损的。因此，为了提高盈利能力，企业正在寻找降低与生产每一件产品相关的投入成本的方法。

Fixed cost. The fixed cost is the cost that is independent of output. These remain constant throughout the relevant range and are usually considered sunk for the relevant range (not relevant to output decisions). Whether producing 1 unit or 10,000 units, fixed costs will be about the same. Fixed costs often include rent, costs of maintaining factory buildings, utilities, machinery, maintenance and salaries of managers, etc. For example, a company producing bottled water needs a physical building and an assembly line that includes specialized equipment. If we assume the building and equipment are leased, there is a monthly payment for each of them. The company is responsible for paying 100% of the monthly payments, whether they produce one case of bottled water or 10,000 cases of bottled water.

固定成本。固定成本是与产出无关的成本。这些值在整个生产过程中基本保持不变，并且通常被认为在相关范围内属于沉没成本（与输出决策无关）。无论是生产 1 台还是 10000 台，固定成本都是一样的。固定成本通常包括租金、维护厂房的成本、水电费、机械费、维修费和管理人员工资等。例如，一家生产瓶装水的公司需要一座实体建筑和一条包含专门设备的生产线。如果我们假设房屋和设备是租来的，那么每个月的租金是固定成本。无论生产一箱瓶装水还是生产一万箱瓶装水，公司都要承担每月 100% 的该项固定成本。

The average fixed cost is the fixed cost per unit produced, calculated by dividing the total fixed cost by the number of units produced. It is an important metric to help you set prices. For example, a small postcard company might have a fixed cost of $100 over one month. If it produces 200 cards in that month, the average fixed cost will be $0.5 per unit; if it produces 2000 cards, the average fixed cost will fall to $0.05 per unit. This would mean that, for each card you make, it costs you $0.05 in fixed cost. The more cards the company makes, the lower fixed cost per unit gets, the lower the price charged to cover the fixed cost, leading to higher profits.

平均固定成本是每生产一个产品的固定成本，用总固定成本除以生产的产品数量来计算。这是帮助定价的一个重要指标。例如，一个小的明信片公司可能在一个月内有 100 美元的固定成本。如果该月生产 200 张明信片，平均固定成本将为每张 0.5 美元；如果生产 2000 张，平均固定成本降至每张 0.05 美元。这意味着，你每做一张明信片，要花费 0.05 美元的固定成本。公司生产的卡片越多，单位固定成本越低，支付固定成本的价格就越低，利润就越高。

Greater production does not necessarily lower fixed costs. Drastically increasing production may increase fixed costs. For example, as accumulation of wealth, the small postcard manufacturer finds itself more powerful and considers to build new factories to expand production scale. The executives' salaries will rise, and more investment will occur in purchasing and upgrading equipment. Therefore, as total costs fluctuate at different level of production, the price charged has to be adjusted accordingly.

扩大生产不一定能降低固定成本。大幅度增加生产可能会增加固定成本。例如，随着财富的积累，明信片小制造商发现自己更强大，并考虑建立新的工厂，扩大生产规模。管理人员的工资将会提高，更多的投资将会用于购买和升级设备。因此，由于总成本在不同生产水平上的波动，所收取的价格也必须做出相应的调整。

2. Cost Analysis 成本分析

① Break-even Analysis 盈亏平衡分析

In economics, business, and specifically cost accounting, "break-even" means that there is no net loss or gain. The break-even point (BEP) is the point at which total cost and total revenue are equal, and break-even analysis is a tool that helps determine how many product units a company needs to sell to recover its costs and start realizing profit.

在经济学、商业特别是成本会计中，"盈亏平衡"意味着没有净损失或净收益。盈亏平衡点（BEP）是指总成本和总收益相等的点，盈亏平衡点分析是帮助确定公司需要销售多少产品才能收回成本并开始盈利的工具。

Over the same time span, three pieces of information are needed to calculate the break-even point: total fixed cost, variable cost per unit, and average price per unit. The price will be at least as high as the production costs, usually higher. Subtracting the variable cost from selling price, we get contribution per unit, also called unit contribution margin. For example, suppose the company sells its pens for $9 each, using the variable cost of $5 per unit that we had before, the contribution per unit is $9–$5 = $4. Using the fixed cost for pen manufacturing of $80,000, the break-even point in units of the product is calculated as:

在相同的时间跨度内，需要 3 个信息来计算盈亏平衡点：总固定成本、单位可变成本和单位平均价格。价格将至少与生产成本一样高，通常更高。从销售价格中减去可变成本，就得到单位贡献，也称为单位边际贡献。例如，假设公司以每支 9 美元的价格出售钢笔，每支的可变成本是 5 美元，单位贡献是 9 美元 – 5 美元 = 4 美元。以生产笔的固定成本 8 万美元计算，产品的盈亏平衡点（以单位计算）为：

Break-even Point (in units) = total fixed cost / contribution per unit to fixed cost = total fixed cost / (average price per unit – average cost per unit) = $80,000 / $4 = 20,000 units.

盈亏平衡点（每单位）= 每单位固定成本总额 / 对固定成本的贡献 = 总固定成本 /（每单位平均价格 – 每单位平均成本）= 80,000 美元 / 4 美元 = 20,000 单位。

The company must sell 20,000 pens at $9 each, or sell $180,000 worth of pens over a year's period, to meet its fixed costs and to break even. Any units sold above 20,000 are profitable.

该公司必须以每支 9 美元的价格出售 2 万支钢笔，或者在一年内出售价值 18 万美元的钢笔，才能满足其固定成本并实现盈亏平衡。任何超过 20000 支的设备都是盈利的。

Companies can adjust prices to change the results. Suppose the pen company decide to raise pen price to $13 each, which means it only needs to sell $80,000 / $(13-5) = 10,000 units of pens per year. If the company has the desire to get some product exposure and decides to lower the price to $7, then it has to sell $80,000 / $(7-5) = 40,000 units of pens per year to make a break-even.

公司可以通过调整价格来改变这一结果。假设这家笔公司决定把每支钢笔的价格提高到 13 美元，这意味着它每年只需要卖出 80000 /（13-5）= 10000 支钢笔。如果公司希望获得一些产品曝光率，并决定将价格降至 7 美元，那么它必须每年卖出 80000 美元 /（7-5）美元 =40000 支钢笔，才能实现收支平衡。

When the company's sales volume surpasses the break-even point, it begins to make a profit. The profit is calculated as:

当公司的销售额超过盈亏平衡点时，就开始盈利了。利润计算如下：

Profit = quantity above break-even point × contribution margin

利润 = 盈亏平衡点以上的数量 × 边际贡献

Suppose the company sells 30,000 units, then it will get a profit of (30,000-20,000) × $4 = $40,000.

假设公司销售 3 万件，那么它将获得（30000 –20000）件 ×4 美元 = 40000 美元的利润。

For most occasions, companies set a profit goal in market planning, demonstrating how much money it wishes to earn. Our break-even analysis can include the profit goal into calculation, which goes:

在大多数情况下，公司会在市场规划中设定利润目标，以表明公司希望赚多少钱。我们的盈亏平衡分析可以将利润目标纳入计算，即：

Break-even Point (in units which target profit included) = (total fixed cost + target profit) / contribution per unit to fixed cost

盈亏平衡点（包括目标利润在内的单位）=（总固定成本 + 目标利润）/ 每单位对固定成本的贡献

Suppose the company wishes to gain a profit of $100,000, then it has to sell ($80,000+ $100,000) / $4 = 45,000 units within a year.

假设公司希望获得 10 万美元的利润，那么它必须在一年内卖出（80000+100000）美元 / 4 美元 = 45000 万件。

Sometimes the profit is expressed as a percentage of sales. Say, the company wants to make a profit of at least 20% on sales, that is, 20% of $9 equals $1.8. The contribution per unit becomes:

有时利润以销售额的百分比表示。比如说，公司想从销售中获得至少 20% 的利润，也就是说，9 美元的 20% 等于 1.8 美元。单位贡献为：

Contribution per Unit = selling price - (variable costs + target profit) = $9 – ($5+$1.8) = $2.2

单位贡献 = 售价 –（可变成本 + 目标利润）= 9 美元 –（5+1.8）美元 = 2.2 美元

Break-even Point (in units) = total fixed cost / contribution per unit to fixed costs = $80,000 / $2.2 = 36,363 units

盈亏平衡点（单位）= 固定成本总额 / 单位对固定成本的贡献 = 80000 美元 / 2.2 美元 = 36363 单位

Plot it on a graph, X axis is quantity demanded (number of units) and Y axis is revenue and costs. The plot of fixed cost will be a line parallel to X axis and above Y axis. The line of total cost would start from the point where line of fixed cost meets the Y axis. It would have a positive slope. The line of sales revenues would start from origin (0,0) and move upward with a slope greater than that of the total cost line. The point where these two lines intersect will be the "Break-even Point".

作图表示的话，X轴是需求量（单位数量），Y轴是收入和成本。固定成本作图是一条与X轴平行且在Y轴以上的直线。总成本线将从固定成本线与Y轴相交的点开始。它的斜率是正的。销售收入线将从原点（0，0）开始，以大于总成本线的斜率向上移动。这两条线相交的点就是"平衡点"。

The break-even formula is used to give answers about the future profitability of a business. Even though, break-even analysis has its limitations. For instance, as output rises, the business may benefit from being able to negotiate inputs at lower prices, so variable costs do vary when output changes. Moreover, demands are unlikely to be the same as output in practice, companies will have stocks of unsold items or wasted output, unless they can work on a purely just-in-time basis.

盈亏平衡公式可用于给出企业未来盈利能力的答案。尽管如此，盈亏平衡分析也有其局限性。例如，当产量上升时，企业可能会受益于能够以较低的价格谈判投入，因此当产量变化时，可变成本也会变化。此外，需求不太可能与产出相同。在实践中，企业将有未售出的产品库存或浪费的产出，除非它们能够在完全准时的基础上工作。

② Marginal Analysis 边际分析

Companies must ensure that the benefit of certain activities outweigh the cost in order to be profitable. Marginal analysis is a decision-making tool examining costs and demands simultaneously. It allows companies to identify the price and output that will generate the maximum profit at the point where marginal revenue equals marginal cost. Marginal analysis is all about weighing marginal revenue (the added income or revenue of having one more unit) against marginal cost (the corresponding expense of that additional unit).

为了盈利，公司必须确保某些活动的收益大于成本。边际分析是一种同时考察成本和需求的决策工具。它使公司确定在边际收入等于边际成本时产生最大利润的价格和产量。边际分析就是将边际收入（增加的收入或增加一个单位的收入）与边际成本（增加一个单位的相应费用）进行权衡。

How, then, do a company decide on a choice? The answer is that it compares, to the best of its ability, the marginal benefits with the marginal costs. From a business' point of view, marginal benefit is the additional revenues received from selling one more item, that is, marginal revenue. An economically rational decision is one in which the marginal benefits of a choice are greater than the marginal costs of the choice. For example, a company produces a product that sells for \$120 each and costs \$100 a piece to produce, and 50 units of those products are produced. This results in a total cost of \$5,000 and a total revenue of \$6,000. Once it produces the 51st unit of this product, the total revenue then goes to \$6,120, and the total cost goes to \$5,150. In this case, the decision to produce the 51st unit would be a bad one because the cost of production per unit increases to \$5,150 / 51 = \$100.98 per unit. The net benefit goes up by \$6,120 – \$6,000 = \$120, while the overall cost increases by \$5,150 – \$5,000 = \$150, meaning that the cost outweighs the benefit and that the production of the additional unit is not worth the extra cost.

那么，一个公司是如何做出选择的呢？答案是，它会尽其所能地将边际效益与边际成本进行比较。从企业的角度来看，边际效益是指多销售一个商品而获得的额外收入，即边际收入。经济上合理的决策是，选择的边际收益大于选择的边际成本。例如，一家公司生产一种产品，每件售价 120 美元，生产成本为 100 美元，生产 50 个这种产品。因此，总费用为 5000 美元，总收入为 6000 美元。生产第 51 个产品后，总收入是 6120 美元，总成本是 5150 美元。在这种情况下，生产第 51 个单元的决定将是一个糟糕的决定，因为每个单元的生产成本将增加到 5150 美元 / 51 = 100.98 美元每单位。净收益增加了 6120 美元 – 6000 美元 = 120 美元，而总成本增加了 5150 美元 – 5000 美元 = 150 美元，这意味着成本大于收益，生产额外的产品的收入比不上额外的成本。

Analysis bases on one additional unit and optimizes until benefit and cost are zero can be applied to multiple business processes. Production processes can range from making more products, to working more hours on a project to improve its quality, to adding more features to a web application or hiring more labor for a work crew. Marginal analysis is also useful in setting prices or evaluating incentives for sales staff. The concept of evaluating what happens with incremental change and how to optimize the relationship between benefit and cost can be applied to most business processes.

分析基于一个额外单元并进行优化，直到效益和成本为零的分析可以应用于多个业务流程。生产过程可以从生产更多的产品，到在一个项目上花费更多的时间来提高其质量，到向网络应用程序添加更多的功能或为工作团队雇用更多的劳动力。边际分析在定价或评估对销售人员的激励方面也很有用。评估增量更改会发生什么，以及如何优化收益和成本之间的关系的概念可以应用于大多数业务流程。

8.2.4　Evaluating the Pricing Environment 评估定价环境

1. Economy 经济

When the economy is weak and many people are unemployed, companies often lower their prices. Because in weak economy, consumers with less purchasing power are more sensitive to prices, and will buy more of daily necessities other than goods and services that allow them to enjoy life. Therefore, marketers should know the nature of their business and products, and choose either to scale down the production or to halt production.

当经济疲软、许多人失业时，公司通常会降低产品价格。因为在经济疲软的情况下，购买力较低的消费者对价格更敏感，他们会购买更多的生活必需品，而不是那些享受生活的商品和服务。因此，营销人员应该知道他们的业务和产品的性质，并选择缩小生产或停止生产。

On the contrary, in good times when the economy prospers, inflation allows companies to raise prices to maintain profitability. Once a company does decide to raise a price they have several options for how to implement that change. If the projected price increase is significant, it may be better to gradually raise the price over time instead of making one large jump. Another option for companies who sell packaged goods is to reduce the amount of products in each package instead of increasing the price that consumers pay for per package.

相反，在经济繁荣的好时期，通货膨胀使公司能够通过提高价格来保持盈利。一旦公司决定提高价格，他们有几个选择来实施这一决定。如果预计的价格上涨幅度很大，那么最好是逐步提高价格，而不是一次性大幅跃升。对于销售包装好的商品的公司来说，另一个选择是减少每包中的产品数量，而不是提高消费者为每包产品支付的价格。

2. Competition 竞争

How competitors set price and sell their products will have a tremendous effect on a company's pricing decisions. Firstly, the availability of substitute products affects a company's pricing decisions. Generally, the less competition a company has, the higher demand there is for its products. However, nowadays, with so many products sold online, consumers can compare the prices of many merchants before making a purchase decision. So, in the era of Internet, competing on prices is becoming a less effective way to fight with rivals.

竞争对手如何定价及如何销售他们的产品，将对公司的定价决策产生巨大的影响。首先，替代产品的可获得性影响公司的定价决策。一般来说，一个公司的竞争越少，对其产品的需求就越大。然而，如今有这么多种产品在网上销售，消费者可以在做出购买决定之前货比三家。因此，在互联网时代，价格竞争正成为一种低效的竞争方式。

Secondly, changes in competition may also impact the price, such as a new competitor entering the market could affect the level of demand for your products or services. The competitors' activities, whether they have a new feature, an advertising campaign running or a price reduction, can also have an impact on the pricing decisions of a company.

其次，竞争对手的变化也会影响价格，例如，新的竞争者进入市场可能会影响你的产品或服务的需求水平。竞争对手的营销活动，无论是增加新特性、广告还是降价活动，都会对公司的定价决策产生影响。

3. Consumer Trends 消费趋势

The marketplace is ever-changing, so marketers need to update their knowledge about consumer behavior at all times. For example, according to an investigation from JD.com, online shoppers in China are more likely to pay for time, personality, and loneliness. Data shows that the Post-80s generation constitutes the main force of online shopping. The order volume of choosing to pay for the service of "delivery, within 2 hours" has a month-on-month growth of 120%, meaning these people place a high value on time, and tend to spend more money on top-speed delivery. Data also shows that people pay for personal consumption, reflected by a year-on-year sales growth of over 100% in products related to hairstyling, hair care, and personal image building. All in all, keeping up with the consumer trends can help marketers adjust their pricing strategies in time.

市场是不断变化的，所以营销人员需要随时更新他们关于消费者行为的知识。例如，根据京东的一项调查，中国的网购者更有可能为了时间、个性和孤独买单。数据显示，80 后是网络购物的主力军。选择支付"2 小时内送达"服务的订单量环比增长 120%，这意味着这些人看重时间，并倾向于将更多的钱花在快速送达上。数据还显示，人们为个人消费买单，与美发、护发和个人形象塑造相关的产品销售额同比增长逾 100%。总而言之，紧跟消费趋势可以帮助营销人员及时调整他们的定价策略。

8.2.5 Choosing a Pricing Strategy 选择定价策略

1. Cost-based Pricing 成本定价法

Just as it sounds, cost-based pricing is a pricing method in which a fixed amount or a percentage of the total cost is added to the cost of product, usually as a margin to make a profit. It is a most frequently used method for its simplicity in calculation. Although the calculation is simple, precisely estimating all the costs can be difficult. For example, indirect costs such as salaries of corporate staff, administration costs, legal costs, office costs, utilities, electricity, and other supports must be accurately projected and built into the cost-based pricing model to ensure the proper pricing. There are basically two methods of calculating cost-based prices.

顾名思义，成本定价法是以产品的可变成本，加上一定比例的固定成本和利润，来确定商品的价格。由于计算简单，成本定价法是最常用的定价方法。然而，精确地估计所有的成本是很困难的。例如，企业必须准确地预测员工工资、行政管理成本、法律成本、办公成本、公用事业、电力和其他项目等间接成本，并将其纳入基于成本的定价模型中，以确保合理的定价。大致有两种计算成本价格的方法。

In cost-plus pricing, a price setter has to identify all the costs involved in producing a given product and add a percentage of the total cost to get a selling price. The formula goes:

在成本加成定价法中，价格制定者必须确定生产某一产品所涉及的所有成本，并与总成本的一定百分比相加，以得到销售价格。这个公式是：

Price = total cost × (1+a percentage of the total cost)

价格 = 总成本 ×（1+ 总成本的百分比）

Mark-up pricing, on the other hand, add a percentage to the selling price:

另一方面，加成定价法使售价增加了一个百分比：

Price = total cost / (1 − mark-up percentage)

价格 = 总成本 /（1 − 加成率）

Cost-based pricing is a straight-forward strategy that ensures all production and overhead costs are covered before profits are calculated. It works well for larger companies, as they can better withstand the race to the bottom. The disadvantage in cost-based pricing for services is that it punishes efficiency. If a service technician has an hourly rate, the faster they are able to solve a problem, the less they earn.

成本定价法覆盖所有的生产成本和间接成本，能够确保利润空间。这对大公司很有效，因为它们可以更好地承受竞争压力。一旦将成本定价法用于服务，则会降低效率。如果服务技术人员按小时收费，他们解决问题的速度越快，挣的钱就越少。

2. Demand-based Pricing 需求导向定价

Demand-based pricing is a pricing method that uses consumer demand at different price points as a central element. Marketers carry out a series of surveys to investigate the quantity of a product the customers would buy at different price levels. Two strategies are commonly implied: target costing and yield management pricing.

需求导向定价法是一种以不同价格点的消费者需求为中心要素的定价方法。市场营销者进行一系列调查，调查顾客在不同价格水平下购买产品的数量。通常有两种策略：目标成本法和收益管理定价法。

Target costing is an approach in which companies set targets for their costs based on the prices perceived in the market segments and the profit margin they want to earn. Before a product is designed, a company conduct a marketing research to identify the quality and the functionality of the product that consumers want, as well as the price they are willing to pay for that product. Together with the information about the total profits that the company, retailers and dealers expect, the company makes a trade-off, that is, if the costs can be controlled to a selling price that ensure the product quality required, the product will be produced, otherwise the plan will be abandoned. The selling price in target costing is calculated as:

目标成本法是公司根据细分市场的价格和他们想要获得的利润率来设定成本目标。在设计产品之前，公司要进行市场调查，以确定消费者想要的产品的质量和功能，以及他们愿意为该产品支付的价格。再加上公司、零售商和经销商所期望的总利润信息，由公司做出权衡，即如果可以将成本控制在一个保证产品质量的销售价格，那么产品就会被生产出来，否则这个计划就会被放弃。目标成本中的销售价格计算如下：

Selling Price = target cost + profit margin = target cost + profit percentage × selling price (where the profit margin is based on cost)

销售价格 = 目标成本 + 利润率 = 目标成本 + 利润百分比 × 销售价格（利润率基于成本）

Yield management pricing is a pricing strategy that charging different prices to different customers in order to manage capacity and maximize the profits. It is originally developed for perishable service sector products. The key variables are: (1) the perishable nature of the product, and (2) different levels of demand from different customer categories or segments. For example, when a hotel finds that it is unlikely to rent its rooms at normal prices, it may choose to reduce the price to a lower level in order to have all their rooms occupied.

收益管理定价法是对不同的客户进行不同的定价，以实现管理能力和利润最大化的一种定价策略。它最初是为易逝性服务业产品所设计的。关键变量是：（1）产品的易逝性；（2）来自不同客户或细分市场的不同需求水平。例如，当一家酒店发现它不太可能以正常价格出租房间时，它可能会选择将价格降低到一个较低的水平，以使酒店满房。

Yield management pricing attempts to understand, anticipate and react to consumer behavior in order to maximize revenue. It examines transactions for goods or services already supplied, or good and services to be supplied in the future, the statistics and information about known future events or unexpected past events such as a terrorist attack. It also considers competitive pricing information, seasonal patterns, and other pertinent factors that affect sales. Yield management opportunities are available everywhere. Smart marketers will see the yield pricing relationship with their own products and services, and adopt creative strategies to maximize profits.

收益管理定价法试图理解、预测和对消费者的行为做出反应，以实现收入最大化。它同时关注过去和将来货物及服务的交易，以及关于已知未来的事件或过去未预料到的事件（如恐怖袭击）的统计和信息。它还考虑到有竞争力的价格信息、季节模式和其他影响销售的相关因素。收益管理的机会无处不在。聪明的营销人员会看到他们自己的产品和服务的收益定价关系，并采取创造性的策略来最大化利润。

3. Competition-based Pricing 竞争导向定价法

Competition-based pricing is a pricing method in which a seller utilizes prices of competing products as a benchmark. A company can decide whether to sell its own product at a price lower or higher than its competitor's price. If the company is trying to appear to be higher-end than its competitors, it may want to price its own product a bit higher. But if the company wants its product to be more affordable, it may choose to price its product lower. This pricing method is fairly simply and low risk. However, in many cases, it is not entirely effective because the company does not know what strategies their competitors are utilizing to select their price. In this case, using each other as a benchmark is like throwing a dart in the dark.

竞争导向定价法是卖方以竞争产品的价格为基准进行定价的一种定价方法。公司决定是否以低于或高于竞争对手的价格出售自己的产品。如果该公司试图表现得比竞争对手更高端，它可能希望自己的产品定价高一点。但是，如果公司想让自己的产品更实惠，它可以选择降低产品的价格。这种定价方法是相当简单和低风险的。然而，在许多情况下，这并不完全有效，因为公司不知道他们的竞争对手采用什么策略定价。在这种情况下，将彼此作为基准无疑是碰运气。

4. Customer-needs Based Pricing 顾客导向定价法

Customer-needs based pricing is a method of pricing in which the seller makes a decision based on what the customer can justify paying. It is not simply what the consumer is willing to pay, but reflects the value of the product or service from the consumer's perspective. A company would make the most money if they could figure out the maximum each customer would pay, and charge them that amount. Pricing decisions are made to justify purchase decisions and are at a level that convinces the customer benefits from the transaction. Successful companies use value pricing and everyday low pricing to ensure consumers' ultimate value. To optimize pricing, companies need to consider how to best segment the market so that prices reflect the differences in value perceived by different types of consumers.

顾客导向定价法是一种定价方法，在这种定价方法中，销售者根据顾客合理支付的价格做出决定。它不仅仅是消费者愿意支付的价格，而是从消费者的角度反映了产品或服务的价值。如果一家公司能够计算出每位顾客的最高消费金额，并按照这个金额定价，那么它就能赚到最多的钱。该定价策略是为了证明购买决策的合理性，并且在一定程度上说服客户从交易中获益。成功的公司使用价值定价和日常低价来确保消费者的最终利益。为了优化定价，公司需要考虑如何最好地细分市场，使价格反映不同类型消费者对价值的感知。

5. New Product Pricing 新产品定价

The first new product pricing strategy is called price-skimming. Price-skimming calls for setting a high price for a new product to skim maximum revenues layer by layer from those segments willing to pay the high price. This means that the company lowers the price step by step to skim maximum profit from each segment. As a result of this new product pricing strategy, the company makes fewer but more profitable sales.

第一个新的产品定价策略叫作撇脂定价。撇脂定价要求为新产品设定一个较高的价格，以便从那些愿意支付较高价格的细分市场逐层攫取最大的收入。这意味着公司会逐步降低价格，以从每个细分市场中获取最大的利润。这种新产品定价策略的结果是，公司的销售额减少了，但利润增加了。

Many companies inventing new products set high initial prices in order to skim revenues layer by layer from the market. An example for a company using this new product pricing strategy is Apple. When it introduced the first iPhone, its initial price was rather high for a phone. The phones were, consequently, only purchased by customers who really wanted the new gadget and could afford to pay a high price for it. After this segment had been skimmed for six months, Apple dropped the price considerably to attract new buyers. Within a year, prices were dropped again. This way, the company skimmed off the maximum amount of revenue from the various segments of the market.

许多发明新产品的公司为了从市场上逐层攫取利润，设定了较高的初始价格。苹果公司就是一家采用这种新产品定价策略的公司。当它推出第一部iPhone 时，它的初始价格对于一部手机来说是相当高的。因此，这些手机只会被那些真正想要这个新玩意，并且有能力支付高价的消费者购买。在这个细分市场撇脂6个月后，苹果大幅降价以吸引新买家。不到一年，价格再次下降。通过这种方式，公司从各个细分市场中攫取了最大的收益。

However, this new product pricing strategy does not work in all cases. The product's quality and image must support the high initial price, and enough buyers must want the product at that price. Also, the costs of producing smaller amount must not be so high that they overshadow the advantage of charging more. And finally, competitors should not be in sight. If they are able to enter the market easily and undercut the high price, price-skimming does not work.

然而，这种新的产品定价策略并不是在所有情况下都有效。产品的质量和形象必须能够支撑初始的高价，而且必须有足够多的买家想要这个价格的产品。此外，低产量生产的成本不能高到吃掉了高价的优势。最后，竞争者不能出现。如果竞争者们能够轻易进入市场，并廉价出售，那么撇脂定价是行不通的。

瑞典家具零售巨头宜家，以低价推出产品，吸引了大量的买家，使宜家成为全球最大的家具零售商。虽然低廉的价格使每一笔销售的利润减少，但高销量带来了更低的成本，并使宜家保持了健康的利润率

The opposite new product pricing strategy of price skimming is penetration pricing. Instead of setting a high initial price to skim off each segment, market-penetration pricing refers to setting a low price for a new product to penetrate the market quickly and deeply. Thereby, a large number of buyers and a large market share are won, but at the expense of profitability. The high sales volume leads to falling costs, which allows companies to cut their prices even further.

与撇脂定价相反的新产品定价策略是渗透定价。市场渗透定价是指为一种新产品设定一个较低的价格，以便迅速而深入地渗透市场，而不是通过设定一个较高的初始价格来收割每个细分市场。这样可以赢得大量的买家和较大的市场份额，但以牺牲利润为代价。高销量导致成本下降，这使公司可以进一步降低价格。

Trial pricing is the act of pricing a new product low for a limited period of time in order to lower the risk for a customer. The idea is to invite the customers to try something new and win their acceptance. For example, cosmetic companies distribute samples of their new products for a free trial, or give a special offer in order to gain recognition by the potential market.

试用定价是在一定时间内为新产品定价以降低客户风险的行为。这个想法是邀请客户尝试新事物并赢得他们的接纳。例如，化妆品公司派发新产品的样品，免费试用，或提供特别优惠，以获得潜在市场的认可。

8.2.6 Pricing Tactics 定价战术

1. Pricing for Individual Products 个别产品的定价

There are two ways of presenting the price of individual products to customers.

有两种方式向客户展示单个产品的价格。

Two-part pricing requires two separate parts of payments to own the product. The first part is usually priced cheap to attract the customer. Once the customer pays for the first part, he or she would find the second and latter parts are of high price when switching is difficult. Theme parks and cinema halls are good examples. Ticket prices at entrance may be attractive. After entering, you find the food and drinks, or lodging at theme parks are over-priced, or they sell specific soft drinks and souvenirs. Consumers are not allowed to bring food and drinks from outside, neither can they leave, because the movie or fantasy rides are right there waiting.

两段定价法需要两个独立的支付部分来拥有产品。第一部分的价格通常很便宜，以吸引顾客。一旦客户支付了第一部分，他会发现第二部分的价格很高，而中途更换很困难。主题公园和电影院就是很好的例子。门票价格可能很有吸引力。进入公园后，你会发现食物和饮料，或在主题公园住宿的价格过高，并且他们出售限定款软饮料和纪念品。消费者不能从外面带食物和饮料，也不能离开，因为电影或奇幻游乐设施已经在那里等着了。

Payment pricing divides the total price into smaller amounts that most consumers consider affordable. Payment pricing is most commonly used in paying for a car. Instead of paying out the full price right at the start, consumers can spread the cost over a longer period of time. Likewise, according to CNet, nearly 50% of smart phones sold in the United States were purchased through monthly installment plans, which allow consumers to purchase a cell phone over the course up to 30 months.

（分期）付款定价将总价格分成多个小金额，让大多数消费者都认为自己是负担得起的。付款定价最常用的例子是购买一辆车。消费者可以在更长的一段时间内分摊成本，而不是一开始就全额支付。CNet 的数据显示，在美国销售的智能手机中，有近 50% 是通过分期付款的方式购买的，这种方式可以让消费者分 30 个月付款购买一部手机。

2. Pricing for Multiple Products 多种产品的定价

When customers buy several products under the same brand at one time, they wish to purchase for a special price. Price bundling means combining several products or services into a single comprehensive package for an all-inclusive reduced price. Despite the fact that the items are sold for discounted prices, it can increase profits because it promotes the purchase of more than one item. For example, if one goes to eat at a western restaurant, and it charges $50 for dinner which includes main course, starters, desserts. If it charges separately—$30 for the main course, $10 for starters, and $15 for desserts, it is obviously at a higher price than price bundling where the restaurant can claim that customer is getting $5 discount if he or she selects the set meal. By using price bundling, a company can sell its weaker or inferior products with its main or stronger products which helps the company in clearing the idle stock available within the company, thus to create the extra source of revenue in the long run for the company.

当顾客同时购买同一品牌的多个产品时，他们希望以特价购买。捆绑定价是指将多种产品或服务组合成一个完整的一揽子产品或服务，并以低于商品单价总和的价格折价销售。尽管这些商品是以折扣价出售的，但它可以增加利润，因为它鼓励消费者购买不止一件商品。例如，如果一个人去西餐厅吃饭，晚餐的费用是 50 美元，包括主菜、开胃菜和甜点。如果它单独收费——主菜 30 美元，开胃菜 10 美元，甜点 15 美元，很明显，单价高于捆绑定价，餐厅可以声称，如果顾客选择套餐，就得到 5 美元的折扣。通过价格捆绑，公司可以将较弱或较差的产品与主要或较强的产品一起销售，帮助公司清理公司现有的闲置库存，从而为公司创造额外的长期收入来源。

Captive pricing is used when the value of the core product is very low, but the value of the supporting product, which is necessary for working of main product is high. For example, when you buy a printer, you need ink in order to actually use the printer effectively; for a razor to work, you need to buy the blades. When you buy a car, after some time parts of it get broken and you have to change them in order to make the car function properly again. In all these situations you realize how expensive all these components of the core products are. Most of the times, the captive product pricing is higher than the core product. Companies tend to provide a lower price for the core product, which is one-time purchase, in order to attract the customers. At the same time, they price higher for captive product, which needs repetitive purchase, to increase their profits.

当核心产品（也称引诱品）的价值很低，而配套产品（俘虏品）的价值很高时，就会采用俘虏品定价法。例如，当你买了一台打印机，你需要墨水才能真正使用它；要让剃刀工作，你需要购买刀片；当你买了一辆车，过了一段时间，它的零部件坏了，你必须更换它们，以使汽车再次正常运行。在所有这些情况下，你会意识到核心产品的组件是多么昂贵。多数情况下，俘虏品（组件）的定价高于核心产品。公司为了吸引顾客，往往会对核心产品制定较低的价格，即一次性购买。与此同时，他们对俘虏品的定价更高，顾客重复购买俘虏品，就能增加公司的利润。

3. Distribution-based Pricing 基于分销的定价

The products are charged for different prices according to distribution costs.

根据分销成本的不同，制定不同的产品价格。

FOB (Free on Board) origin pricing is a geographically-focused pricing strategy in which goods are shipped free on board and the customer pays the price of freight between the factory and the point of delivery. Assume that there is a jelly dealer X in California purchasing 10,000 jars of jelly from Company Y in Japan. If the purchase contract says "FOB, San Francisco, ABC warehouse", it means Company Y will pay the loading and shipping costs to get the 10,000 jars of jelly from its Japanese factory to the ABC warehouse in San Francisco. FOB delivered pricing, on the other hand, is a pricing tactic in which the cost of loading and transporting the product to the customer is included in the selling price and is paid by the manufacturer.

FOB 原产地定价是一种以地理为中心的定价策略，该策略在装运港船上交货，客户支付从交货点到工厂的费用。假设有一个加利福尼亚的果冻经销商 X 从日本的 Y 公司购买了 1 万罐果冻。如果采购合同上写着 "FOB, San Francisco, ABC warehouse"，这意味着 Y 公司将支付从日本工厂运 1 万罐果冻到旧金山 ABC 仓库的装箱和运输费用。另一方面，FOB 交货价格是将装箱和运输产品的成本包含在售价中，由制造商来支付的价格。

Basing-point pricing is a pricing tactic in which the customer must pay the base price of the product and the freight charges for delivering the product, no matter how near or distant. These freight charges or transportation costs are determined from a "base point" which may not actually be the manufacturing location. Depending on the distance of the buyer from the base point, the transportation costs have to be paid by the buyer of the product.

在基点定价中，客户必须支付产品的基本价格和交付产品的运费，无论距离远近。这些运费或运输成本是由一个 "基点" 确定的，这个基点可能不是实际的制造地点。根据买方与基点的距离，运输费用必须由买方支付。

In uniform delivered pricing (UDP), the seller pays for all the transportation charges and keeps the price same for each customer, regardless of the customer's location. For example, if there is a shoe factory in Guangzhou, then irrespective of which province the customers are in, no matter what the actual cost of shipping to that province, the price will be the same for all.

在统一交付定价（UDP）中，卖方支付所有的运输费用，并对每个客户保持相同的价格，而不管客户的位置如何。例如，如果在广州有一家鞋厂，那么不管客户在哪个省，不管实际运费是多少，到那个省的价格都是一样的。

In case of highly competitive markets, or high-priced products when the cost of freight is a negligible amount comparing to its selling price, a company may use freight absorption pricing. It is a pricing tactic where the manufacturer bears parts or all of the freight or transportation costs involved in transporting the goods to the customer, in order to capture the business. It helps the firm to expand its market far beyond its normal reach and acquire more customers.

在市场竞争激烈的情况下，或者在运输成本与销售价格相比微不足道的情况下，公司可以采用运费吸收定价。这种定价策略中，制造商承担部分或全部运费或运输成本，将货物运输给客户，以获取业务。这有助于公司扩大其市场范围，获得更多的客户。

4. Discounting for Channel Members 渠道会员优惠

① Trade or Functional Discounts 贸易或功能折扣

Trade discounts are usually provided to intermediaries for the functions they perform in the distribution of commodities, such as selling, storage, and transportation. The different functions they perform should be compensated accordingly. A wholesaler might be entitled to a 40% trade discount for high-volume purchase, while a medium-volume wholesaler is given a 30% trade discount. Such successive discounts represent a system of graded incentives.

贸易折扣通常是针对中间商在商品销售、储存和运输等方面所发挥的作用而给予的奖励。中间商发挥的各种作用应该得到相应的补偿。对于大批量采购，批发商可能享有 40% 的贸易折扣，而中等规模的批发商则享有 30% 的贸易折扣。这种逐层的折扣执行了分级奖励的制度。

② Quantity Discounts 数量折扣

Quantity discounts are made where prices are reduced for purchases of large quantities. Cumulative quantity discount (CQD) is a price reduction offered to a buyer in which the amount of the discount increases over time with the volume purchased. The larger the order, the larger the discount. Marketers use these tactics to encourage customers to stay with them. For example, a wholesaler may offer a CQD of 5% if more than 5,000 units are purchased in a month. Each week, store G purchases 2,500 units. Although none of the orders individually total 5,000 units, at the end of the month store G has ordered 10,000 units, and is eligible for the CQD. In its most basic form, a CQD can be thought of as a simple bulk discount. The more units one buys, the more money he or she saves. This type of discount promotes loyalty between a retailer and their wholesale distributor. It also gives retailers the incentive to buy a lot of goods from their wholesalers, so they can become eligible for the discount. For each large purchase, marketers offer a type of discount that based on the volume of the individual purchase, which is called non-cumulative quantity discount.

数量折扣是指购买大量商品而降低价格。累计数量折扣（CQD）是向买方提供的价格折扣，折扣的金额随购买量的增加而增加，订单越多，折扣越大。营销人员使用这些策略来鼓励客户与他们保持联系。例如，如果一个月内购买了 5000 件以上，批发商可以提供 5% 的累计数量折扣。又例如，G 店每周购买 2500 件商品。虽然没有一个订单总数为 5000 个，但是到了月底，G 商店累计订购了 10000 个，并且有资格获得累计数量折扣。基本上，累计数量折扣可以被认为是简单的批量折扣。一个人买的东西越多，省的钱就越多。这种折扣可以提高零售商和批发商之间的忠诚度。它还鼓励零售商从批发商那里购买大量商品，这样他们就有资格享受折扣。对于每一次大规模的购买，营销人员都会根据单次购买的数量提供折扣，这种折扣被称为非累积数量折扣。

③ Cash Discounts 现金折扣

A cash discount is a reward for the payment of an invoice or account within a specified time period. It encourages buyers to pay their bills quickly. From the seller's viewpoint, immediate payment is preferred so that the seller can invest the money for the period to gain the interest. Thus, the seller may offer a discount for a quick cash payment.

现金折扣是对在规定时间内付款的发票或账户所给予的奖励。它鼓励买家迅速支付账单。从卖方的角度来看，立即付款是最好的，这样卖方就可以拿钱进行投资，并在一段时间内获得利息。因此，卖方可以为快速的现金支付提供折扣。

④ Seasonal Discounts 季节性折扣

A seasonal discount is a discount which is offered on seasonal goods or at particular seasons. It has become a common practice for companies whose intention is to spread demand over the year. A company who does not offer discounts during slack seasons will probably lose out their customers to its competitors. Airline companies usually offer a discount to consumers who purchase the flight tickets during off seasons. Electric power companies use seasonal discounts to encourage customers to shift consumption to off-peak periods to reduce the pressure of power supply.

季节性折扣是对季节性商品或特定季节提供的折扣。对于那些打算在一年内分散需求的公司来说，这已成为一种常见的做法。在淡季不打折的公司可能会把顾客拱手让给竞争对手。航空公司通常为那些在淡季购买机票的消费者提供折扣。电力公司利用季节性折扣来鼓励客户将消费转移到非高峰时段，以减少电力供应的压力。

◎ **阅读推荐**

杰克·赫舒拉发，阿米亥·格雷泽，大卫·赫舒拉发. 价格理论及其应用 [M]. 李俊慧，周燕，译. 北京：机械工业出版社，2009.

蒂姆·史密斯.定价策略 [M].周庭瑞，张恩忠，赵智行，等译.北京：中国人民大学出版社，2015.

汤姆·赖利.增值销售：从价格战中突围，用价值真正赢得客户 [M].林腾，译.北京：中国人民大学出版社，2014.

詹姆斯·C.安德森，尼尔马利亚·库马尔，詹姆斯·A.那鲁斯.向价格战说不：价值销售的赢之道 [M].孔辛，译.北京：商务印书馆，2011.

威廉·庞德斯通.无价：洞悉大众心理玩转价格游戏 [M].闫佳，译.杭州：浙江人民出版社，2013.

9

整合营销传播

知识解锁 Knowledge Unlocked

以下问题的答案，可在本章寻找：

1. 整合营销传播是什么意思？其有何意义？

2. 营销传播模型中各要素如何运作？

3. 促销活动有什么样的策略？

4. 如何完整地进行一次广告宣传？

9.1　IMC: Definition and Functions 整合营销：定义和功能

As we know, promotion is one of the 4Ps in the marketing mix. It has its own communication tools. It is more powerful integrating all the promotional tools together than using any single one of them. The strategic planning process designed to optimize the communication of a company's brands by coordinating all promotional tools, and delivering a single consistent message is called integrated marketing communications, or IMC for short. IMC is a concept that has emerged in the recent past. The new strategy seeks to fuse modern and traditional marketing strategies with the intention of creating an efficient, reliable tool to convey a company's brand value propositions to its potential audience.

众所周知，促销是营销组合中的 4P 之一，它有自己的传播工具。将所有的促销工具整合在一起，比使用任何一种单一的工具都更强大。通过协调所有的促销工具来优化公司品牌传播的战略规划过程，并传递单一且一致的信息，这种过程被称为整合营销传播，简称 IMC。IMC 是近几年才出现的概念。这种新战略试图将现代和传统营销策略结合起来，创造一种高效、可靠的工具，向潜在受众传达公司的品牌价值主张。

IMC takes several basic functions such as:

整合营销有几个基本功能，如：

（1）Informing consumers about new products. When a company puts up advertisements, no matter on TV, magazines or social networks, it tries to tell consumers about the information and benefits of its new products and where they can be purchased.

告知消费者新产品。当一家公司在电视、杂志或社交网络上发布广告时，它试图告诉消费者有关其新产品的信息和好处，以及在哪里可以买到这些产品。

（2）Persuading consumers to choose one brand over others. By comparing the dominant features of its products with that of the competitors' in the same category, a brand pushes itself forward to convince customers of its advantages over others.

说服消费者选择一个品牌。一个品牌通过比较其产品的主要特点并与同类产品进行比较，来推销自己，使顾客相信它比别的产品更有优势。

世界自然基金会（WWF）呼吁人们关注气候变化问题

（3）Reminding consumers to continue using certain products. Repeating exposure of a brand in different channels reinforces the memory in customers. Many brands retain fresh to customers by putting inviting messages for a further discovery, creating top of mind awareness.

提醒消费者继续使用某些产品。品牌在不同渠道的反复曝光，强化了消费者的记忆。许多品牌为消费者进行进一步的探索而放置有吸引力的信息，来保持客户的新鲜感，从而打造第一提及知名度。

（4）Building relationships with potential clients. Marketers use IMC to develop and maintain positive and lasting relationships with customers and stakeholders, both internally and externally.

与潜在客户建立关系。市场营销人员借助整合营销来发展和维持与客户及利益相关者之间的积极持久的关系，包括内部和外部的关系。

（5）Assisting with other elements of the marketing mix. IMC must not be seen in isolation, it must fit within the entire marketing mix, such as assisting sales representatives and promoting pre-sell products.

辅助营销组合中的其他要素。整合营销不能被孤立地看待，它必须适合整个营销组合，如协助销售代表和促进预售产品的销售。

9.2 Communications Model 营销传播模型

Marketing communication is explained by the communication model. Following the basic concept, communication model describes the process of sending and receiving messages or transferring information from one part (source) to another (receiver). Between parties, communication is viewed as a means of sending and receiving information.

营销传播可以用营销传播模型来解释。根据基本概念，该模型描述了从一个部分（信息源）向另一个部分（接收方）发送和接收消息或传输信息的过程。在当事人之间，沟通被视为发送和接收信息的一种方式。

9.2.1 Source 来源

Source refers to an organization or individual that produces a message. It is also called the encoder or sender, for it translates an idea formed by marketers into a commutable message that will convey the desired meaning accepted by the audience. In marketing communications, this is where advertising agencies play an important role. The format depends on the type of media vehicle being used to deliver the communication message. A radio message, a TV message or a print message is encoded differently as all of them have their own pros and cons. Whatever message format one may use, the core idea needs to be the same.

来源指的是产生消息的组织或个人。它也被称为编码器或发送者，因为它将市场营销人员的想法转化为可交流的信息，传达给目标消费者（并让他们）能够理解。在营销传播中，这就是广告代理商扮演重要角色的地方。格式取决于用于传递通信消息的媒体载体的类型。广播信息、电视信息或印刷信息的编码都不同，因为它们都有各自的优缺点。但不管使用怎样的形式，核心理念应该是相同的。

9.2.2　Message 消息

The message is a verbal or non-verbal information transmitted from sender to receiver in the communication process. Communication is effective only when the message is understood and when it stimulates action or encourages the receiver to think in new ways. Message can be delivered in forms of public relations, advertisements, press releases, sales promotions, a personal sales pitch, or word-of-mouth communication .

信息是在传播过程中由发送者传递给接收者的一种言语或非言语信息。只有当信息被理解，当它能刺激购买行动或鼓励接收者以新的方式思考时，信息传播才有效。营销信息可以通过公关、广告、新闻稿、促销、个人推销或口头传播等形式传递。

9.2.3　Medium 媒介

The encoded message must now be delivered to its audience via a message channel, which is known as medium. A medium is a term that refers to the message channel that carries the message from the sender to the receiver. In marketing, the medium may be television, print, radio, newspaper, banner advertising, or a sales person. The objective here is that the message should reach as large target audience as possible. A proper message can immediately connect a company with its target group, build a better brand positioning, and thereby give an immediate boost to the organization.

编码后的信息现在必须通过一个称为媒介的信息通道传递给受众。媒介是一个营销术语，指的是将消息从发送方传送到接收方的消息通道。在市场营销中，媒介可以是电视、印刷品、广播、报纸、横幅广告或销售人员。使用不同媒介的目的是让信息到达尽可能多的目标受众。恰当的信息可以立即将公司与其目标群体联系起来，建立更好的品牌定位，从而给组织带来即时的推动。

9.2.4　Receiver 接收者

The receiver is the one making the decision after decoding the message. In other words, the receiver is the end customer. Ideally, the receiver should act on the message he or she has received. To make sure that the receiver acts on the message, IMC sends messages in different formats through various media vehicles. The receiver receives the same message in differently encoded format and decodes it. Decoding is how the receivers interpret the message and come to an understanding about what the source is communicating. So decoding is in the hands of receivers. All the sender can do is to encode the message as best as he can and ensure that it reaches the receiver.

接收者是在解码信息后做出决定的人。换句话说，接收者就是最终客户。理想情况下，接收者应该根据收到的消息采取行动。为了确保接收方对消息给出回应，整合营销传播通过各种媒体载体以不同的格式发送消息。接收者以不同的编码格式接收相同的消息并对其进行解码。解码是指接收者如何解读信息，以及如何理解信息的来源。所以解码就掌握在接收者的手中。发送方所能做的就是尽其所能地对消息进行编码，并确保它到达接收方。

9.2.5　Noise 噪声

Noise is the term given to anything that disrupts and interferes the communication. That is, anything that prevents the audience from receiving the message the way the source intended to. It does not necessarily involve an audible distraction. Noise could be applications that allow audiences to skip advertisements, poorly placed billboards, advertisements in print that are too small or poorly placed. It can occur in any stage of the communication flow and influence all elements of the model. Marketers try to minimize noise by placing information where the least distraction takes place.

噪声是指任何干扰和介入营销信息传播的东西，即任何阻止听众以他们所希望的方式接收信息的东西。它不一定是声音干扰。噪声可以是让观众跳过广告的应用，放置不当的告示，太小或位置不当的印刷广告。它可以发生在信息流的任何阶段，并影响传播模式中的所有元素。营销人员试图通过将信息放置在干扰最少地方来将噪声最小化。

9.2.6　Feedback 反馈

Feedback refers to any response the receiver offers to the message. This could be communication or behavior, that is, the way that consumers respond to promotional campaigns. Measuring feedback is extremely important in a promotions campaign because it allows for a measure of the success of the marketing campaign. For example, negative feedback such as no increase in sales would show that adjustments need to be made in the promotional strategy.

反馈是指接受者对信息的一切反应。它可以是口头沟通或行为表现，也就是消费者对促销活动的反应。反馈在促销活动中是非常重要的，因为它可以衡量营销活动成功与否。例如，负面的反馈，如销售额没有增加，表明促销策略需要调整。

9.3　The Promotion Mix 促销组合

The promotion mix is one of the 4Ps of the marketing mix. It refers to the strategies that combine a range of marketing communication methods to execute marketing activities. The promotion mix mainly consists of advertising, sales promotion, public relations, personal selling, data-driven marketing, and online marketing communication. Different methods have distinct advantages and complexities, and it requires skills and experiences to utilize them effectively. In a sense, each form of promotional activities applied by marketers in the mix is a way of marketing communication, since it tells consumers the characteristics of the product and where its value lies. The elements in the promotion mix evolve over time and new methods are applied along with the changes of consumers in the target segments. Some commonly used methods of promotion mix are described below.

促销组合是营销组合的 4P 之一。它是指结合一系列营销传播手段来执行营销活动的策略。促销组合主要包括广告、促销、公关、个人销售、数据驱动营销和网络营销传播。不同的方法有其独特的优点和复杂性，有效地利用它们则需要技巧和经验。从某种意义上说，营销人员在组合中应用的每一种促销活动都是一种营销传播方式，因为它告诉消费者产品的特性及其价值所在。促销组合中的元素会随着时间的推移而变化，新的方法也会随着目标细分市场中消费者的变化而应用。以下是一些常用的促销组合方法。

Advertising: Advertising is the presentation and promotion of ideas, goods, or services by an identified sponsor in a mass medium. Advertising uses every possible medium to get its message through. It does this via television, print (newspapers, magazines, journals etc.), radio, press, internet, direct selling, hoardings, mailers, contests, sponsorship, direct mails, posters, mobile apps, and even people (endorsements). In advertising campaigns, the marketer has control over what the message will say, when it will appear, and who is likely to see it. However, it costs much to produce and distribute, and it is so commonly used that most of advertisements are neglected by the audience and some of them lose credibility.

广告：广告是由明确的赞助商在大众传媒中展示和推广创意、商品或服务。广告使用一切可能的媒体来传递信息。它通过电视、印刷品（报纸、杂志、期刊等）、广播、报刊、互联网、直销、广告牌、邮件、竞赛、赞助、直邮、海报、移动应用，甚至是人（代言）来实现这一目标。在广告活动中，营销人员可以控制信息的内容、何时出现及谁可能会看到它。然而，它的制作和传播成本很高，它的应用如此普遍，以至于大多数广告被消费者忽视，其中一些还失去了信誉。

Sales promotion: It refers to all media and non-media marketing communication for a limited amount of time. Consumer sales promotion techniques include price pack deals, reward programs, coupons, point-of-sale displays. A consumer sales promotion targets the customer while a trade sales promotion focuses on organizational customers that can stimulate immediate sales. Trade promotion techniques include special pricing, trade shows, demonstrations, no-obligation gifts, etc. Sales promotion is especially effective for new product release and products with high perceived risks and it encourages repeat purchase.

销售推广：指在一定时间内进行的所有媒体和非媒体的营销传播。消费者促销技巧包括价格优惠、奖励计划、优惠券、销售点展示。消费者促销针对的是顾客，而贸易促销针对的是能够立即刺激销售的公司客户。促销手段包括特价、展销、示范、免费赠品等。促销对于新产品的发布和高感知风险的产品尤其有效，它鼓励重复购买。

Public relations: Public relation is an excellent tool because it gives additional exposure to a company for which it does not have to pay directly. It is also more reliable and effective than advertising, for the reason that the information about a firm or product is carried by a third party in an indirect way. Newspapers and magazine articles, TV and radio presentations, charitable contributions, speeches, seminars are examples of implementing public relations. For the reason of lacking control over the message transmitted, companies should pay attention to avoid negative public relations, since dirty secrets and misleading facts or legitimate claims are destroying and discrediting.

公共关系：公共关系是一个不错的工具，因为它为公司提供了额外的曝光机会，而不需要直接付费。它比广告更可靠也更有效，因为关于公司或产品的信息是由第三方以间接的方式提供的。报纸和杂志文章、电视和广播演讲、慈善捐款、演讲、研讨会都是实施公关活动的例子。由于对所传递的信息缺乏控制，公司应该注意避免负面的公关信息，因为肮脏的秘密和误导性的事实或一些正当要求正在败坏信誉。

Personal selling: Personal selling is a one-on-one promotional technique that allows marketers to convince customers in purchasing a product or service. It takes forms of face-to-face interaction, telemarketing, sales presentations, etc. A successful personal selling includes knowledgeable salespersons, their good understanding of customer needs and strong communication skills, together with the judgement of the qualification of potential buyers. In spite of high costs, personal selling gives marketers the opportunity to contact with the customers directly, so that they can collect first-hand information and get quantifiable results and feedback immediately. The most difficult part here is the reliability of the salespeople to the audience, for trust building always takes time.

个人推销：个人推销是一对一的推销技巧，它使营销者能够说服顾客购买产品或服务。它采取面对面互动、电话营销、销售报告等形式。成功的个人销售包括销售人员应具备渊博的知识，他们对客户需求能很好地理解，具备强大的沟通技巧，以及对潜在买家的判断。尽管个人销售的成本很高，但它给了营销人员与客户直接接触的机会，使他们能够收集第一手信息，并立即获得可量化的结果和反馈。该技巧最具挑战性的是销售人员的可信度，因为建立信任总是需要时间的。

Data-driven marketing: It refers to strategies built on insights pulled from the analysis of big data, collected through consumer interactions and engagements, to form predictions about future behaviors. Evidence based on data encourages knowledge to be updated. The advantage of data-driven marketing is that it enhances and personalizes the customer experience. But sharing customer data between organizations without customers' permission leads to a great concern.

数据驱动营销：数据驱动营销是指基于大数据分析，通过消费者互动和参与，收集数据并深刻分析，从而形成对消费者未来行为的预测。基于大数据的结论促进了营销认知的及时更新。数据驱动营销的优点是增强和个性化的客户体验。但是，在没有客户许可的情况下在组织之间共享客户数据会引发极大的担忧。

Online marketing: Online marketing reaches wider audiences at a lower cost than traditional advertising budgets. Its flexibility and convenience allow consumers to purchase products anytime and anywhere. It also facilitates consumer data collection for further study, such as tracking customers' preferences. Online marketing carries negative aspects too. Customers may experience unethical and fraudulent practices in online marketing, as cyber crime occurs more frequently. Along with the fundamental marketing knowledge, it requires understanding of search engine technology, advertising techniques, content creation, and logics, all special expertise to master the online marketing.

网络营销：与传统广告预算相比，网络营销能以更低的成本接触到更广泛的受众。它的灵活性和方便性使消费者可以随时随地购买产品。它还有助于收集消费者数据以供进一步研究，如跟踪消费者的偏好。网络营销也有负面影响。随着网络犯罪的频繁发生，消费者可能会在网络营销中遇到不道德和欺诈行为。除了基本的市场营销知识外，营销人员还需要了解搜索引擎技术、广告技术、内容创作和逻辑，所有这些都是掌握网络营销的专业知识。

9.4　Steps in Developing Communication Campaigns 开展宣传活动的步骤

9.4.1　Identify the Target Audience 确定目标受众

All successful marketing efforts begin with a thorough understanding of the target audience. What do they need, want, and expect? Researches should be carried out to investigate the demographics, geographics, psychographics, and purchase behavior of potential customers, as well as insights into when, where, and how do they buy your products. At the same time, marketers need to make efforts to let the message reach the intended audience and be understood by them.

所有成功的营销活动都是从彻底了解目标受众开始的。他们需要什么，想要什么，期望什么？营销人员应研究潜在客户的人口统计、地理、心理和购买行为等特征，观察分析他们何时、何地、如何购买你的产品。同时，营销人员需要努力让信息到达目标受众并被他们理解。

9.4.2　Establishing the Communication Objectives 建立沟通目标

1. Creating Awareness 创造品牌知名度

When initially enter the market, a company has to let people know the existence of its products or services. This is a challenging step, for capturing customers' attention does not mean they will notice the brand name. Creating awareness might include broadcast commercials or print advertisements that depict the image of a company and constant repetition of a brand name, slogans, and jingles. The whole objective is to become known and memorable. Established companies often use a closely-related goal of building or maintaining top-of-mind awareness, which means customers think of you first when considering your product category.

当公司刚进入市场时，它必须让人们知道它的产品或服务的存在。这是一个具有挑战性的步骤，因为吸引客户的注意力并不意味着他们会注意到品牌名称。提高知名度包括广播广告或印刷广告，描绘公司的形象，不断重复品牌的名称、口号和广告语。在这个阶段，一切目标就是让大家知道并记住品牌。成熟的公司通常有一个紧密相关的目标，那就是建立或保持第一提及知名度，这意味着客户在考虑你的产品类别时首先想到的是你。

2. Provide Knowledge 提供知识

Customers with newly built awareness of the product but lack knowledge begin to do research about the product for example through the internet, retail advisors, and product packaging. In today's digital world, this step has become more important as consumers expect to gather product knowledge at the click of a button. Consumers will quickly move to competitor brands if they do not get the information they want. So this stage is where comprehension of the brand name and what it stands for become important. What are the brand's specific appeals and unique benefits? In what way is it different from the competing brands? Who is the target market? The marketer's job is to ensure that these types of questions are answered fully and properly, and the product information is easily accessible.

刚建立起对产品的认知但不了解产品相关知识的客户，开始研究产品，例如利用互联网、零售顾问和产品包装等来建立认知。在当今的数字世界，这一步变得越来越重要，因为消费者希望通过点击鼠标来收集产品知识。一旦消费者得不到他们想要的信息，他们会迅速转向竞争对手的品牌。因此，在这个阶段，理解品牌名称及其代表的含义变得非常重要。品牌的具体诉求和独特优势是什么？它与竞争对手的品牌有什么不同？谁是目标市场？营销人员的工作是确保这些类型的问题得到充分和适当的回答，并且产品信息很容易获得。

3. Creating Desire and Preference 创造欲望和偏好

The next communication objective is to create an emotional connection between the product and its consumers. How customers feel about the product, or the attitudes towards the product implies the consequent buying decisions. At this stage, marketers will expect the consumer to disconnect from rival products and focus on their own particular product. Sports drink commercials showing athletes competing, getting hot and sweaty and then taking a drink afterward is a common approach to drive purchase intent. These advertisements normally include benefits of the drink related to taste or nutrients.

下一个沟通目标是在产品和消费者之间建立情感联系。顾客对产品的感觉或对产品的态度暗示了随后的购买决定。在这个阶段，市场营销人员将期望消费者与竞争对手的产品分离，专注于自己的特定产品。运动饮料的商业广告中，运动员们在比赛中热得大汗淋漓，接着来一杯运动饮料，运动员们立马神清气爽。这是一种常见驱动购买意向的方式。这些广告通常会宣传饮料的美味或营养。

4. Encouraging Purchase and Trail 鼓励购买和试用

Two separate but closely related communication objectives are to stimulate trial use and drive repeat purchases. Free trials or product samples are common techniques to persuade customers to try a product for the first time. Inviting consumers to take a car for a test drive or offering consumers a free sample of a food product are commonly seen around us. The goal is to get the customer to experience a certain product and reassures them that the purchase will be a safe one. Once getting them on the first purchase, a marketer has to figure out how to convert that into a follow-up purchase. Discounts on the next purchase or frequency programs are ways to turn one-time users into repeat buyers, and ultimately, loyal customers.

两个独立但密切相关的沟通目标是刺激试用和鼓励重复购买。免费试用或产品样品是说服客户第一次试用产品的常用技巧。邀请消费者开车试驾，或者为消费者提供免费的食品样品，这些在我们周围都很常见。目标是让客户体验某种产品，并向他们保证购买的产品是安全的。一旦让他们达成第一次购买，营销人员必须将其转换成后续购买。下次购买时的折扣或频率计划是将一次性用户转变为回头客并最终成为忠实顾客的方法。

5. Build Loyalty 赢得忠诚

Customers today have more choices than ever before. Switching between brands even they have favorite ones does not mean they are flip floppers, just because trying new items is an interesting experience. Premium products with good quality will attract customers, but brand loyalty is created by insistence in brand quality and philosophy of running a business. Ongoing communication with current users, developing a strong customer community, personalization of the customer experience are some of the effective promotional efforts that can keep customers coming back.

今天的顾客比以往任何时候都有更多的选择。即使人们有最喜欢的品牌，也会在不同品牌之间切换，这不意味着他们是易变的人，只是因为尝试新产品是一种有趣的体验。优质的产品会吸引顾客，但品牌忠诚是坚持品牌品质和经营理念的结果。与现有用户进行持续的沟通，发展强大的客户社群和个性化的客户体验都是有效的促销努力，可以保留回头客。

9.4.3 Determining the Budget 确定预算

1. Setting the Total Communication Budget 确定总预算

Top-down budgeting is where a company develops or sets the total or top budget and then breaks it down into the component parts within that budget.

自上而下预算是指公司制定或设定总预算或最高预算，然后将其划分为预算中的各个组成部分。

The most commonly used top-down technique is the percentage-of-sales method, an advertising expense budgeting method based on allocating a fixed percentage, either coming from the previous period's sales or an industry average reported by trade associations, to marketing communication campaigns.

最常用的自上而下的方法是销售百分比法，这是一种基于固定比例的广告费用预算方法，来自前一时期的销售或行业协会报告的行业平均数，划拨给营销传播活动。

On the other hand, the competitive-parity method is based on what the competitors are estimated to be spending. This method assumes the other firms have the same marketing objectives and same amount of money spent on marketing communications will cause the same effect. It is a defensive strategy that can help a business protect its brand or product's competitive position in the marketplace without overspending.

另一方面，竞争平价法是基于对竞争者支出的估计。这种方法假设其他公司有相同的营销目标，在营销传播上投入相同的资金也会产生相同的效果。这是一种防御策略，可以帮助企业保护其品牌或产品在市场上的竞争地位，而不需要过度支出。

Bottom-up budgeting starts with a list or plan or schedule of the things to do prepared by managers from all departments, and then totals it up to arrive at an overall budget number. For example, your sales department has project goals amounting $10,000, $25,000, and $40,000 for the coming year. Overall, your sales department's budget would be $75,000.

自下而上的预算首先是由各个部门的经理列出要做的事情的清单、计划或时间表，然后汇总得出总的预算数字。例如，你的销售部门在下一年的项目目标分别是 10000 美元、25000 美元和 40000 美元，那么你的销售部门的总预算是 75000 美元。

2. Using Push or Pull Strategy 采用推拉策略

A push strategy means taking the product directly to the customer via whatever means, ensuring the customer is aware of a brand at the point of purchase. It may involve setting up distribution channels and persuading middlemen and retailers to stock the product. The push technique can work particularly well for lower value items such as fast moving consumer goods, when customers are standing at the shelf ready to drop an item into their baskets and are ready to make their decision on the spot. This term now broadly encompasses most direct promotional techniques such as encouraging retailers to stock your product, designing point of sale materials or even selling face to face. New businesses often adopt a push strategy for their products in order to generate exposure and a retail channel.

推式战略是指通过各种方式将产品直接卖给顾客，确保顾客在购买时了解某个品牌。其中可能包括建立分销渠道，说服中间商和零售商进货。当顾客站在货架前，准备把一件商品投进他们的购物篮，并准备当场做出决定时，特别适合采取这种办法。这种推法尤其适用于价格较低的商品，比如快速消费品。这个术语现在广泛地包含了最直接的促销技巧，比如鼓励零售商为你进货，设计销售点材料，甚至面对面销售。新企业通常会对他们的产品采取促销策略，以增加曝光度和开辟零售渠道。

Once a brand has been established, companies may turn to a pull strategy. A pull strategy involves customers seeking out the brand in an active process, and retailers placing orders for stock due to direct consumer demand. A pull strategy requires a highly visible brand which can be developed through advertising and consumer sales promotion. Stimulated by promotion activities, consumers will pull the product into their shopping baskets.

一旦品牌建立起来，公司可能会转向拉式策略。拉式策略包括顾客主动寻找品牌，零售商根据顾客的直接需求下订单。拉式策略要求品牌家喻户晓，可以通过广告和消费者促销来形成品牌的高度认知。在促销活动的刺激下，消费者会把产品拉进购物篮。

3. Allocating Budget 分配预算

Allocation of budget is to decide how much is to spend on each IMC campaign that a company has chosen for promoting its products. It is affected mainly by three factors. First of all, organizational factors such as complexity of an organization's structure, and preferences for various media will be a major consideration. Secondly, the market potential has a significant influence. Segments with the strongest purchasing power will attract the greatest amount of budget allocation. Thirdly, the cost of buying marketing communication is considered. Using celebrities endorsement for a product that is unrelated to their images can be a costly decision.

预算分配是决定在每个被公司选中的产品进行整合营销活动时的开销。它主要受到 3 个因素的影响。第一，组织因素，如组织结构的复杂性，对各种媒体的偏好将是一个主要的考虑因素。第二，市场潜力的显著影响。购买力最强的细分市场将吸引最多的预算拨款。第三，购买营销传播的成本。使用名人来代言与他们形象无关的产品可能是一个烧钱的决策。

9.4.4　Designing the Communication 设计传播

1. Advertising Appeal 广告诉求

Advertising appeal is the persuasive pressure that stimulates a person to buy a product or service by speaking to an individual's needs, interests, or wants. Companies put a lot of effort into their creative advertising strategies and use various types of appeals to influence purchasing decisions.

广告诉求是一个卖点，会对消费者产生强烈的吸引力，它通过个人需求、兴趣或愿望，来刺激人们购买产品或服务的欲望。公司在创意广告策略上投入了大量精力，并利用各种各样的吸引力来影响购买决策。

Rational appeals focus on the consumer's need for practicality and functionality in a product. Rational appeal sends messages focusing on product features and functional benefits. The advertiser then provides proof to back up the claims. An automobile advertisement focuses on gas efficiency, mileage and prices to reach consumers who want a cost-efficient, reliable vehicle. Household appliance manufacturers may place emphasis on features that lower home utility costs and protect the environment.

理性诉求关注的是消费者对产品的实用性和功能性的需求。理性诉求发布关注产品特性和功能优点的消息。接着，广告商提供证据来支持这些说法。汽车广告关注的是燃油效率、行驶里程和价格，以吸引那些想购买一辆性价比高、性能可靠的汽车的消费者。家电制造商可能会把重点放在降低家庭使用成本和保护环境的功能上。

Emotional appeal, on the contrary, is to stimulate emotions in order to appeal to the psychological, emotional or social needs of the consumer. It involves creativity, visual cues that contribute to a specific mood or feeling. Common rational approaches include showing a personal story that relates to the product, such as user testimony.

An emotional appeal for a hotel chain, for example, might include phrases like "family friendly". It makes a consumer want to buy something simply because they like it rather than they have knowledge about it.

相反，感性诉求是为了迎合消费者的心理、情感或社会需求而激发情感。它涉及创造力和视觉线索，激起特定的情绪或感觉。常见方法包括显示与产品相关的个人故事，例如用户现身说法。对连锁酒店的感性诉求可能包括像"适合家庭出行"这样的短语。它使消费者仅仅因为喜欢某样东西而想买它，而不是因为了解它。

There are also fear appeals, sex appeals, musical appeals, humorous appeals, slogans, and jingles as well.

另外还有恐惧诉求、性诉求、音乐诉求、幽默诉求、口号和歌曲诉求等。

高露洁牙线利用人对不美观的恐惧来做广告

2. Creative Strategy 创意策略

Creative strategy is the process that turns an idea into an advertisement. Marketers need to update their knowledge by pay attention to social and cultural trends, and keep practicing creativity. One may have to generate 1,000 wacky ideas before he finds a strategic homerun, but a single great creative strategy can be worth the time and investment of those wasted ideas.

创意策略是把一个想法变成广告的过程。营销人员需要通过关注社会和文化趋势来更新他们的知识，并不断实践创新。一个人可能要想出 1000 个古怪的点子才能找到一个战略上的"本垒打"，但是一个伟大的创意策略是值得投入时间和想法的。

口碑传播（word of mouth）包括人与人之间的口头、书面或电子交流，这些交流与购买或使用产品或服务的优点或经验有关

Two main types of creative strategy are the unique selling proposition (UPS) and brand image strategies. A unique selling proposition (USP) is the reason people do business with you and not someone else. For example, Charles Revson, founder of Revlon, always used to say he sold hope, not makeup. Some airlines sell friendly service, while others sell on-time service. Neiman Marcus sells luxury, while Wal-Mart sells bargains. While UPS is based on the functional differences between brands, brand image strategy creates a psychological differentiation for the product. A brand image associates the products with unique symbols and logos reflecting an organization's image, perceived as distinctive features. The idea behind brand image strategy is that the consumer is not purchasing just the product but also the image associated with that product. Brand images can be strengthened using brand communications like advertising, packaging, word of mouth, publicity, other promotional tools, etc.

创意策略主要有两种类型：独特的销售主张和品牌形象策略。独特的销售主张是人们和你做生意而不是和别人做生意的原因。例如，露华浓的创始人查尔斯·雷夫森总是说，他卖的是希望，而不是化妆品。一些航空公司提供亲切的服务，而另一些则提供准时的服务。内曼·马库斯卖奢侈品，而沃尔玛卖便宜货。独特的销售主张基于品牌之间的功能差异，而品牌形象策略为产品创造了一种心理差异化。品牌形象将产品与独有的符号和标识联系起来，这些符号和标识反映了组织的形象，被视为独有的特征。品牌形象战略背后的理念是，消费者不仅购买产品，还购买与该产品相关的形象。品牌形象可以通过广告、包装、口碑、宣传等品牌传播手段来强化。

9.4.5 Developing the Marketing Communication Strategy 制定营销传播策略

1. Marketing Communication through Product Lifecycle 全生命周期营销传播

Marketing communications strategies will change over the lifecycle of a product. Some of them are more effective than others in different stages of the product's life cycle.

营销传播策略会随着产品的生命周期而改变。在产品生命周期的某个阶段，一些策略可能比其他的更有效。

The objective of introduction stage is to build customer awareness and encourage trial of the product. This is accomplished by clearly understanding the customers' requirements and expectations, and involving them from the beginning of the product development. The process will be time-consuming, and companies should be prepared that the sales growth of the product will be minimal. A press conference, a speech, an article or face-to-face discussion, are specific marketing communications that companies may use. Regardless of what forms of communication is used, the essential factor for the future development of the brand is winning the trust of the target audience.

引入期的目标是建立客户意识，鼓励他们试用产品。此举通过清楚地了解顾客的需求和期望，并从产品的开发阶段开始就让消费者参与进来这一方式实现。这个过程很耗时，公司应该做好准备，因为在引入期，产品的销售增长最小。新闻发布会、演讲、文章或面对面的讨论，都是公司可能使用的具体营销传播方式。无论采用何种传播形式，品牌未来发展的关键是赢得目标受众的信任。

At the growth stage, the objective is to strengthen the brand position in the market. Consumers have become more aware and demanding about a brand. Companies should continue to maintain communications with the double focus, that is, a certain part of the messages sent by the company should be aimed at informing and educating consumers and for market developments, and the other part be at brand building by emphasizing on its position. At the second stage, customers have already established interests and trust in the brand, and the company must find substantial benefit by which to distinguish it from the competitors.

在成长期，目标是加强品牌在市场中的地位。消费者对品牌的意识和要求越来越高。企业应继续保持传播的双重重点，即公司发布的一部分信息应旨在告知、教育消费者，立足市场的发展，另一部分则应放在强调其地位的品牌建设。在第二阶段，顾客已经对品牌建立了兴趣和信任，公司必须从中获得实质性的利益，从而将自己与竞争对手区分开来。

At the third stage known as maturity stage, customers are already well informed about the product or service, and the key tasks for the company are to retain current customers. It requires the company to focus its efforts on generating customers' desire to purchase the brand. This can be obtained by sales promotions and well-planned special events.

在第三个阶段，即成熟期，客户已经对产品或服务有了充分的了解，公司的主要任务是留住现有的客户。这时，公司应把精力集中在激发顾客购买该品牌的欲望上。这可以通过促销和精心策划的特别活动来实现。

When competitive companies are using new technologies to satisfy consumer needs, the brand is stepping into the stage of decline. The main objective the company should reach at the decline stage of brand management is to maintain a strong connection with customers for survival, or, let the product die out gradually. At this stage, the brand must be very flexible and responsive to the changes in the market. The company should either spend its promotional budget on sales promotions, personal sales, and relationship marketing, or reduce investing on all elements of the promotion mix.

当其他有竞争力的公司采用新技术来满足消费者需求时，品牌就进入了衰退期。在品牌管理的衰退期，公司应该达到的主要目标是为了生存而与客户保持紧密的联系，或者让产品逐渐消亡。在这个阶段，品牌必须非常灵活，对市场的变化做出及时反应。公司应该把促销预算花在促销、个人销售和关系营销上，或者减少对促销组合的所有要素的投资。

2. Message Structure 消息结构

One of the purposes of marketing is to persuade consumers to buy the products or services. In doing so, how communication message is delivered is a vital issue. Persuasive communication that presents only one point of view is called one-sided message. Most mass media advertising messages are one-sided. A one-sided message is more appropriate for an audience that is favorably disposed toward the view being presented or is unlikely to be exposed to the other side. A religious fund-raising appeal is usually one-sided on the assumption that the targeted audience is favorably disposed toward the view being expounded and is unlikely to be receptive to other religious beliefs.

营销的目的之一是说服消费者购买产品或服务。在此过程中，如何传递通信消息是一个至关重要的问题。只表达一种观点的说服性交流为片面信息。大多数大众媒体的广告信息都是片面的。一边倒的信息更适合对所呈现的观点有好感或不太可能接触到另一面信息的观众。宗教筹款的诉求通常是片面的，因为它假定目标受众对所阐述的观点有好感，不太可能接受其他宗教信仰。

In delivering two-sided messages, marketers present both positive and negative information. Usually the marketers will begin their persuasive speech by demonstrating favorable issues about the product. Later they will present opposing viewpoints or counterarguments. It works best with an educated audience that tends to make informed choices like industrial buyers.

在传递双面信息的过程中，营销人员同时传递正面和负面信息。通常情况下，营销人员会通过展示产品的优点来开始他们的说服性演讲。之后他们会提出相反的观点或反驳。它最适合受过教育的受众，他们往往会像产业买家一样做出明智的选择。

9.4.6 Pretest What the Communication Will Say 传播内容预测试

Pretesting is a form of customized research that predicts in-market performance of an ad, before it airs, It allows a company to ensure its campaign products are understood, attractive, acceptable, identifiable, and persuasive by the target audiences. In doing so, a company gains great insights for future campaign development. Ideally, a third party research agency with experience in conducting and analyzing focus group discussions is invited to do the pretest. All important campaign materials need to be pretested, including slogans, taglines, logos.

预测试是一种定制化的研究形式，在广告播出前预测其在市场上的表现。它能够使公司确保其推出的产品被目标受众理解、吸引、接受、识别和说服。这样做，公司可以获得对未来活动发展的深刻见解。最理想的情况是，邀请具有引导和分析焦点小组讨论经验的第三方研究机构进行预测试。所有重要的竞选材料都需要预先测试，包括品牌口号、标语和标识。

When move on to the production stage, copy testing is used to evaluate different executions of an advertising campaign. Copy tests are useful for selecting one out of many different ad executions, or for making adjustments to improve comprehension or the tone of the ad.

在进入生产阶段时，广告文案测试用于评估广告活动的不同执行情况。该测试对于从许多不同的广告提案中挑选其一非常有效，或者可用来提高对广告理解和提升广告的调性。

9.4.7 Choosing the Media 选择媒体

Media planning is the process of establishing the exact media vehicles to be used for advertising. The goal of media planning is to find that combination of media vehicles that enables the message to be communicated to the largest group of the target audience at the most effective cost. A good media plan defines the marketing problem, translates the marketing requirements into attainable media objectives. There are pros and cons for each type of media, and choosing the most appropriate mix of marketing media is important. The following are the traditional media that are most commonly used.

媒介规划是为广告投放搭建精确的媒介载体的过程。媒介规划的目标是找到媒介载体的组合，使信息以最经济的成本传播给最大群体的目标受众群。一个良好的媒体计划定义了营销问题，将营销需求转化为可实现的媒体目标。每种媒体都有利弊，选择最合适的营销媒体组合是很重要的。以下是最常用的传统媒体。

Television. Television is one of the greatest achievements of the 20th century. It is the most popular part of mass media with wide geographic coverage and broad audience reach. Paid membership of network TV are allowed to channel surf and skip commercials. Television gives limited length of exposure, as most ads are only thirty seconds long or less, which limits the amount of information you can communicate. It is also difficult to measure response through television commercials.

电视。电视是 20 世纪最伟大的成就之一。它是大众传媒中最受欢迎的一种，具有广泛的地域覆盖和广泛的受众范围。有线电视通常比网络电视便宜，但付费的网络电视会员可以在频道上冲浪并跳过广告。电视广告的曝光时间有限，因为大多数广告只有 30 秒或更少，这就限制了可以交流的信息量。通过电视广告来衡量观众的反应也很困难。

Radio. In regards to media buying and creative production, radio is less expensive. Commercials on radio are repeated throughout the day and evening. Because radio listeners are spread over many stations, companies may have to advertise simultaneously on several stations to reach the target audience. Radio is a background medium. Most listeners are doing something else while listening, which means that the ad has to work hard to get their attention. But listeners who are interested in the product cannot go back to the ads to go over important points.

广播。对于媒体购买和创意制作来说，它比电视更实惠。广播里的商业广告一天到晚都在滚动播放。由于电台听众遍布在各个电台，公司可能不得不在几个电台同时做广告以到达目标听众。广播是背景媒体。大多数听众在听的时候都在做别的事情，这意味着广告必须努力吸引他们的注意力。但是对产品感兴趣的听众不能回到广告中去看重要的内容。

Newspapers. Newspapers are one of the traditional media used by businesses, both big and small alike, to advertise their businesses. It allows companies to reach a huge number of people in a given geographic area. Larger papers reach a large local audience, and smaller community papers can be effective in reaching specific communities. It is especially good for older markets above age 50, and the emergence of new media has caused newspaper circulation to decline in most markets.

报纸。报纸是企业（无论大小）用来宣传其业务的传统媒体之一。它使公司能够接触到特定地理区域内的大量人口。发行量大的报纸可以接触到大量的本地读者，而较小的社区报纸可以有效地到达特定的社区。这对 50 岁以上的老年市场尤其有利，因为新媒体的出现导致大多数市场的报纸发行量下降。

Magazines. Magazine advertising is more focused and more expensive compared to newspaper advertising. It allows for better targeting of audience, as companies can choose magazine publications that cater to their specific audience or whose editorial content specializes in topics of interest to the audience. It has high readership and reader loyalty so that more attention will be paid to the advertisement. However, long read times require planning weeks or months in advance.

杂志。与报纸广告相比，杂志广告更有针对性，也更贵。它能更好地瞄准受众，因为公司可以选择迎合特定受众的杂志出版物，或其内容专门针对受众感兴趣的主题。它有很广泛的读者群和较高的读者忠诚度，因此杂志有更多的精力放在广告上。然而，长时间的阅读需要提前几周或几个月进行计划。

Outdoor media. Outdoor media such as signs, billboards, and placards are used in several places to spread a common message. It has the lowest CPM (cost per thousand, "M" is the Roman numeral for one thousand) yet the widest reach among all media. Outdoor media are usually large and creative with 24/7 exposure, so it can cause good consumer awareness. It is suitable especially for short and simple messages. The disadvantage is that the audience is disengaged and their responses are difficult to measure.

户外媒体。户外媒体如标志、广告牌和标语牌在一些地方被用来传播共同的信息。它拥有最低的千人成本（CMP，"M"是指罗马数字1000，千人成本是一种媒体送达1000人或"家庭"的成本计算单位），但在所有媒体中覆盖面最广。户外媒体通常规模大，创意多，7天24小时曝光，能有效建立消费者意识。它特别适用于简短的信息。它的缺点是受众是自由分散的，他们的反应很难衡量。

Directories. Directory advertising is a directed, information-focused form of advertising. Yellow Pages advertising is a typical type of directories. It has specific categories or headings in which advertisers can place an advertisement. The 24-hour availability can be particularly beneficial to the advertiser, when households use their Yellow Pages frequently. A key disadvantage of the Yellow Pages is that it can be extremely costly.

目录。目录广告是一种定向的、以传播信息为中心的广告形式。黄页广告是一种典型的目录类型。它有特定的类别或标题，广告商可以在其中放置广告。当用户频繁使用他们的黄页时，24小时的可用性对广告商尤其有利。黄页的一个主要缺点是它可能非常昂贵。

9.4.8 Developing a Media Schedule 制订媒体计划

Next step of media planning comes with a media schedule. Media schedule refers to the pattern of advertising timing. Usually marketers draw a chart indicating which media channels will be used for the advertising campaign, along with the projected run dates and the frequency of showing communication messages. There are factors to consider when comparing various types of advertising media. In marketing industry, these factors are usually presented as specific terminologies.

媒体计划的下一步是媒体时间表。媒体计划是指广告投放的时间安排模式。

通常情况下，市场营销人员会画一张图表，说明广告活动将使用哪些媒体渠道，以及预计的项目开展时间和传播信息的频率。在比较不同类型的广告媒体时，有一些因素需要考虑。在市场营销行业中，这些因素通常以特定术语的形式出现。

Advertising exposure, the degree to which the target audience will be exposed to a brand message from a specific medium, is often used to assess the different promotional tools in order to achieve advertising objectives. More specifically, the total number of households or persons exposed to an advertising schedule is called impressions. For example, a TV commercial that is aired one time during a program watched by 10 million people, then we can say it receives 10 million gross impressions. If the advertisement is displayed three times during the program, the gross impression count will be 30 million.

广告曝光率，即目标受众从特定媒介中获得品牌信息的程度，通常被用来评估不同的促销手段，以实现广告目标。更具体地说，接触广告时间表的家庭或个人的总数称为印象。例如，一个电视广告在一个有 1000 万观众的节目中播放了一次，那么我们可以说它获得了 1000 万的总印象。如果广告在节目中出现 3 次，总印象数为 3000 万。

Reach and frequency are terms generally used when planning advertising campaigns. Media planners use reach for it represents the total number of people exposed to the marketing communication. Reach is one of the most important terms in media planning and has three characteristics. First, reach is a percentage, although the percentage sign is rarely used. For example, if a media plan targets the roughly 5 million of women who are 20-25 years old, then a reach of 50 means that 50% or 2.5 million of the target audience will exposed to some of the media vehicles in the media plan. Second, reach measures the accumulation of audience over time. Reach may grow from 20 (20%) in the first week to 60 (60%) in the fourth week. Third, reach does not double-count people exposed multiple times if the media plan involves repeated ads in one media category or ads in multiple media categories.

到达率和频率是规划广告活动时通常使用的术语。媒体策划者使用"到达率"这个词，因为它表示接触到营销传播的总人数。到达率是媒体策划中最重要的术语之一，它有 3 个特点：首先，到达率是一个百分比，尽管百分比符号很少使用。例如，如果一个媒体计划针对大约 500 万名 20~25 岁的女性，那么到达率为 50 意味着 50%，即 250 万目标受众将接触到媒体计划中的部分媒体载体。其次，到达率衡量的是受众随时间的积累，它可能从第一周的 20（20%）增加到第四周的 60（60%）。最后，如果媒体计划涉及一个媒体类别的重复广告或多个媒体类别的广告，到达率不会重复计算多次曝光的人数。

Frequency is the number of times that the average household or person is exposed to the schedule among those persons reached in the specific period of time. Reach indicates the media dispersion while frequency shows the media repetition. Because it is an average number, dispersion of frequency will differ between specific schedules and daypart mixes.

广告频次是指平均每户或每个人在特定时间段内接触到该计划的次数。到达率表示介质分散，而广告频次表示介质重复。因为它是一个平均数字，广告频次的散布将根据特定的时间表和时段的不同而不同。

By multiplying reach times frequency, we get gross rating points (GRPs), which is a shorthand measure of the total amount of exposure used to compare the effectiveness of different media vehicles. For example, the 2014 World Cup received a frequency of 1.5, meaning that, on average, audience members of the World Cup game had one-and-a-half opportunities to watch the advertisement. If the reach was 58, the GRPs would be $58 \times 1.5 = 87$.

通过将到达率和广告频次相乘，我们得到了总收视点（GRPs），用来比较不同媒体载体有效性的总曝光量。例如，2014 年世界杯的广告频次为 1.5 次，这意味着，观看世界杯比赛的观众平均有 1.5 次机会观看广告。若到达率为 58，则 GRPs 为 $58 \times 1.5 = 87$。

The classic scheduling models are continuity, flighting, and pulsing. Continuity scheduling spreads media spending evenly across months. For example, with an annual budget of $1,200,000 a year, continuity scheduling would allocate exactly

$100,000 per month. This method ensures steady brand exposure over each purchase cycle for individual consumers. It also takes advantage of volume discounts in media buying. However, because continuity scheduling usually requires a large budget, it may not be practical for small advertisers.

传统的排期模型有持续型排期、起伏式排期和间隔式排期。持续型排期将媒体支出平均分配到每个月。例如，如果年度预算为每年 120 万美元，连续型排期每月将正好分配 10 万美元。这种方法确保了稳定地将品牌曝光给每个购买周期的个体消费者。它还可以利用媒体购买的批量折扣。然而，由于连续性排期通常需要较高的预算，它可能不适合小广告客户。

The flight scheduling approach alternates advertising across months, with heavy advertising in certain months and no advertising at all in other months. For example, a board game maker like Parker Brothers might concentrate its advertising in the fall when it knows that many people buy board games as gifts for the holidays. Or, with the same budget of $1,200,000, for example, a different brand could spend $200,000 per month during each of six months—January, March, May, July, September, and December—and spend nothing during the other months, in hopes that the impact of advertising in the previous month can last into the following month.

起伏式排期按月投放广告，在某些月份投放大量广告，而在其他月份完全不投放广告。例如，像帕克兄弟这样的桌游制造商可能会在秋天集中做广告，因为他们知道很多人会购买桌游作为假期礼物。同样年预算为 120 万美元，某品牌可以在以下 6 个月——1 月、3 月、5 月、7 月、9 月和 12 月，每月花 20 万美元，其余 6 个月份则不花一分钱，希望广告的影响在前一个月可以持续到下个月。

Pulse scheduling combines the first two scheduling methods, so that the brand maintains a low level of advertising across all months but spends more in selected months. For example, an airline like United Airlines might use a low level of continuous advertising to maintain brand awareness among business travelers. United Airlines might also have seasonal pulses to entice winter-weary consumers to fly to sunny climes. In budget allocation terms, a consumer goods brand may spend $5,000 in each of the twelve months to maintain the brand awareness and spend an additional $10,000 in January, March, May, July, September and December to attract brand switchers from competing brands. The pulse scheduling method takes advantage of both the continuity and flight scheduling methods and mitigates their weaknesses.

间隔式排期将以上两种方法结合在一起，因此该品牌在所有月份都保持较低的广告水平，但在选定的月份花费更多。例如，像联合航空公司，可能会使用低水平的持续性广告来保持其品牌知名度。而它也有季节性的波动，以吸引那些厌倦了冬天的旅行者，飞到阳光充足的地方。在预算分配方面，一个消费品品牌在 12 个月中，可能每个月花费 5000 美元来维持品牌知名度，而在 1 月、3 月、5 月、7 月、9 月和 12 月额外花费 10000 美元来吸引从竞争品牌转向本品牌的消费者。间隔式排期充分利用了持续型排期和起伏式排期的优点，弥补了它们的不足。

尼尔森 2019 发布的《全球媒体信任报告》（Global Trust in Media Report）显示，消费者信任朋友的可能性是信任品牌的两倍。调查发现，全球有 92% 的消费者信任口碑，口碑是最值得信任的媒介，其次是 70% 的网络评论。相比之下，人们对传统媒体广告的信任度较前几年有所下降

9.4.9　Evaluating the Campaign 评估活动

The evaluation should be taken before, during, or after the execution of the campaigns. As opposed to pre-testing, post-testing is carried out during and after running the campaign to monitor the market responses. Some popular metrics assessed in post testing include brand awareness, consumer attitudes, usage rate, sales performance, and product usage.

评估应在活动执行之前、期间或之后进行。与前测不同，后测是在活动期间和之后进行的，目的是监测市场反应。在事后测试中评估的一些流行指标包括品牌知名度、消费者态度、使用率、销售业绩和产品使用率。

Unaided recall and aided recall are common methods in evaluation of advertising results, to bring back information from consumers' memory. Unaided recall is a research technique to determine how well a consumer remembers an advertisement without any external help such as clues, or visuals. In unaided recall, a team of test audience is shown an advertisement and then quizzed about the brand. The effectiveness is gauged by the response that the tester gets from the respondents participating in the experiment. Usually, the questions asked in unaided recall are more open-ended. For example, the moderator may ask: "What brands of athletic shoes come to mind?" However, it should be noted that unaided recall is a relative term, since recall seldom happens spontaneously and some amount of cueing is necessary to conduct the research.

独立回忆和辅助回忆是评价广告效果的常用方法，从消费者的记忆中提取信息。独立回忆是一种研究技术，用于确定消费者在没有任何外部帮助（如线索或视觉效果）的情况下对广告的记忆程度。在独立回忆中，一组测试对象首先看到一则广告，然后被问及该品牌。通过测试人员从实验参与者那里得到的响应来衡量有效性。通常，在独立回忆中所问的问题都是开放式的。例如，主持人可能会问："你想到了什么牌子的运动鞋？"然而，需要注意的是，独立回忆是一个相对的概念，因为回忆很少是自发发生的，需要一定的暗示才能进行。

Aided recall is a research technique used to test audience memory retention of advertisements. The respondents are prompted by being shown a particular advertisement and then asked to remember their previous exposure to it. Verbal aids are also used to prompt recall. The moderator may ask questions like "Please look at these brands: A, B, C, and D. Which one do you use?" When conducting a survey, usually unaided recalls are asked before aided.

辅助回忆是一种用来测试观众对广告记忆程度的研究方法。被调查者会被提示看一个特定的广告，然后被要求回忆他们之前看过的广告。口头上的帮助也被用来刺激回忆。主持人可能会问这样的问题："请看看这些品牌：A、B、C和D。你用哪一种？"在进行调查时，通常先不提供帮助，要求（被调查者）回忆。

◎ **典藏推荐**

肯尼斯·E. 克洛，唐纳德·巴克 . 整合营销传播——广告、媒介与促销 [M]. 谭咏风，等译 . 上海：格致出版社，2014.

Bernd H. Schmitt. 体验营销 [M]. 刘银娜，高靖，梁丽娟，译 . 北京：清华大学出版社，2004.

唐·舒尔茨，海蒂·舒尔茨 . 整合营销传播：创造企业价值的五大关键步骤 [M]. 王茁，顾洁，译 . 北京：清华大学出版社，2013.

丹尼尔·罗尔斯 . 移动营销：移动互联网技术带给营销、销售和传播的巨变 [M]. 黄丽茹，屈云波，译 . 北京：企业管理出版社，2015.

特雷西·L. 塔腾，迈克尔·R. 所罗门 . 北京大学新媒体研究院社会化媒体研究中心 . 社交媒体营销 [M]. 上海：格致出版社，2017.

10

Placement Strategy

渠道策略

知识解锁 Knowledge Unlocked

以下问题的答案，可在本章寻找：

1. 价值链和供应链是什么？渠道起着什么样的作用？

2. 有哪些不同类型的中间商？

3. 如何选择不同的营销传播渠道？

4. 物流业能为我们做什么？

In the previous chapters, we have learnt how to understand consumers' value, create the value proposition, communicate the value proposition by advertising. Now we move on to the last part of the marketing mix—to put the products or services in the right place where consumers have easy access, in another word, to deliver the value proposition. One of the most common reasons for the failure of a business, no matter large or small, is its inability to deliver to customers in the physical distribution stage. The delivery of superior value—through higher benefits, lower prices, or some combination of the two—lies at the heart of any winning business strategy.

在前几章中，我们学习了如何理解消费者的价值，如何创造价值主张，如何通过广告来传达价值主张。现在我们进入营销组合的最后一部分——把产品或服务放在消费者容易获得的地方，换句话说，传递价值主张。一家企业，无论大小，失败最常见的原因之一是它无法在分销阶段把产品有效地交付给客户。通过更高的收益、更低的价格或两者结合来提供更高的价值，是任何成功商业战略的核心。

10.1 Distribution of the Product 产品的分销

10.1.1 The Value Chain 价值链

A complete process of business running involves receiving raw materials, adding value to the raw materials through various activities to create a finished product, and selling that end product to customers. This can be demonstrated by a value chain, a series of interrelated activities through which a company convert inputs into outputs. Organizations use value chain analysis to remove waste, identify efficiencies, and spot activities which can provide competitive advantage.

完整的公司运营过程包括接收原材料，通过各种活动为原材料增值来创造出成品，然后将成品卖给顾客。这可以通过价值链反映出来。价值链是一系列相互关联的活动，公司通过这些活动将投入转化为产出。组织使用价值链分析来消除浪费，识别效率和发现可以提供竞争优势的活动。

A value chain consists of five primary activities, they are: inbound raw materials, production, distribution of finished products, marketing, and customer service. Each link in a value chain consists of a bundle of value activities, and these bundles are performed by a firm to "design, produce, market, deliver, and support its product".

价值链由 5 个主要活动组成，它们是：供应原材料、生产、成品分销、市场营销和售后服务。价值链中的每一个环节都包含一组价值活动，这些活动由公司执行，以"设计、生产、营销、交付和支持其产品"。

The first activity in the value chain is inbound raw materials, which includes all receiving, warehousing, and inventory management of raw materials ready for production. The second activity is production which encompasses all efforts needed to convert raw materials into a finished product or service. Distribution of finished products is the third activity and occurs after all operations are completed and the end product is ready for the customer. Marketing is the fourth part of the value chain and include all strategies used to get potential customers to purchase a product, such as channel selection, advertising, and pricing. Service is the fifth and final step that describes all activities that create better consumer experiences. Companies have similar value chains but how they add value to each link is the key of making great differences among competition.

价值链的第一项活动是供应原材料，包括所有准备生产的原材料的接收、仓储和库存管理。第二项活动是生产，包括将原材料转化为成品或服务所需的一切努力。成品分销是第三项活动，发生在所有操作完成，最终产品为客户准备好之后。市场营销是价值链的第四部分，包括所有用来吸引潜在客户购买产品的策略，如渠道选择、广告和定价。售后服务是第五步，也是最后一步，它描述了创造更好的消费者体验的所有活动。企业拥有相似的价值链，但如何为每个环节增值是在竞争中产生巨大差异的关键。

10.1.2 The Supply Chain 供应链

While the value chain focuses on creating or adding value to the product, the supply chain is the integration of all the external activities involve the transformation of natural resources, raw materials, and components into a finished product that is delivered to the end customer. The concept of supply chain management (SCM) was developed to express the need to integrate the key business processes, from end user through original suppliers, in order to maximize total profitability. The organizations that make up the supply chain are linked together through physical flows and information flows. The objectives of supply chain management is to minimize total system cost, improve quality, optimize transportation and logistics, satisfy customer service requirements, and face global competition. By forming strong trusting supply chain relationships and working toward best practices in distribution, companies aim for long-term stability.

价值链专注于为产品创造或增加价值，而供应链是所有外部活动的集成，包括自然资源、原材料和组件转换为成品，并交付给最终客户。供应链管理概念的提出是为了整合关键业务流程，满足从最终用户到原始供应商的需求，以使总利润率最大化。供应链中的组织通过物理流和信息流联系在一起。供应链管理的目标是最小化系统总成本，提高质量，优化运输和物流，满足客户服务要求，以面对全球竞争。通过建立强有力的相互信任的供应链关系和在分销方面的最佳实践，实现长期稳定的目标。

10.2　Types of Distribution Channels 分销渠道的类型

Channel of distribution provides a narrower focus within the supply chain. It is the physical flow where companies move products from the producer to the end customers. Due to that a channel partner works in collaboration with an organization in a way that assists the sale, distribution, storage, and production process, maintaining a strong relationship with various channel partners within the industries can be a central concern of a marketer's responsibilities.

分销渠道是供应链中更具体的概念。它是公司将产品从生产者转移到最终消费者的实体流程。由于渠道合作伙伴以协助销售、分销、存储和生产过程的方式相互协作，因此与行业内的各种渠道合作伙伴保持紧密的关系可能是营销人员职责的核心关注点。

10.2.1　Levels of Distribution Channels 分销渠道层次

Businesses need the help of marketing intermediaries, like wholesalers, and retailers, to make their products reach to the ultimate consumers. These intermediaries serve as channels. With the different number of intermediaries involved, there are basically four levels of distribution. They exist for both consumer goods and industrial goods.

企业需要营销中介的帮助，比如批发商和零售商，使他们的产品到达最终消费者手中。这些中间人充当了渠道的功能。由于涉及的中介数量不同，基本上有 4 个级别的渠道，同时适用于消费品和工业产品。

（1）Zero-level channel: Distribution happens directly from manufacturer to end consumer. This might mean door to door sales, direct mails or telemarketing. One example is a factory outlet store selling clothes directly to its customers.

零级渠道：分销直接从制造商到终端消费者。这可能意味着门到门销售、直接邮件或电话营销。比如工厂直销店直接卖衣服给顾客。

（2）One-level channel: Distribution happens with a single agent in between, usually from manufacturer to retailer, then to end consumers. For example, a vegetable farmer sells carrot and lettuce to a vegetable market, who sells to individual customers.

一级渠道：分销过程中只有一个代理人，通常是从制造商到零售商，再到最终消费者。例如，一个菜农向菜市场出售胡萝卜和生菜，菜市场又向个人顾客出售。

（3）Two-Level channel: Distribution happens with two business entities in between. For example, goods flowing from manufacturer to wholesaler and retailer to end consumers. A poultry farmer sells chicken and eggs to a restaurant supplier, who sells to restaurants, who then serve the customers.

二级渠道：分销发生在两个业务实体之间。例如，商品从制造商流向批发商和零售商，再流向最终消费者。家禽养殖户将鸡和蛋卖给餐厅供应商，餐厅供应商再将鸡和蛋卖给餐厅，餐厅再为顾客服务。

（4）Three-level channel: Distribution happens with three business entities in between. For example, goods flowing from manufacturer to a distributor on top of a dealer and a retailer, before it goes to end consumers. Ice cream makers transport the ice creams to local distributors who have refrigerated cold rooms. The distributors then transport to local dealers who will have less and small freezers, and then to the retailer who will have only one or two freezers. Finally, the customers buy the ice creams from the supermarkets or convenient stores.

三级渠道：发生在 3 个经营主体之间的分销。例如，商品从制造商流向位于经销商和零售商之上的分销商，然后流向最终消费者。冰激凌制造商将冰激凌运送到当地经销商那里，由他们放入冷藏室。然后，分销商将产品运送给本地的经销商，而这些经销商拥有更少且更小的冰柜，然后再将产品运送给零售商，而零售商只有一两个冰柜。最后，顾客从超市或便利店购买冰激凌。

10.2.2　Direct and Indirect Channels 直接及间接渠道

Direct distribution takes place when the product or service leaves the producer and goes directly to the customer with no middlemen involved. This occurs, more often than not, with the sale of services. For example, both the car wash and the barber utilize direct distribution because the customer receives the service directly from the producer. This can also occur with organizations that sell tangible goods, such as the jewelry manufacturer who sells its products directly to the consumer.

直接分销是指产品或服务离开生产者，直接进入消费者手中，而不涉及任何中间商。这种情况经常发生在服务类产品的销售中。例如，洗车和理发都采用直接分销，因为顾客直接从生产者那里得到服务。这也可能发生在销售有形商品的公司中，比如直接向消费者销售产品的珠宝制造商。

消费者购买戴尔产品，可以从戴尔的官网直接订货

Indirect distribution occurs when there are intermediaries within the distribution channel. In the wood example, the intermediaries would be the lumber manufacturer, the furniture maker, and the retailer. The larger the number of intermediaries within the channel, the higher the price is likely to be for the final customer. This is because of the value adding that occurs at each step within the structure.

当分销渠道中存在中间商时，就会出现间接分销。在木材的例子中，中间商是木材制造商、家具制造商和零售商。渠道内的中介数量越多，最终客户的价格可能就越高。这是因为价值在供应链中的每一个步骤都会增加。

10.2.3　Consumer Channels 消费品分销渠道

Manufacturers may reach out to consumers either directly, that is, without using distribution channels, or by using one or more distribution channel members.

制造商可以直接接触消费者，也就是说，不使用分销渠道，或不使用一个或多个分销渠道成员。

Manufacturer to consumer: This is the simplest channel, direct marketing. Some manufacturers sell directly to consumers for it can provide the lowest possible prices. Fresh food is more welcome when bought directly from farmers, rather than in the supermarkets. In this way, manufacturers can have better control over the product quality and sales conditions. Avon cosmetics and Amazon.com are examples of companies engaged primarily in direct marketing.

制造商—消费者：这是最简单的渠道，即直接营销。一些制造商直接向消费者销售，因为它可以提供尽可能低的价格。直接从农民手中购买的新鲜食品比从超市购买的更受欢迎。这样制造商就可以更好地控制产品的质量和销售情况。例如，雅芳化妆品公司和亚马逊网站是主要从事直销的公司。

Manufacturer to retailer to consumer: For most of the products, consumers are more familiar with the retailers than the manufacturers. Supermarket chains and corporate retailers exercise considerable power over manufacturers because of their enormous buying capabilities. Wal-Mart uses its enormous retail sales to pressurize manufacturers to supply products at frequent intervals directly to their store at concessional prices.

制造商—零售商—消费者：对于大多数产品，相比制造商，消费者对零售商更熟悉。连锁超市和企业零售商在制造商那里拥有相当大的权力，因为其拥有巨大的购买能力。沃尔玛利用其庞大的零售销售额向制造商施加压力，要求它们以优惠价格，每隔一段时间就直接向其门店供应产品。

Manufacturer to wholesaler to retailer to consumer: For small retailers with limited order quantities, the use of wholesalers makes economic sense. Wholesalers buy in bulk from producers and sell smaller quantities to numerous retailers. But large retailers in some markets have the power to buy directly from manufacturers and to provide favorable prices, thus cut out the wholesalers. Wholesalers dominate where retail oligopolies or monopolies are not dominant.

制造商—批发商—零售商—消费者：对于订单数量有限的小型零售商，利用批发商更具有经济效益。批发商从生产商那里大批量采购，然后少量出售给许多零售商。但是，一些市场上的大型零售商有直接从制造商那里购买产品并提供优惠价格的权力，这样就把批发商排除在外了。在零售寡头或垄断企业不占主导地位的地方，批发商占主导地位。

Manufacturer to agent to wholesaler to retailer to consumers: A company uses this channel when it enters new markets. It does not have enough sales to warrant the setting up of a sales and distribution infrastructure, and therefore, it delegates the task of selling its products to an agent who does not take title to the goods. Companies want to sell to larger number of customers, and hence are increasingly using multiple channels to distribute their products.

制造商—代理商—批发商—零售商—消费者：公司会在进入新市场时使用这种渠道。它没有足够的销售额来保证一个销售和分销基础设施的建设。因此，它把销售其产品的任务委托给一个不具备所有权的代理人。公司想要销售给更多的客户，因此越来越多地使用多种渠道来分销他们的产品。

10.2.4　Industrial Channels 工业品分销渠道

In the distribution of industrial goods, there are fewer middlemen and shorter channel of distribution. Direct selling is prevalent due to closer relationship between the manufacturer and the customer, as well as due to the nature of the product sold.

在工业产品的分销过程中，中间商更少，分销链更短。由于制造商和客户之间关系更加密切，以及销售的产品性质，在工业品分销中，直销更为盛行。

Manufacturer to industrial customers: This is a common channel for expensive industrial products like heavy equipments and machines. The seller has to participate in many activities like installation, commissioning, quality controls and maintenance jointly with the buyer. The seller is responsible for many aspects of the operations of the product long after the product is sold. The nature of the product requires a continuing relationship between the seller and the buyer. The large size of the order makes direct selling and distribution economical.

制造商—工业客户：这是常见的昂贵的工业产品（如重型设备和机器）的销售渠道。卖方与买方共同参与安装、调试、质量控制和维护等工作。卖方负责产品销售后很长一段时间内产品的多方面的维护。工业产品的性质要求买卖双方保持持续的关系。大量的订单使直销和分销变得经济实惠。

Manufacturer to agent to industrial customers: A company that sells industrial products can employ the services of an agent who may sell a range of products from several producers on a commission basis. It helps companies who do not have the resources to set up their own sales and distribution operation. The arrangement allows the seller to reach a large number of customers without having to invest in a sales team. But the company does not have much control over the agent, who does not devote the same amount of time and attention as a company's dedicated sales team.

制造商—代理商—工业客户：销售工业产品的公司可以使用代理商的服务，代理商根据佣金制销售来自多个生产商的系列产品。这种方式能帮助那些没有资源的公司建立自己的销售和分销业务。卖方不必投资建设一个销售团队，就能接触到大量客户。但是公司对代理商并没有太多的控制权，因为代理商们没有像公司的销售团队那样投入那么多的时间和精力。

Manufacturer to distributors to industrial customers: For less expensive, more frequently purchased products, distributors are used. The company has both internal and field sales staff. They find new customers, get product specifications, distribute catalogues, and gather market information. They also visit distributors to address their problems and keep them motivated to sell the products. Distributors enable customers to buy small quantities locally.

制造商—经销商—工业客户：对于较便宜、较频繁购买的产品，公司一般采用经销商模式。公司既有内部销售人员，也有现场销售人员。他们寻找新客户，获取产品规格，分发产品目录，收集市场信息。他们也会拜访经销商，解决他们的问题，并激励他们销售产品。分销商使顾客能够在当地实现少量购买。

Manufacturer to agent to distributors to industrial customers: The manufacturer employs an agent rather than a dedicated sales force to serve distributors mainly because it is less expensive to do so. The agent may sell the goods of several suppliers to an industrial distributor, who further sells it to the business user. This type of channel may be required when business customers require goods rapidly, and when an industrial distributor can provide storage facilities.

制造商—代理商—分销商—工业客户：制造商雇用代理商而不是专门的销售团队来为分销商服务，主要是因为这样做成本更低。代理可以将多个供应商的货物销售给一个工业分销商，后者再将其销售给公司用户。当公司客户急需货物时，或当工业分销商可以提供存储设施时，可能需要这种类型的通道。

10.3　Functions of Distribution Channels 分销渠道的功能

If selling from the manufacturer to the consumer were always the most efficient way, there would be no need for channels of distribution. Intermediaries, however, provide several benefits to both manufacturers and consumers: improved contact efficiency through bulk-breaking, a better assortment of products, transportation and storage of goods, facilitating transactions, and easier communication with customers.

如果从制造商到消费者的销售总是最有效的方式，那么就不需要分销渠道了。然而，中介对制造商和消费者来说都有好处：通过分件提高了接触效率，能更好地对产品进行分类，运输和存储货物，促进交易，更容易地与客户沟通。

亚马逊货位系统的特点：（1）检货区与存货区分离；（2）货位与库存数量绑定

A manufacturer only works with its channel partners, who respectively deal with a large number of customers. The improved contact efficiency that results from adding intermediaries in the channels of distribution can be illustrated by the following example. Supposing there are 5 different manufacturers and 20 retailers. If each manufacturer sells directly to each retailer, there are 100 contact lines. The complexity of this distribution arrangement and the number of required transactions can be reduced by adding wholesalers as intermediaries between manufacturers and retailers. If a single wholesaler serves as the intermediary, the number of contacts is reduced from 100 to 25—5 contact lines between the manufacturers and the wholesaler, and 20 contact lines between the wholesaler and the retailers. Reducing the number of necessary contacts brings more efficiency into the distribution system by eliminating duplicate efforts in ordering, processing, shipping, etc.

制造商只与渠道合作伙伴合作，渠道合作伙伴各自处理大量的客户。通过以下示例可以说明在分销渠道中添加中间商所带来的接触效率的提高。假设有5个不同的制造商和20个零售商。如果每个制造商直接向每个零售商销售，则有100条接触线。通过增加批发商作为制造商和零售商之间的中间人，可以减少这种分销安排的复杂性和所需的交易数量。如果由一个批发商作为中介，那么联系线路就从 100 条减少到 25——其中，制造商和批发商之间有 5 条联系线，批发商和零售商之间有 20 条联系线。减少一定的联系数量可以减少订购、加工、运输等方面的重复工作，从而提高分配系统的效率。

10.3.1　Bulk-breaking and Creating Assortments 分件和创建分类

Manufacturers typically produce many similar products, while consumers want small quantities of many different products. In order to smooth the flow of goods and services, there are two functions that intermediaries can perform. First, retailers buy in bulk quantities from the manufacturer or wholesaler, and resell in smaller quantities to their customers. This phenomenon is known as bulk breaking. Second, channel intermediaries bring together items from a number of different manufacturers to provide wider selection for their customers, so that customers can conveniently buy different items from one retailer at one time. This is known as creating assortments.

制造商通常生产许多相似的产品，而消费者需要少量的各类产品。为了使商品和服务的流动更加顺畅，中间商可以完成两项功能。首先，零售商从制造商或批发商那里大批量购买，然后再少量转售给他们的客户。这种现象被称为分件。其次，渠道中间商将许多不同制造商的产品组合在一起，为客户提供更广泛的选择，使客户可以方便地同时从一个零售商那里购买不同的产品。这就是所谓的创建分类。

10.3.2　Transportation and Storage of Goods 货物的运输和储存

The transportation and storage of goods is another function that distribution channel performs. As wholesalers buy goods in bulk quantity, they help producers and retailers minimize transportation cost. Wholesalers and retailers create place utility of goods by transporting them from production point to places where customers can reach, with fast speed and skills. They also provide inventory service until the product is needed.

货物的运输和储存是分销渠道的另一个功能。由于批发商大量购买货物，他们能帮助生产商和零售商将运输成本降到最低。批发商和零售商将货物从生产地运送到顾客容易获取的地方，通过快速和技术手段创造地点效用。他们还提供库存服务，直到产品被提走。

亚马逊 FBA（Fulfillment by Amazon），指卖家把自己在亚马逊上销售的产品库存直接送到亚马逊当地市场的仓库中，客户下订单，就有亚马逊系统自动完成后续的发货

10.3.3　Facilitating Functions 提供便利功能

Channel members provide a range of facilitating functions that support sales of the products for both manufacturers and consumers, including post-purchase service and maintenance, financing, information dissemination, and channel coordination. They use their sales force to deal with customers, negotiate sales and provide customer service. The sales force also gathers market intelligence, which can help to market products more effectively. In some cases, channel members may provide credit and other forms of financing to make it easier for customers to buy.

渠道商提供一系列便利功能，为制造商和消费者提供产品销售支持，包括售后服务和维护、金融服务、信息传播和渠道协调。他们利用自己的销售团队与客户打交道，对销售额进行谈判，提供客户服务。销售人员还收集市场情报，以便更有效地推销产品。在某些情况下，渠道商可以提供信贷和其他形式的融资，使客户更容易购买。

10.3.4   Communication and Transaction Functions 通信及交易功能

Intermediaries can help reduce the cost of distribution by making transactions routine. Exchange relationships can be standardized in terms of lot size, frequency of delivery and payment, and communications. Sellers and buyers no longer have to bargain over every transaction. As transactions become more routine, the costs associated with those transactions are reduced.

中间商可以通过使交易常规化来帮助降低分销成本。交换关系可以根据批量规模、交付和支付的频率及通信进行标准化。买卖双方不再需要在每笔交易上讨价还价。随着事务变得更加常规，与这些事务相关的成本也降低了。

10.4   Role of the Internet in Distribution 互联网在分销中的作用

The Internet is an important new channel for commerce in a wide range of industries. It is changing distribution channels as never before. Thirty years ago, a retail store without a physical storefront was all but unheard of. But today, you can buy almost anything from the Internet by visiting online shopping websites. From tangible goods like food, clothing, airline tickets, to intangibles such as music, top up cards, the Internet makes possible the direct provision of products and services from producers to customers. Online businesses benefit from selling more products without the cost of a physical storefront, which is especially attractive for start-ups who want to keep operating costs low. As a result, many traditional intermediaries will die out, while new channels and intermediaries will take their place.

互联网在许多领域都是重要的贸易新渠道。它正在以前所未有的方式改变分销渠道。30 年前，没有实体店面的零售商店几乎是闻所未闻的。但是今天，你几乎可以通过访问在线购物网站购买任何东西。从食品、服装、机票等有形商品，到音乐、充值卡等无形资产，互联网使生产者直接向消费者提供产品和服务成为可能。在线业务可以在不需要实体店面的情况下销售更多产品，这对希望降低运营成本的初创企业尤其有吸引力。因此，许多传统的中介机构将会消亡，而新的渠道和中介机构将会取而代之。

The removal of intermediaries in economics from a supply chain is called disintermediation. Disintermediation may decrease the total cost of servicing customers in regards of rental space, employment, store decoration, etc., thus allowing the manufacturer to increase profit margins and reduce prices. In some cases, however, companies find themselves fail to perform many tasks economically, whereas intermediaries such as distributors have better facilities, specialized competencies, and have the relevant scale to do a more efficient job on many value-added activities.

在经济学中，将中介机构从供应链中移除，称为"去中介化"。去中介化可能会降低服务客户的总成本，包括出租空间、雇佣、店面装修等，从而使制造商能够提高利润率，降低价格。然而，在某些情况下，公司发现自己无法在经济上完成许多任务，而分销商等中介机构拥有更好的设施和专业能力，并具有相应的规模，可以在许多增值活动中更有效地开展工作。

Many companies use the Internet to implement knowledge management in managing the supply chain. Knowledge management (KM) is a multidisciplinary approach of creating, sharing, using, and managing the knowledge and information of an organization. Real-time data and technological devices improve the effectiveness of knowledge management.

许多公司利用互联网来实施知识管理来管理供应链。知识管理是创建、共享、使用和管理组织的知识和信息的多学科方法。实时数据和技术设备提高了知识管理的有效性。

10.5 Types of Channel Intermediaries 渠道中介

Wholesaling intermediaries are businesses that distribute products or services from producers to retail intermediaries, who then sell the products to individual consumers. Some wholesale intermediaries are independent, while others are attached to manufacturers and retailers.

批发中间商是将产品或服务从生产商分销给零售中间商的企业，零售中间商再将产品销售给个人消费者。一些批发中间商是独立的，而另一些则依附于制造商和零售商。

10.5.1　Independent Intermediaries 独立的中介机构

Many wholesaling intermediaries are independently owned. Independent intermediaries are channel intermediaries who do business with many different manufacturers and customers without being controlled or owned by any manufacturer. These firms are divided into two major categories: merchant wholesalers and agents or brokers.

许多批发中间商是独立所有的。独立中间商是渠道中间商，他们与许多不同的制造商和客户做生意，而不由任何制造商的控制或拥有。这些公司分为两大类：批发商、代理商或经纪人。

1. Merchant Wholesalers 独立批发商

Merchant wholesalers are the first of two basic types of wholesalers within the industry. These wholesalers are the ones who buy directly from the manufacturer, store the product and then sell it to retailers or business customers for a profit. They carry all sorts of different items of different types. However, they do not have specialized knowledge about the types of products you like or they cannot be expected to make recommendations on what your customers will want most. With a merchant wholesaler, much of the research job is left to the retailers.

独立批发商是行业内两种基本批发商中的第一种。这些批发商直接从制造商那里购买、储存产品，然后卖给零售商或公司客户以获取利润。他们有各种不同类型的商品。然而，他们不了解你喜欢的产品的相关专业知识，也不能期望他们给客户最想要的产品提出建议。独立批发商把大部分的调研工作都留给了零售商。

Merchant wholesalers take title to the goods. In other words, they have the legal ownership of the goods. Therefore, they have the right to set prices and develop their own strategies. But if there is any loss between the buying and selling of the product, it must be borne by the merchant wholesaler.

独立批发商拥有货物的所有权。换句话说，他们合法拥有货物的所有权。因此，他们有权制定价格和发展自己的战略。但是，在产品购买和销售过程中如果有任何损失，都必须由该独立批发商承担。

2. Merchandise Agents or Brokers 商品代理或经纪人

The second type, merchandise agents or brokers, makes up the other major portion of the wholesale trade industry. Agents or brokers differ from merchant wholesalers in that they do not purchase or take ownership of the goods they buy and sell. Instead, the agent or broker will arrange for the sale of goods between the merchant wholesaler and the retailer and will generally earn the money by receiving commissions for the arrangement of the sale.

第二种类型是商品代理或经纪人，它也是批发贸易行业的主要类型。代理商或经纪人与独立批发商的不同之处在于，他们不购买或占有他们买卖的货物。取而代之的是，代理人或经纪人将安排批发商和零售商之间的货物销售，通常会通过销售安排来收取佣金。

食品经纪人，是帮助食品生产商或制造商推销其产品的人。他可以作为独立承包商或食品经纪公司工作。其客户通常包括零售店、独立批发商和连锁批发商

The manufacturers' agent, or manufacturers' representative, is an individual, sales agency or company that sells products on the manufacturer's behalf to wholesalers and retailers. Manufacturers' agents generally represent several different companies that offer compatible but not competing products to the same industry. This approach reduces the cost of sales by spreading the agent's costs over the different products that he or she represents. As a result, manufacturers' agents are viewed as a cost-effective alternative to full-time salaried sales forces.

制造商代理或制造商代表，是代表制造商向批发商和零售商销售产品的个人、销售代理或公司。制造商代理通常代理几个不同的公司，这些公司向同行业提供相互兼容但不存在竞争的产品。这种方法通过将代理商的成本分摊到他所代理的不同产品上来降低销售成本。因此，制造商代理被视为全职受薪销售队伍的具有成本效益的一个方法。

巴东国际贸易有限公司，代理进出口业务

Usually, a contract between the two parties is signed to define the rights to sell, the price of the products, and the territory of selling. They are not under the immediate supervision of the manufacturers that they sell for, so their relationship generally falls into client-customer pattern. Most part of the reward is consisted of a commission, which varies according to the market and the product type.

通常情况下，双方会签订合同来确定销售权、产品价格和销售地。他们不受所销售产品的制造商的直接监督，所以他们的关系通常是客户—顾客关系。

大部分的报酬由佣金组成，佣金多少根据市场和产品类型的不同而有所不同。

The sales agent, as a marketing intermediary, is an independent individual or company whose main function is to act as the primary selling arm of an importing or exporting company (principal), introducing its products to potential buyers in the external market, in exchange for a commission based on the value of the business deals arranged and paid to the principal. Sales agents do not take title to the products, yet they enjoy unlimited territories and the right of pricing, promotion and distribution of the products–usually a complete product line or one manufacturer's total output.

销售代理作为营销中介，是一个独立的个人或公司，其主要功能是作为进出口公司的主要销售部门（委托人），把自己的产品介绍给外部市场的潜在买家以换取佣金，该佣金根据安排并支付给委托人的商业交易的价值而得出。销售代理并不拥有产品的所有权，但他们享有无限的可销售区域和产品的定价、促销和分销权——通常是一个完整的产品线或一个制造商的总产出。

Commission agents purchase and sell items on behalf of a principal. Commission agents conduct business under their own names, which affords a measure of anonymity to their principals while allowing the agents a certain degree of autonomy. As experts in their field, commission agents can assist small businesses in making the most of their limited budgets. Usually, principals outline their material needs and a project's purchase budget, or the desired price of sale, along with a set of preferred conditions for a deal. The commission agent is responsible for meeting the ideal conditions requested by the principal, and must stay within the provided budget or the price of sale. As long as commission agents conform to these stipulations, they possess the freedom to act and make deals as they choose.

佣金代理商代表委托人买卖物品。佣金代理商以自己的名义开展业务，这给他们的委托人提供了一定程度的匿名性，同时也给代理人一定程度的自主权。作为该领域的专家，佣金代理商可以帮助小企业充分利用有限的预算。通常，委托人会列出他们的材料需求和项目的采购预算，或者期望的销售价格，以及一系列交易的优先条件。佣金代理商负责满足委托人所要求的理想条件，并且必须保持在所提供的预算或销售价格之内。只要佣金代理商符合这些规定，他们就有选择行动和交易的自由。

Merchandise broker is a negotiator between the buyer and the seller of goods. A merchandise broker is strictly a go-between, who puts the merchandise buyer and seller together for the purposes of a sale without taking possession of the goods. They are paid commissions or fees for negotiating sales of specific lots of goods once the deal is completed.

商品经纪人是买卖双方之间的谈判者。商品经纪人是严格意义上的中间人，他为了销售而把商品的买方和卖方撮合在一起，但不占有货物。一旦交易完成，他们就会因谈判特定批次商品的销售而获得佣金或费用。

10.5.2 Manufacturer-owned Intermediaries 制造商的营销经理

A manufacturer's marketing manager may decide to distribute goods directly through company-owned facilities to realize complete control over distribution and customer service.

制造商的营销经理可以决定通过公司拥有的设施直接配送货物，以实现对配送和客户服务的完全控制。

Sales branches stock the products they distribute and fill orders from their inventories. They also provide offices for sales representatives. Sales branches are common in the chemical, petroleum products, motor vehicle, and machine and equipment industries.

销售分支机构储存他们要分销的产品，并从他们的库存中提货。他们还为销售代表提供办公室。销售分支机构普遍存在于化工、石油产品、汽车、机械设备等行业。

A sales office is an office for a producer's salespeople. Manufacturers set up sales offices in various regions to support local selling efforts and improve customer services. Some kitchen and bath fixture manufacturers maintain showrooms to display their products. Builders and decorators can visit these showrooms to see how the items would look in place. However, unlike sales branches, sales offices do not store any inventory. When a customer orders from a showroom or other sales office, the merchandise is delivered from a separate warehouse.

销售办公室是产品销售人员的办公室。制造商在各地设立销售办事处,以支持当地的销售工作,改善客户服务。一些厨房和浴室设备制造商保留展厅来展示他们的产品。建造者和装修人员可以参观这些展厅,看看这些物品摆起来会是什么样子。然而,与销售分支机构不同的是,销售办公室没有任何产品库存。当客户从陈列室或其他销售办公室订购商品时,商品从一个另外的仓库交付。

Manufacturers' showrooms are owned or leased by the manufacturer where customers can pay a visit to the products on display. Fully-equipped showrooms give customers the chance to touch and feel, and make the properties of products as straightforward as possible. Once customers get to the showroom, they feel more in command of the buying process. Usually, a company sets its showrooms in a merchandise mart where competing brands in the industry are concentrated, and trade shows are held on a regular basis. Other times, a company builds its own permanent showrooms for visitors to come. Retailers can make business-to-business purchases from these showrooms.

制造商的展厅由制造商拥有或租用,在那里顾客可以参观展出的产品。设备齐全的展厅让顾客有机会触摸和感受,并尽可能简单明了地知晓产品的性能。一旦顾客来到展厅,他们就会对购买过程有更多的掌控感。通常,一个公司会把它的展厅设在一个商品市场上,那里集中了行业内的竞争品牌,并且定期举行贸易展览会。其他时候,公司会建立自己的永久性展厅,供游客参观。零售商可以在这些展厅进行企业对企业的采购。

10.6 Planning a Channel Strategy 规划渠道策略

A distribution channel strategy enables a firm to sell to customers in geographical areas or market sectors that its direct sales team cannot reach. To ensure that distributors operate effectively on the manufacturer's behalf, the strategy is better to incorporate the right steps of control and support.

分销渠道策略使公司能够向其直销团队无法到达的地理区域或市场部门的客户销售产品。为了确保经销商有效地代表制造商运作，该策略应按照正确的管理步骤执行，并获得各方支持。

10.6.1 Developing Distribution Objectives 制定分销目标

The channels of distribution are designed to achieve objectives such as: (1) to make available the product to the consumer who wants to buy it; (2) to meet customers' service requirement and create differentiation over competitors; (3) to get strong promotional support from the channel member for the firm's product, including the use of local media, in-store displays, and cooperation in special promotion events; (4) to get feedback with regard to sales trends, inventory levels, competitors' moves and customers' reactions from intermediaries; (5) trade off cost against speed of delivery and intensity to be cost-effective; (6) to make it flexible to switch channel structures or add new types of middlemen without generating costly economic or legal conflicts with existing channel members. In a word, the overall objective of a distribution plan is to make products available to the place, at the time, in the quantity and at the lowest price that customers are satisfied with.

分销渠道的设计是为了实现以下目标：（1）向想要购买产品的消费者提供该产品；（2）满足客户的服务需求，创造与竞争对手的差异化；（3）获得渠道成员对公司产品的大力推广支持，包括使用当地媒体、店内展示、配合特别推广活动；（4）从中间商那里获得关于销售趋势、库存水平、竞争对手动向和客户反应等反馈；（5）在成本与交付速度和强度之间进行权衡，以达到成本效益；（6）灵活转换渠道结构或增加新型中间商，避免与现有渠道成员产生重大经济损失或法律冲突。总而言之，分销计划的总体目标是使产品在当地、在同一时间、以顾客满意的最低价格提供给他们。

10.6.2 Evaluateing Internal and External Environmental Influences 评估内部和外部环境的影响

Every channel is influenced by environmental forces or variables such as types of intermediaries, channel member preferences, firm marketing efforts, channel attributes, channel integration, economic, political and legal factors, technological changes, and international macro influences. Due to the dynamic nature of these factors, companies must frequently evaluate and monitor the performance of their distribution channels. Rapidly changing environments are forcing distribution firms to seek more creative and flexible means for meeting competition. Many producing companies have responded to these challenges by building collaborative relationships with the distribution firms.

每个渠道都受到环境因素或变量的影响，如中介机构类型、渠道成员偏好、企业营销努力、渠道属性、渠道整合、经济、政治、法律因素、技术变革、国际宏观影响等。由于这些因素的不确定性，公司必须经常评估和监控其分销渠道的性能。快速变化的环境迫使分销公司寻求更有创造性和更灵活的方式来应对竞争。许多生产企业通过与分销公司建立合作关系来应对这些挑战。

10.6.3　Choose a Distribution Strategy 选择分销策略

Distribution strategy is a plan to make a product or a service available to the target customers through its supply chain. Distribution strategy designs the entire approach for availability of the offering starting taking inputs from what the company communicated in marketing campaigns to what target audience is to be served.

分销战略是指通过供应链将产品或服务提供给目标客户的计划。分销策略设计了整个产品的可用性的整个方法，从公司在营销活动中传播信息开始，到弄清楚目标受众的特点。

1. Distribution Marketing Systems 分销营销系统

A conventional distribution system is a multiple-level distribution channel that is the most commonly seen. It comprises of a producer, a wholesaler, and a retailer, all acting under independent ownership. Each member is a separated business seeking to maximize its own profits, even at the expense of profits for the network as a whole. No channel members have much control over the other members, and no formal means exist for assigning roles and resolving channel conflict. Although most conventional channels are successful, coordination between these three parties is the major challenge for such a system, especially during the economic downturn. Fail to reach a desired revenue level would end the cooperation of the wholesalers, retailers, and distributors. Due to this, companies are now going towards developing integrated channels which may be horizontal or vertical.

传统的分销系统是最常见的多级分销渠道。它由生产商、批发商和零售商组成，均在独立所有权下运作。每个成员都是独立的企业，寻求各自的利润最大化，即使是以牺牲整个网络的利润为代价。供应链成员对其他成员没有太多的控制，也没有分配角色和解决渠道冲突的正式方法。虽然大多数传统渠道是成功的，但三方之间如何合作是这个系统所面临的主要挑战，特别是在经济低迷时期。如果不能达到预期的收入水平，批发商、零售商和分销商之间的合作就会终止。正因为如此，公司现在正在发展综合渠道，可能是横向的，也可能是纵向的。

A horizontal marketing system is the merger of two or more unrelated companies who have come together for a common purpose to exploit the market opportunities. Generally, this type of marketing system is followed by companies who lack in capital, human resources, production techniques, marketing programs, and are afraid of incurring the huge losses. In order to overcome these limitations, the companies join hands with other companies who are big in size either in the form of joint venture—that can be temporary or permanent, or mergers to sustain in the business. Horizontal marketing system has gained popularity in the recent times due to an immense competition in the market where everybody is striving to gain a good position in the market along with huge profits. For example, a bank and a hospital agree to have the bank's ATMs located at the hospital's locations, two companies combining to achieve economies of scale. Two giants, Nike and Apple, have entered into a partnership, with the intent to have a Nike+ footwear in which the iPod can be connected with these shoes that will play music along with the display of information about time, distance covered, calories burned, and heart pace on the screen.

横向营销系统是指两个或两个以上不相关的公司为了一个共同的目的而合作，以利用市场机会。一般来说，这种类型的营销系统是由那些缺乏资金、人力资源、生产技术、营销方案和害怕招致巨大损失的公司所采用的。为了克服这些限制，这些公司与其他规模较大的公司联合起来，这些公司可以是临时的，也可以是长期的，或者是通过合并来维持业务。近年来，由于市场竞争激烈，每个人都想在利润丰厚的市场中占有一席之地，所以横向营销体系得到了普及。例如，一家银行和一家医院同意将银行的自动取款机设在医院所在地，两家公司联合以实现规模经济。两大巨头耐克和苹果已经达成合作，推出了一款耐克＋的鞋子，iPod 可以与这些鞋子连接，播放音乐，并在屏幕上显示时间、路程、卡路里消耗和心率等信息。

A vertical marketing system (VMS) is a distribution channel structure in which producers, wholesalers, and retailers act as a unified network. Members in vertical marketing systems tend to recognize the symbiotic nature of the relationship between all channel members and aim to maximize benefits through cooperation. There are three types of vertical marketing systems: administered, contractual, and corporate.

垂直营销系统（VMS）是一种分销渠道结构，使生产者、批发商和零售商成为统一的网络。垂直营销系统的成员往往认识到所有渠道成员之间关系的共生性质，并通过合作实现利益最大化。垂直营销系统有三种类型：管理式、合同式和公司式。

Under administered VMS, there is no contract between the members of production and distribution channel but their activities are influenced by the size and power of any one of the member. In other words, any powerful and influential member of the channel dominate the activities of other channel members. For example, big brands like Wal-mart, Procter& Gamble, command a high level of cooperation from the retailers in terms of display, shelf space, pricing policies, and promotional schemes. Most smaller business cannot exert the necessary influence to run such a system but may find it necessary to deal with a wholesaler or producer that operates under such a system.

在管理式垂直营销系统下，生产和分销渠道的成员之间不存在合同，但是他们的活动受到成员中所有成员的规模和能力的影响。换句话说，任何有影响力的渠道成员都会主导其他渠道成员的活动。例如，像沃尔玛、宝洁这样的大品牌，在陈列、货架空间、定价政策和促销方案等方面都能获得零售商的高度配合。大多数小公司会发现有必要施加影响来运行这一系统，但却无能为力。

Under contractual VMS, the pieces of the distribution channel continue to operate as individual entities. The businesses enter into contractual relationships with other elements in the distribution channel with their respective obligations and benefits spelled out ahead of time. This approach allows all of the participants to leverage economies of scale that enable more competitive pricing. Variations on contractual vertical marketing systems exist, such as retail cooperatives that only deal with a wholesaler. For example, if 15 independently owned restaurants enter into an agreement with a produce wholesaler, the total costs go down for everyone thanks to bulk ordering and shipping.

在合同式垂直营销系统下，分销渠道的各个部分作为单独的实体继续运行。企业与分销渠道中的其他要素建立合同关系，并预先说明各自的责任和利益。这种方法允许所有的参与者利用规模经济来实现更有竞争力的定价。不同的合同垂直营销系统也存在，比如只与批发商打交道的零售合作社。例如，如果 15 家独立经营的餐厅与农产品批发商达成协议，由于批量订购和运输，所有餐厅的总成本都会下降。

麦当劳：采用多渠道合作的特许经营

A corporate VMS streamlines the process by bringing all of the elements of the distribution channel, from manufacturing to the stores, under the ownership of a single business. Firestone, for example, manufactures tires and owns the service centers that sell the tires to customers. The ownership of the distribution channel can happen from any point in the chain. A well-financed retail outlet might buy a wholesaler and production facilities, or a producer could purchase its main wholesaler and retail outlets.

公司式垂直营销系统简化了这个过程，它将分销渠道的所有元素（从制造到商店）都置于单个公司的所有权之下。例如，费尔斯通制造轮胎，并拥有向客户销售轮胎的服务中心。分销渠道的所有权可以产生于价值链中的任何节点。一个资金充足的零售门店可能会购买一个批发商和一些生产设施，一个生产商可能会购买它的主要批发商和零售门店。

塔吉特百货是美国仅次于沃尔玛的第二大零售百货集团，拥有全产业链

2. Channel Distribution Intensity 渠道分销强度

Intensive distribution strategy tries to sell their products in as many outlets as possible. Under the intensive distribution strategy, all the possible outlets can be used by a company to distribute the product. It creates brand awareness of the product as well as boosts sales. Intensive distribution strategies are often used for convenience offerings such as soda, snacks, household items, newspapers. Consumers can find them sold in all kinds of different places. Redbox, which rents DVDs out of vending machines, has made headway using a distribution strategy that is more intensive than Blockbuster's: The machines are located in fast-food restaurants, grocery stores, and other places people go frequently. The strategy has been so successful, Blockbuster has had to respond with its own line of vending machines, though it may be too little too late.

密集型分销渠道策略试图在尽可能多的网点销售他们的产品。在密集型分销策略下，公司利用所有可能的网点来分销产品。它创造了产品的品牌知名度，并促进了销售。密集型分销策略通常用于提供便利，如汽水、零食、家居用品、报纸等。消费者可以在各种不同的地方找到它们。从自动贩卖机中出租 DVD 的 Redbox 公司，利用这种比百视达公司更集约的分销策略取得了成功：这种机器安装在快餐店、杂货店和人们经常去的一些地方。这一策略非常成功，促使百视达不得不推出自己的自动售货机生产线，尽管可能为时已晚、收效甚微。

By contrast, selective distribution involves selling products at selective outlets in specific locations. Starbucks, Armani, Zara or any other such branded company will have selective distribution. Sony TVs can be purchased at a number of outlets such as Suning Appliance, GOME, or Wal-mart, but the same models are generally not sold at all the outlets. The lowest-priced Sony TVs are at Wal-mart, the better Sony models are more expensive and found in stores like Suning or specialty electronics stores. By selling different models with different features and price points at different outlets, a manufacturer can appeal to different target markets. For example, customers would not expect to find the highest-priced products in Walmart, they are looking for the lower-priced goods.

相比之下，选择性分销指的是在特定地点的特定销售点销售产品。星巴克、阿玛尼、Zara 等类似品牌都会有选择性的分销渠道。索尼电视可以在苏宁电器、国美或沃尔玛等多家门店售卖，但相同型号的电视通常不会在所有门店销售。价格最低的索尼电视在沃尔玛有售，质量更好的索尼电视更贵，在苏宁或特殊电子产品商店有售。通过在不同的销售地点销售具有不同功能和价位的不同型号的产品，制造商可以吸引不同的目标市场。例如，顾客不会期望在沃尔玛找到价格最高的商品，他们会寻找价格较低的商品。

Exclusive distribution sells products through one or very few outlets. Exclusive simply means limiting distribution to only one outlet in any area, and can be a strategic decision based on applying the scarcity principle to creating demand. For example, the popular TV show *Where Are We Going, Dad?* is exclusively owned by Mango TV. To control the image of their products and the prices at which they are sold, the makers of upscale products often prefer to distribute their products more exclusively. Distributing a product exclusively to a limited number of organizations under strict terms can help prevent a brand from deteriorating, or losing value. Retailers are teaming up with these brands in order to create a sense of quality based on scarcity, a sense of quality that will not only apply to the brand but also to the store. Exclusive distribution strategies work best for firms that focus on low volume, high margin sales.

独家经销通过一个或极少量的网点销售产品。独家仅仅意味着在任何地区只有一个分销渠道，并且可以是基于应用稀缺性原则来创造需求的战略决策。比如，很受欢迎的电视节目《爸爸去哪儿》由芒果电视独播。为了控制产品的形象和销售价格，高档产品的制造商往往更倾向于独家地销售其产品。在严格的条件下，将产品独家分销给有限数量的公司，可以帮助防止品牌恶化或失去价值。零售商与这些品牌合作，以创造一种稀缺性产生的质感，这种质感不仅适用于品牌，也适用于商店。独家分销策略最适合那些专注于低销量、高利润率的公司。

10.6.4 Developing Distribution Tactics 制定分销战术

The final step of distribution planning includes tactics that are used to implement the plan. Specifically, it relates to which channel partners to select and how to manage the channel.

分销计划的最后一步是用于实施计划的战术。具体来说，它与选择哪个渠道合作伙伴及如何管理渠道有关。

1. Selecting Channel Partners 选择渠道合作伙伴

Manufacturers rely on channel partners to deliver products and know-how to customers and help them control costs and risks. Channel partnerships can prove hugely beneficial for many businesses, boosting sales, creating new revenue streams, and opening a company up to a wealth of shared resources. However, before any business can access these benefits they must ensure that they choose their channel partner wisely. The right partnership can truly demonstrate the benefits of business collaboration, but the wrong one can leave a firm stuck with a business that is ill-suited to its needs and ambitions.

制造商依赖渠道合作伙伴向客户提供产品和技术，帮助他们控制成本和风险。渠道合作对很多企业来说都是非常有益的，可以促进销售，创造新的收入来源，并为公司打开资源共享的大门。然而，在任何企业能够获得这些好处之前，他们必须明智地选择他们的渠道合作伙伴。正确的伙伴关系可以真正展示出商业合作的好处，但错误的伙伴关系可能会让企业陷入无法满足其需求、无法实现抱负的境地。

In selecting channel partners, collaboration is absolutely vital for any channel partnership strategy to be effective. Partnerships allow resources to be shared between both parties, including consultancy, education, and expertise, as well as more tangible resources like technology, capital, and marketing materials. Effective channel partnerships have enabled businesses to generate new revenue streams, leverage powerful IT solutions and brand influence, and gain access to professional business tools that may have otherwise been out of reach.

在选择渠道合作伙伴时，合作对于任何渠道合作战略的有效性都是至关重要的。伙伴关系允许双方共享资源，包括咨询、教育和专业知识，以及更多的有形资源，如技术、资本和营销材料。有效的渠道伙伴关系使企业能够产生新的收入流，利用强大的 IT 解决方案和品牌影响力，来获得专业的商业工具。

The development of criteria for the selection of specific intermediaries is of great necessity. The criteria generally includes factors as financial soundness, local government contacts, business reputation, distribution network, technical support, and infrastructural facilities (especially relating to heavy industrial goods), business experience and managerial expertise, and commercial terms.

制定选择特定渠道中间商的标准非常必要。其标准一般包括财务稳健、与地方政府有联系、商业信誉、分销网络、技术支持和基础设施（特别是重工业产品）、商业经验和管理经验以及商业条款等。

2. Managing the Channel 管理渠道

After selecting channel members, the process of managing the channel begins. Distribution channel management is a collective set of activities and operations employed to get the product to market via channel partners as efficiently and effectively as possible. The channel leader assumes the main task of distribution channel management, as it is considered to have more channel power over other members. The channel power refers to the ability of any one channel member to alter or modify the behavior of other members in the distribution channel, due to its relatively strong position in the market. It mainly comes from three sources:

在选择了渠道成员后，管理渠道的过程便开始了。分销渠道管理是通过渠道合作伙伴尽可能有效地将产品推向市场的一系列活动和操作的集合。渠道领导者承担分销渠道管理的主要任务，因为它被认为对其他成员有更多的渠道权力。渠道权力是指任何一个渠道成员，由于其在市场上的相对强势地位，能够改变或修改分销渠道中其他成员的行为。它主要有 3 个来源：

（1）Economic power: When the intermediary has the ability to control resources.

经济权利：当中间商具有控制资源的能力时。

（2）Legitimate power: When a company has legal authority to keep a check on the channel partners in terms of their signed agreement.

合法权利：公司依法有权对渠道合作伙伴签署的协议进行核查。

（3）Reward or coercive power: When a producer provides several additional benefits to the other intermediaries, with the intention to motivate them to perform certain activities as required.

奖励或强制权：生产者向其他中间商提供若干额外利益，以激励其按要求进行某些活动的行为。

Traditionally, producers assume the responsibility of channel leader, by establishing operating norms, overseeing the channel partners, and dealing with channel conflict and related issues that arise. Nowadays, with more advanced technology-based management and the control of forefront customer information, large retailers begin to take over the role of channel leader. They are having louder voice in dictating their needs to manufacturers rather than controlled by them.

以往生产者承担渠道领导者的责任，建立运营规范，监督渠道合作伙伴，处理渠道冲突及相关问题。如今，随着更先进的以技术为基础的管理和对重点客户信息的控制，大型零售商开始承担起渠道领导者的角色。在向制造商说明自己的需求方面，他们的声音越来越重要，而不是被制造商控制。

Another issue raises much of the concern is the channel conflict. It may arise when the channel partners have different goals, have different perceptions about the market conditions, lack of communication, or dominated by manufacturers. For example, if the manufacturer changes the promotional scheme of a product with the intention to cut the cost, the retailer may find it difficult to sell the product without any promotional scheme and hence the conflict arises.

另一个值得关注的问题是渠道冲突。当渠道合作伙伴有不同的目标，对市场情况有不同的看法，在缺乏沟通或者被制造商控制时，就会出现这种情况。例如，如果制造商为了降低成本而改变产品的促销方案，零售商可能会发现没有任何促销方案来销售产品，从而产生冲突。

Channel conflict management takes various forms. The channel partners must decide a single goal in terms of either increased market share, survival, profit maximization, high quality, customer satisfaction, etc. with the intention to avoid conflicts. Some channels escape conflicts by swapping employees between different levels. That is, two or more persons can shift from the manufacturer level to the wholesaler or retailer level on a temporary basis, for better understanding of the roles every level plays. For sharp conflicts, trade associations are formed and even take legal actions.

渠道冲突管理有多种形式。渠道合作伙伴必须在提高市场份额、生存、利润最大化、高质量、客户满意度等方面确定单一目标以避免冲突。一些渠道通过在不同渠道级别之间交换员工来避免冲突。也就是说，两个或两个以上的人可以临时地从制造商转到批发商或零售商，以便更好地理解每个级别所扮演的角色。对于尖锐的冲突，会形成行业协会，甚至会采取法律行动。

10.7 Logistics Functions 物流功能

Logistics involves planning, delivering, and controlling the flow of physical goods, marketing materials, and information from the producer to the markets in order to achieve the highest level of customer's wants and needs satisfaction. The goal of logistics is "having the right item in the right quantity at the right time at the right place for the right price in the right condition to the right customer".

物流包括计划、交付和控制从生产者到市场的实物、营销材料和信息的流动，以获得最高水平的客户需求满意度。物流的目标是"在正确的时间、正确的地点、正确的数量、正确的价格、正确的条件下，为正确的客户提供正确的商品"。

10.7.1 Order Processing 订单处理

Order processing starts with the receipt of an order from a customer. It may be obtained by a salesperson, be telephoned in, or arrived by mail. Regular buyers and sellers are often linked electronically. As the inventories become low, an electronic purchase order is generated. It is communicated to the seller, whose computers will determine that the goods are available, and the seller will inform the buyer that the order will be filled and shipped by a certain date. The first step in most order-processing systems is to verify the accuracy of the order—that is, to make certain that the document contains no internal errors that might mean the customer was uncertain about what he or she was ordering. The next step is to verify the customer's credit or ability to pay. After determining from which inventory point to ship the goods, instructions are sent to that warehouse to fill the order. At the warehouse an "order picking list" is given to a warehouse worker, who assembles the specific order. In the packing area, it is checked and packed for shipment, and the package is labeled. The traffic manager prepares the transportation documents and notifies a carrier to pick up the shipment. An invoice for the goods is sent to the buyer, and various inventory and financial records are updated. The shipper uses the term "order cycle" to indicate the span of time between receiving and shipping the order. The buyer uses the phrase to indicate the span of time between placing and receiving the order.

订单处理从接收来自客户的订单开始。订单可以由销售人员获得，可以通过电话获得，也可以通过邮件获得。老顾客和卖家经常以电子通信的方式联系。当库存降低时，就会生成一个电子采购订单。系统通知卖方，卖方的计算机将确认货物是否已备妥，卖方将告知买方订单将在某一日期完成并发出。在大多数订单处理系统中，第一步是验证订单的准确性——也就是说，要确保文档中没有内部错误，这些错误可能意味着客户不确定他或她正在订购什么。下一步是验证客户的信用或支付能力。在确定从哪个库存点装运货物后，指令被发送到该仓库以完成订单。在仓库，"订单领料单"被交给仓库工人，由工人来装配特定的订单。在包装区，订单接受检查，准备装运货物，并贴上标签。货运主管准备运输单据并通知承运人来取货。货物的发票被发送给买方，各种库存和财务记录得到更新。发货人使用"订货周期"这个术语来表示从收到订单到发货之间的时间跨度。买方使用这个术语来表示从下单到收到订单之间的时间跨度。

10.7.2　Warehousing 仓储

Warehousing is the storing of finished goods until they are sold. It plays a vital role in logistics operations of a firm. The effectiveness of a company's marketing depends on the appropriate decisions on warehousing, such as location of warehousing facilities, the number, size, and ownership of warehouses, design and layout of the building.

仓储是将成品储存起来，直到它们被销售出去。它在企业的物流运作中起着至关重要的作用。公司营销的有效性取决于仓储方面的适当决策，如仓储设施的位置、仓库的数量、大小和所有权、建筑的设计和布局。

Warehousing basically takes two forms: storage warehouses and distribution centers. Storage warehouse means a facility for the storage of furniture, household goods, or other commercial goods of any nature. Distribution centers are highly automated and larger that are designed for the receipt of goods from various suppliers and plants. Orders from customers are received and processed efficiently and quick distribution of the ordered goods is made in these centers. In modern technological age, new, highly automated warehousing replaces the older warehousing system. Effective computerized material handling systems are used that are centralized. There is a very little number of human employees working, and most of the work is done through computerized machines and robotics.

仓储大概有两种形式：储存仓库和配送中心。仓储仓库是指存放家具、家居用品或其他任何性质的商品的设施。配送中心是高度自动化的，而且规模更大，专为接收来自不同供应商和工厂的货物而设计。客户的订单在这些中心被有效地接收和处理，所订购的商品在这些中心被迅速分发。在现今科技时代，新的、高度自动化的仓储系统取代了旧的仓储系统。有效的电脑化物料处理系统是中心化的。只需要很少的员工在工作，大部分工作是通过计算机和机器人完成的。

10.7.3　Materials Handling 材料处理

The speed of the inventory movement across the supply chain depends on the material handling methods. An improper method of material handling will add to the product damages and delays in deliveries and incidental overheads. Mechanization and automation in material handling enhance the logistics system productivity. Other considerations for selection of a material handling system are the volumes to be handled, the speed required for material movement, and the level of service to be offered to the customer.

库存在供应链上的移动速度取决于物料处理方法。不适当的材料处理方法会增加产品的损坏、交货的延误和额外的费用。物料搬运的机械化和自动化提高了物流系统的生产力。在选择物料处理系统时，还需要考虑物料的体量、物料搬运所要求的速度和向客户提供的服务水平。

10.7.4 Transportation 运输

For movement of goods from the supplier to the buyer, transportation is the most fundamental and important component of logistics. Transportation function is important because it affects the delivery performance, pricing of product, and condition of the arrived goods, etc. This would ultimately affect the satisfaction of the customers. When an order is placed, the transaction is not completed till the goods are physically moved to the customer's place. The physical movement of goods is through various transportation modes. Companies choose the mode of transportation depending on the infrastructure of transportation in the country or region. Considerations are costs, urgency of the needs, etc.

对于货物从供应商到买家之间的移动来说，运输是物流中最基本、最重要的组成部分。运输功能很重要，因为它影响了交货性能、产品的价格，以及到货条件等，最终会影响客户的满意度。从下订单开始，直到将货物实际搬运到客户的位置，交易才算完成。货物的物理运输是通过各种方式进行的。公司根据国家或地区的交通基础设施来选择运输方式。要考虑的因素有成本、需求的迫切性等。

Railways: The largest carrier of any nation is the railways. Large amounts of bulk and nonperishable product can be delivered to the distant locations in a cost effective way through railway transportation mode like sand, coal, farm and forest items, and mineral.

铁路：任何国家最大型的运输工具都是铁路。通过铁路运输方式，可以将大量的散装和不易腐烂的产品以低成本的方式运送到遥远的地方，如沙子、煤炭、农林产品、矿物等。

Water: Water or shipping is the oldest mode of transporting goods from one region to another. It is a low-cost mode but it is time-consuming transportation than other modes. Trade of iron ore and coal often uses water transportation.

水路：水路或航运是把货物从一个地区到另一个地区最古老的运输方式。这是一种低成本的运输方式，但与其他方式相比，它非常耗时。铁矿石和煤炭的贸易经常使用水运。

Trucks: In recent years, in the transportation mode trucks have played a significant role in transportation of goods from one place to another. The routing and timing schedules of trucks are highly flexible and their service is much faster than railways. High value goods of short hauls are effectively transported through trucks.

卡车：近年来在运输方式中，卡车在货物运输过程中起着重要的作用。卡车的路线和时间安排非常灵活，它们的服务比铁路快得多。短途运输的高价值货物多是通过卡车进行有效运输的。

Air: The air mode of transportation is the least popular among the business organizations, and only about 1% of the total cargo is transported through the means of air. The cost of air transportation is much higher due to high freight rates, but it is the quickest mode of transporting products, especially perishable goods and smaller quantity of highly valuable products.

航空运输：航空运输是商业组织中最不常用的运输方式，只有大约 1% 的货物是通过航空运输的。航空运输的成本由于运费高而高得多，但它是运输产品最快的方式，尤其适合运输易腐货物和少量的高价值产品。

Pipeline: For the shipment of petroleum, chemicals, and natural gas from source markets, specialized means of transportation is used which is called pipelines. Pipelines are mostly used by the owners for the delivery of their own products.

管道：为了从石油、化工和天然气的来源市场运输这些特殊能源所使用的专门工具，称为管道。管道主要用于业主运输自己的产品。

The Internet: Services such as banking, news, and entertainment are distributed via the Internet. The Internet enjoys the advantage of high speed of delivery and low cost.

互联网：银行、新闻和娱乐等服务是通过互联网发布的。因特网的优点是传送速度快，费用低。

10.7.5　Inventory Control 库存控制

The inventory is the greatest culprit in the overall supply chain of a firm because of its huge carrying cost, which indirectly eats away the profits. It consists of the cost of financing the inventory, insurance, storage, losses, damages, and pilferage. The major issue in this function is to keep a complicated balance between carrying less inventory and carry too much of it. Carrying too much inventory results in stock idleness and high inventory carrying costs. On the other hand, carrying of little inventory results in costly production and emergency shipment, stock-outs, and finally customer dissatisfaction.

库存是一个公司整个供应链中影响利润最大的罪魁祸首，因为库存耗费了巨额的成本，间接地消耗了利润。库存成本包括库存、保险、仓储、损失、损害和盗窃的融资成本。库存控制的关键是在保有过少的库存和过多的库存之间这一复杂问题上取得平衡。库存过多会导致库存闲置和高库存持有成本。另一方面，如果存货过少，会导致生产成本高，面临紧急出货或缺货情况，最终将导致客户不满。

◎　阅读推荐

伯特·罗森布洛姆.营销渠道：管理的视野 [M]. 宋华，等译. 北京：中国人民大学出版社，2014.

尼克·约翰逊.新营销，新模式 [M]. 刘凤瑜，译. 北京：中信出版社，2016.

绪方知行，田口香世.零售的本质——7-Eleven 便利店创始人的哲学 [M]. 陆青，译. 北京：机械工业出版社，2016.

颜艳春.第三次零售革命：拥抱消费者主权时代 [M]. 北京：机械工业出版社，2014.

参考文献

[1]   Solomon M R, Greg W M, Elnora W S. Marketing Real People Real Choices[M].7th Edition. Upper Saddle River: Prentice Hall, 2014.

[2]   Pride G. Foundations of Marketing[M]. Harrow:Houghton Mifflin, 2008.

[3]   Schiffmann L G, Kanuk L L. Consumer Behaviour[M]. New Jersey: Pearson International Edition, 2009.

[4]   Kotler P. Marketing Management: Millenium Edition[M]. Upper Saddle River: Prentice Hall,1999.

[5]   Carl S, Hal R V. Versioning: The Smart Way to Sell Information[J]. Harvard Business Review, 1998(November-December):106–14.

[6]   Kaplan R S, David P N. Strategy Maps: Converting Intangible Assets into Tangible Outcomes[M]. Watertown: Harvard Business Press, 2004:10.

[7]   Perreault Jr. W, J Cannon J W, McCarthy E J. Basic Marketing[M]. New York: McGraw-Hill Higher Education, 2013: 24.

[8]   Robins R. Does Corporate Social Responsibility Increase Profits?[J].Business Ethics,2011(12).

[9]   Economist Intelligence Unit. Corporate Citizenship: Profiting from a Sustainable Business[R]. The Economist Intelligence Unit Limited, London,2008.

[10]   Kotler P, Armstrong G. Principles of Marketing[M]. London: Pearson Education Limited, 2010.

[11]   Trout J. Branding Can't Exist Without Positioning[J]. Advertising Age, March 14, 2005:28.

[12]   Krishnan J. Lifestyle—A Tool for Understanding Buyer Behavior[J]. International Journal of Economics and Management 2011(5): 283-298.

[13]   Jones R J B. Routledge Encyclopedia of International Political Economy:

Entries A-F[M]. Boca Raton: Taylor & Francis，2001：161.

[14]　Schiffman L, Kaunk L. Social Class and Consumer Behavior[M].Ninth Edtion. New York: Prentice hall, ,2007:356-382.

[15]　Bourne F S. Group Influence in Marketing and Public Relations[M]// Likert, R. and Hayes, S. P.(eds.). Some Applications of Behavioral Research. Paris: UNESCO,1957.

[16]　Everett M R. Diffusion of Innovators[M]. 3rd Edition. New York: The Free Press, 1983.

[17]　Allison, N K, Golden L L, Mullet G M, Coogan D. Sex-typed Product Images: The Effects of Sex, Sex Role, Self-Concept and Measurement Implications[J]. Advances in Consumer Research, 1980(1).

[18]　Keelson S A. The Evolution of the Marketing Concepts: Theoretically Different Roads Leading to Practically Same Destination[J]. Online Journal of Social Sciences Research, 2012(May): 35-41.

[19]　McCarthy I, Anagnostou A. The Impact of Outsourcing on the Transaction Costs and Boundaries of Manufacturing[J]. International Journal of Production Economics, 2004,88 (1): 61–71.

[20]　Jonna H，James W G. Ethnic Consumer Reaction to Targeted Marketing: A Theory of Intercultural Accommodation[J]. Journal of Advertising, 1999, 28(1): 65-77.

[21]　Ahmad R. Benefit Segmentation: A Potentially Useful Technique of Segmenting and Targeting Older Consumers[J]. International Journal of Market Research,2003,45(3):3773-388,411.

[22]　Andrei P, Ecaterina B R, Ionut T C. Does Positioning Have a Place in the Minds of our Students?[C]. Annals of the University of Oradea, Economic Science Series,2010.

[23]　Al R, Jack T. Positioning: The Battle for Your Mind. New York: McGraw Hill,2001:2.

[24]　Evans, J R, Barry B. Marketing in the 21st Century[M]. Upper Saddle River:

Prentice Hall, 2002.

[25]　Fry J N Family Branding and Consumer Brand Choice[J]. Journal of Marketing Research,1967,4(3).

[26]　Manton S. Integrated Intellectual Asset Management[M]. London: Routledge,2005.

[27]　Czepiel J A, Michael R S. The Service Encounter: Managing Employee/ Customer Interaction in Service Businesses[M].Lanham:Lexington Books, 1985.

[28]　Dikmans L. SOA Made Simple[M]. Mumbai: Packt Publishing Ltd., 2012.

[29]　Parasuraman A,Berry, L L, Zeithaml V A. Understanding Customer Expectations of Service[J]. Sloan Management Review, 1991, 32(3):39-48.

[30]　Parasuraman A P, Valarie A Z, Leonard L B. A Conceptual Model of Service Quality and Its Implications for Future Research[J]. The Journal of Marketing,1985,49(4): 41-50.

[31]　Valarie A Z, Berry L L, Parasuraman A A. Communication and Control Processes in the Delivery of Service Quality[J].Journal of Marketing,1987,52(2).

[32]　Michael V M, Robert L R. Managing Price, Gaining Profit[J]. Harvard Business Review 1992,70(5): 84-94.

[33]　Hanna N, Dodge H R. Pricing and the Legal Issues[M]// Pricing. London: Palgrave, 1995.

[34]　Craig R T. Communication Theory as a Field[J]. Communication Theory,1999, 9(2):119–161.

[35]　Courtland L B, John V T, Barbara E S. Business Communication Essentials[M]. New York: Pearson, 2004.

[36]　Harrell G D. Marketing: Connecting with Customers[M]. Chicago: Chicago Education Press,2008:286.

[37]　Goranova P, Steliana V. Integrated Marketing Communications at Different Stages of the Product Life Cycle in the Context of Brand Management[C]. The

Priority Directions of National Economy Development: International Scientific Conference, 2016.

[38] Porter M E. Competitive Advantage: Creating and Sustaining Superior Performance[M]. Riverside: Simon and Schuster, 2008.

[39] Nagurney A. Supply Chain Network Economics: Dynamics of Prices, Flows, and Profits[M]. Cheltenham: Edward Elgar,2006.

[40] Oliver R K, Webber M D. Supply-chain Management: Logistics Catches up with Strategy[M]//Christopher M(ed.). Logistics: The Strategic Issues. London: Chapman Hall,1992:63–75.

[41] Harland C M. Supply Chain Management, Purchasing and Supply Management, Logistics, Vertical Integration, Materials Management and Supply Chain Dynamics[M]//Slack N (ed.). Blackwell Encyclopedic Dictionary of Operations Management. Oxford: Blackwell,1996.

[42] Girard J P, Girard, JoAnn L. Defining Knowledge Management: Toward an Applied Compendium. Online Journal of Applied Knowledge Management,2015,3(1): 1-20.

[43] Rolnic K. Managing Channels of Distribution[M]. New York: Amacom Books, 1998.

[44] Dwyer F R, Paul H S, Sejo O. Developing buyer-seller Relationships[J]. The Journal of marketing,1987,51(2): 11-27.

[45] Mallik S. Customer Service in Supply Chain Management[M]// Hossein Bidgoil. The Handbook of Technology Management: Supply Chain Management, Marketing and Advertising, and Global Management, Vol 2 (1st ed.). Hoboken: John Wiley & Sons,2010:104.